Deciphering India's Services Sector Growth

This book addresses a range of issues relating to the nature and implications of growth of India's services sector, including factors contributing to the rise of services, output measurement and heterogeneity, growth of services exports, and employment in services sectors. From service tax, exchange rate and services exports, policy interest, employment potential and diversity of the sector to challenges in financial inclusion, trajectories of ICT services and contribution of education to GDP, it brings together diverse themes to highlight major concerns in the wake of the prominent role that services have played in placing India among the fast-growing economies in the world in recent years.

The services sector in India accounts for more than 60 per cent of the GDP of the country and 28.6 per cent of its employed across government, private or state corporations and non-government organisations. The volume explores whether the services sector (beyond agriculture and industry) holds the promise of fulfilling the benefits from India's demographic dividend for its economic transformation through sustainable growth.

With key empirical analyses of household, enterprise and macroeconomic data for India within both formal and informal sectors, this topical book will be useful to scholars and researchers of economics, Indian economy, political economy, development economics, development studies, public policy and South Asian studies and also to development professionals, policy makers and industry specialists.

Shashanka Bhide is Senior Advisor, National Council of Applied Economic Research, New Delhi and was Director, Madras Institute of Development Studies, Chennai, India. He has contributed to research in agriculture, macroeconomic modelling and poverty analysis.

V.N. Balasubramanyam is Professor (Emeritus) of Development Economics, Management School, Lancaster University, UK. He has published widely and his current research is on foreign investment, diaspora and development.

K.L. Krishna is Chairperson, Madras Institute of Development Studies, Chennai; former Professor, University of Delhi; and Member, Centre for Development Economics, Delhi School of Economics, Delhi, India. He has published in applied econometrics, industrial economics, productivity analysis and trade.

Deciphering India's Services Sector Growth

Edited by Shashanka Bhide, V.N. Balasubramanyam and K.L. Krishna

Routledge
Taylor & Francis Group
LONDON AND NEW YORK

First published 2021
by Routledge
2 Park Square, Milton Park, Abingdon, Oxon OX14 4RN

and by Routledge
52 Vanderbilt Avenue, New York, NY 10017

Routledge is an imprint of the Taylor & Francis Group, an informa business

British Library Cataloguing-in-Publication Data
A catalogue record for this book is available from the British Library

Library of Congress Cataloging-in-Publication Data
A catalog record for this book has been requested

ISBN: 978-0-367-14617-7 (hbk)
ISBN: 978-1-003-04513-7 (ebk)

Typeset in Sabon
by Apex CoVantage, LLC

Dedicated to the Memory of
Prof. T.N. Srinivasan

Contents

Figures

Tables

Appendices

Contributors

M. Suresh Babu is Professor of Economics, Department of Humanities and Social Sciences, Indian Institute of Technology Madras, Chennai, India. His research interests include applied macroeconomics, industrial economics, trade and development. His book titled *Hastening Slowly: India's Industrial Growth in the Era of Economic Reforms* was published by Orient BlackSwan in 2018.

Ahalya Balasubramanyam is at the Department of Management School, Lancaster, UK. She has published several articles on India's software industry. She has a doctorate from Temple University, USA, teaches mathematics at the Lancaster Management School and has published a number of articles on India's software sector.

V.N. Balasubramanyam, Emeritus Professor of Development Economics in the Department of Economics, Management School, Lancaster, UK, is with British Northern Universities-India Forum, a research partnership among economists, social scientists and management experts at the University of Leeds, the University of Lancaster and the University of Manchester. He was educated at the University of Mysore, Chicago University and the University of Illinois. He specialises in international trade, international investment and economic development. He has published widely, and his current research is on foreign investment, the diaspora and development.

Shashanka Bhide is Senior Advisor, National Council of Applied Economic Research (NCAER), New Delhi, and Former Director, Madras Institute of Development Studies (MIDS), Chennai (2014–18), India. He was Senior Research Counsellor at NCAER before joining MIDS. He was Professor and Head at the RBI unit of Institute of Social and Economic Change in Bangalore (2003–04). He obtained his PhD in agricultural economics from Iowa State University, USA. His research interests include macroeconomic modelling, infrastructure, agriculture and development. He has published books, journal articles, project reports and newspaper columns.

P. Duraisamy was Vice-Chancellor, University of Madras, Chennai, India. Prior to that, he was Sir Sarvapalli Radhakrishnan National Fellow of the ICSSR and affiliated to the Madras Institute of Development Studies, Chennai. He was Professor in the Department of Econometrics in the University of Madras. He served for over 28 years at the University of Madras and was Head of the Department of Econometrics for over 10 years. He was a senior visiting fellow at Yale University for 3 years and visiting professor at the University of Paris I – (Pantheon-Sorbonne) and Paris II (Panthéon-Assas) during 2007–14. He was also consultant to the World Bank and Population Council. With a PhD, D EconSc (Paris), he has been working in the areas of economics of education, health, labour, macroeconomic issues, applied econometrics, political choice and voting behaviour and has published over 60 papers in highly reputed journals.

K.L. Krishna is Chairperson, Madras Institute of Development Studies; Former Professor, Centre for Development Economics, Delhi School of Economics; and former Director at Delhi School of Economics, India. His field of specialisation includes econometrics, methodology and applications, industrial economics, economics of productivity, regional inequality and empirics of trade. His research work has been widely published in journals.

A.C. Kulshreshtha has served as Additional Director General, Central Statistics Organisation, New Delhi, and as a member of faculty in the UN Statistical Institute for Asia and the Pacific, Japan. He has published more than 100 research papers in the design of experiments, national accounts statistics and official statistics. He is recipient of the P.V. Sukhatme National Award in Statistics from Ministry of Statistics and Programme Implementation, New Delhi, and the Sankhyiki Bhushan Award from the Indian Society of Agricultural Statistics. He was a member of the Advisory Expert Group of Intersecretariat Working Group on National Accounts of the United Nations Statistical Commission that brought out the latest international Standard, the System of National Accounts, 2008. He has been associated with several government advisory committees on National Accounts/Official Statistics. He has been Editor of the *Journal of Indian Association for Research in National Income and Wealth* and is currently the President of the Indian Association for Research in National Income & Wealth.

Jesim Pais is Director, Society for Social and Economic Research, Delhi, India, and works on issues related to industry and employment with a focus on small enterprises and the informal sector. He has previously worked at the Institute for Studies in Industrial Development, Delhi, and the Indian Statistical Institute, Kolkata. He has a PhD from the Indira Gandhi Institute of Development Research, Mumbai. His research work includes studies of migrant workers in industrial cities such as Mumbai, Ludhiana and Faridabad. He has done field-based industry-level research on the manufacture of combine harvesters in Punjab and the leather accessories manufacture in Dharavi, Mumbai.

Balaji Parthasarathy is Professor at the International Institute of Information Technology Bengaluru and a co-founder of the Institute's Centre for Information Technology and Public Policy, India. His research and teaching interests focus on the relationship among technological innovation, economic globalisation, and social change, especially the impacts of public policy and firm strategies on the organisation of production in the information and communications technology (ICT) industry alongside ICTs for development in economically underprivileged contexts. His recent work has examined the political economy of e-governance, e-waste, digital platforms and gig work, and smart cities. He has an undergraduate degree from the Indian Institute of Technology Kharagpur and a PhD from the University of California Berkeley.

Meenakshi Rajeev is Reserve Bank of India Chair Professor at the Institute for Social and Economic Change, Bengaluru. She graduated from Indian Institute of Technology Kanpur in Statistics and earned her PhD in Mathematical Economics from the Indian Statistical Institute, Kolkata. She has worked as a faculty member and taught at the University of California at San Diego, Central Michigan University, Centre for Studies in Social Sciences, Kolkata, and Presidency College, Kolkata. She has also visited and taught in a number of other universities and institutions in the USA, UK, Germany, France and Norway, including Cornell University and Central Bank of Norway. She has published more than 100 articles in reputed journals and as book chapters and working papers. Her recent books are *Emerging Issues in Economic Development* and *Financial Exclusion in Urban Regions: A Story of Exclusion from Springer*. Her areas of research include game theory, banking and credit market, industrial economics and development economics.

K.V. Ramaswamy is Professor at Indira Gandhi Institute of Development Research, Mumbai, India, and works in the area of development economics, labour and industry studies. He was Shastri Indo-Canadian Visiting Fellow at University of Toronto, Canada, and Senior Visiting Fellow at the Institute of South Asian Studies, National University of Singapore, Singapore and at the Institute of Developing Economies, Tokyo. He has edited the book *Labour, Employment and Economic Growth in India*. His current areas of research interest include labour markets, globalisation and regional inequality in India.

Manoranjan Sahoo is Assistant Professor of Economics at Kalinga Institute of Industrial Technology, Bhubaneswar, India. He received his PhD in Economics from Indian Institute of Technology Madras, Chennai.

Shika Saravanabhavan is a PhD scholar at the Institute for Social and Economic Change, Bangalore, India. Her research interests lie in the areas of development credit, financial inclusion and financial literacy. She has published on formal and informal lending and financial inclusion.

R. Srinivasan is Registrar and Professor in the Department of Econometrics, University of Madras, Chennai, India. He has served on a number of academic administrative and advisory bodies. He has published articles and books on economics and development. He was also a Member of the Tamil Nadu State Planning Commission, Chennai.

Brinda Viswanathan is Professor at the Madras School of Economics, Chennai, India, and her research interest is in development economics and applied econometrics. She teaches courses in Indian economic development, development economics and quantitative economics for postgraduate students. She has published in journals on nutrition security, green economy, migration, poverty and vulnerability, gender and labour market and contributed chapters in several edited books as well as edited a couple of books on similar topics. She regularly contributes as a resource person for workshops and training programmes for college teachers, PhD students and government officials on statistical and econometric techniques and on evidence-based policy making.

Foreword

Dr C. Rangarajan
Chairman, Madras School of Economics, Chennai and
Former Governor, Reserve Bank of India

The growth of services, especially since the 1990s, has played a significant role in sustaining the acceleration in India's overall growth. The recent slowdown in the economic growth, even before the shock of the coronavirus pandemic, has seen that services growth, while slowing down from its earlier trajectory, remained well above that of agriculture and manufacturing. These trends suggest that services growth is expected to be the main source of economic growth for India in the years to come, as the economy transforms itself to benefit from the technological changes in a variety of areas such as information processing, telecommunication, artificial intelligence and robotics. All producing sectors of the economy, whether agriculture, manufacturing or construction, are undergoing major changes in the way their products are produced, moved and marketed. The financial services have also been revolutionised in the wake of technologies related to IT and telecommunications. The technology revolution in these services has been driving the expansion of services.

There are concerns relating to the employment generation potential for the sector in which the so-called modern services, the IT, IT-enabled services and telecommunications, have played the crucial role in moving India's exports to be of sizable value. If these modern services require a highly skilled work force, there is a challenge to the economy to produce such a work force to derive benefits from the high-growth sector.

The present volume of chapters on different aspects of the services sector addresses a wide range of issues in the specific context of India but have implications to the other developing economies also, as they explore both explanations for growth and measurement issues at a general and sector-specific context such as the education sector. The services now account for over 70 per cent of GDP in the advanced economies and suggest much potential for the further growth of the sector in countries like India. There is a need to understand how the modern services can benefit the domestic economy and not rely entirely on the export demand for its future growth. In fact, the role of modern services in bringing the domestic manufacturing to produce at global standards of efficiency has often been emphasised. India's move to expand the digital footprints of its financial sector may help reduce costs of financial transactions to the businesses and households.

While services have brought multiple benefits to the economy, India should also consider the need to ensure that the technology benefits that are driving services are also absorbed in all the sectors, whether manufacturing or agriculture. Infrastructure needed for the expansion of services needs to be built. Investments in health, education and skills are needed. Without this comprehensive approach, the fast growth of a small segment of the economy may have limited impact.

The present volume has grown out of a conference held at the Madras Institute of Development Studies. As the editors note in the Introduction, while the subject has received significant contributions by researchers, there is still much to be learnt from India's experience of sustained high rates of growth of the services sector. The volume fills a need for well-documented explanations of India's services growth felt by both researchers and students of economic development.

Acknowledgements

The editors are grateful to all the contributing authors of this volume for their work and patience with this long process of bringing their articles into a book, which we believe would be of greater value to the readers in a collection of related chapters. Except for the chapter by Dr. A.C. Kulshreshtha and the Introduction by the editors, all chapters are based on the papers presented by the authors in a conference organised by the Madras Institute of Development Studies, Chennai, and the British Northern Universities India Forum on January 3–4, 2017.

We also thank Dr. C. Rangarajan, Chairman, Madras School of Economics, Chennai, and former Governor of Reserve Bank of India and former Chairman of Prime Minister's Economic Advisory Council for agreeing to write the Foreword to this volume. Dr. Rangarajan had also delivered the inaugural address at the conference.

The ideas discussed at the conference 'Future of India's Services Growth: Potential and Constraints' provided motivation for this volume. Besides the chapters included here, the distinguished scholars and participants at the conference contributed immensely to the discussion, some of which is also reflected in the Introduction to this book. We are particularly grateful to Dr. Poonam Gupta, Adviser, World Bank; Mr. S. Krishnan, then Principal Secretary, Planning and Development, in the Government of Tamilnadu; Dr. Gaurav Nayyar, Economist, World Bank; and late Professor. T.N. Srinivasan, among a number of distinguished speakers at the conference for their active participation. Proceedings of the conference were brought out by the Madras Institute of Development Studies subsequently.

We would like to acknowledge the constant encouragement we received from late Professor T.N. Srinivasan in our work.

The book would not have been possible without the encouragement and understanding by the publisher, Routledge, who agreed to publish the book. We are grateful to them for their support throughout the process of bringing out this volume.

The editors acknowledge the support of Madras Institute of Development, Chennai, and the British Northern Universities India Forum in bringing out this collection of chapters. They would also like to acknowledge the support of the National Council of Applied Economic Research, New Delhi, Lancaster University Management School and Madras Institute of Development Studies, Chennai, with which Shashanka Bhide, V.N. Balasubramanyam and K.L. Krishna, respectively, are presently associated.

Abbreviations

ADR	American Depository Receipts
AIC	Akaike Information Criterion
AIDIS	All India Debt and Investment Survey
AISHE	All India Survey of Higher Education
APEC	Asia Pacific Economic Cooperation
ARDL	Autoregressive Distributed Lag Model
ASI	Annual Survey of Industries
ASSOCHAM	Associated Chambers of Commerce and Industry of India
BC	Business Correspondents
BoP	Bottom of the Pyramid
BPO	Business Process Outsourcing
BRICS	Brazil, Russia, India, China and South Africa
CAG	Comptroller and Auditor General
CE	Compensation to Employees
CENVAT	Central Value Added Tax
CFC	Consumption of Fixed Capital
CGST	Central Goods and Services Tax
CGTMSE	Credit Guarantee Fund Trust for Micro and Small Enterprises
CII	Change in Inventories
CMM	Capability Maturity Model
Coef	Coefficient
CRILC	Central Repository of Information on Large Credits
CRTS	Constant Returns to Scale
CSO	Central Statistical Office
CSR	Corporate Social Responsibility
CUSUM	Cumulative Sum of Recursive Residuals
CUSUMsq	Cumulative Sum of Recursive Residual Squares
DoE	Department of Electronics
DPEP	District Primary Education Programme
EUS	Employment Unemployment Survey
FCE	Final Consumption Expenditure
FDI	Foreign Direct Investment
FINDEV	Financial development

FISIM	Financial Intermediary Services Indirectly Measured
FWPR	Female Workforce Participation Rate
GDP	Gross Domestic Product
GDR	Global Depository Receipts
GER	Gross Enrolment Ratio
GEXP	Goods Exports
GFCE	Government Final Consumption Expenditure
GFCF	Gross Fixed Capital Formation
GLOBAL	Globalisation Index
GNDI	Gross National Domestic Income
GNI	Gross National Income
GNP	Gross National Product
GO	Gross Output
GOI	Government of India
GST	Goods and Services Tax
GVA	Gross Value Added
GVO	Gross Value of Output
HEI	Higher Education Institutions
HFCI	Household Final Consumption Expenditure
IC	Intermediate Consumption
ICT	Information and Communication Technology
ILO	International Labour Organisation
ISIC	International Standard Industrial Classification
IT	Information Technology
ITES	Information Technology Enabled Services
KLEMS	Capital, Labour, Energy, Materials and Services
LDC	Less Developed Countries
LEB	Life Expectancy at Birth
MBA	Master of Business Administration
MeiTy	Ministry of Electronics and Information Technology
MGNREGA	Mahatma Gandhi National Rural Employment Guarantee Act
MI	Mixed Income
ML	Professional Money Lender
MMF	Money Market Funds
MNC	Multinational Corporations
MPCE	Monthly Per Capita Consumer Expenditure
MSE	Modern Service Exports
MSR	Microsoft Research
MUDRA	Micro Unit Development and Refinance Agency
NAS	National Accounts Statistics
NASSCOM	National Association of Software and Services Companies
NBFC	Non Banking Financial Corporations
NGO	Non Government Organisation

NIC	National Industrial Classification
NNI	Net National Income
NPISH	Non-profit Institutions Serving Households
NREGA	National Rural Employment Guarantee Act
NRHM	National Rural Health Mission
NSDP	Net State Domestic Product
NSS	National Sample Survey
NSSO	National Sample Survey Organisation
OBC	Other Backward Caste
ODC	Offshore Development Centres
OECD	Organisation for Economic Co-operation and Development
PFCE	Private Final Consumption Expenditure
PI	Profit Income
PLFS	Periodic Labour Force Survey
R&D	Research and Development
RBI	Reserve Bank of India
REER	Real Effective Exchange Rate
RRR	Relative Risk Ratio
RTE	Right to Education
RUSA	Rashtriya Uchchatar Shiksha Abhiyan
SC	Scheduled Caste
SE	Standard Error
SEI	Software Engineering Institute
SES	School Education Survey
SGST	State Goods and Services Tax
SHGBL	Self-Help Groups Bank Linked
SHGNBFC	Self-Help Groups Non-Banking Finance Corporation Linked
SIDBI	Small Industries Development Bank of India
SIMP	World Demand for Service Exports
SNA	System of National Accounts
SS	Subsidiary Status
SSA	Sarva Shiksha Abhiyan
SSC	Service Sector Contribution
ST	Scheduled Tribe
STP	Software Technology Park
TDCCs	Technology-Driven Commodity Chains
TFP	Total Factor Productivity
TFPG	Total Factor Productivity Growth
T-S	Taxes *minus* Subsidies
TSE	Total Service Exports
TV	Television
US	United States
UK	United Kingdom
UPS	Usual Principal Status

UPSS	Usual Principal and Subsidiary Status
VAT	Value Added Tax
WDI	World Development Indicators
WEF	World Economic Forum
ZA	Zivot-Andrews

1 Introduction

Shashanka Bhide, V.N. Balasubramanyam and K.L. Krishna

1.1 The rising share of services in the economy: explanations and implications

The rapid expansion of the services sector in the Indian economy, raising and sustaining the growth rate of the overall economy in the period since the 1990s, has led to many questions seeking to improve our understanding of the explanations for the phenomenon, implications to the development goals and the future scenarios for the economy. Between the first three years of the 1950s and the first three years of the decade of 2010–20, a period of six decades, measured by the gross value added (GVA) in constant prices, India's overall economy expanded by a little more than 16 times and the service sector of the economy expanded by 39 times, industry by 29 times and agriculture by four times. This remarkable rapid growth of the services sector, especially since the decade of the 1990s, has been a subject of wonder and dismay for analysts and researchers. The wonder is from the sustained and accelerating growth of the sector. While the average annual services growth measured by value added in real terms exceeded the growth of agriculture or industry from the decade of 1970s onwards, the average annual growth rate during the 1990s exceeded 8 per cent and 7.5 per cent in the 2000s and is expected to surpass it in the next decade.

The dismay is on account of the less emphatic contribution of the service sector to employment, the pace at which new jobs are created.

Gains for the economy from this growth, including revenue for the government and contribution to export earnings, have been many. Service tax emerged as an important source of indirect tax revenues for the government. The rise in tax revenues may have helped the government spend more on welfare programmes than otherwise.

The drivers of growth of services in the economy have remained strong in the recent years when the Indian economy has witnessed sharp decline in growth. Between 2015–16 and 2018–19, the overall annual economic growth, measured by the GVA in constant prices, declined from 7.9 per cent to 4.9 per cent. While the services also registered a decline from 9.6 to 6.9 per cent, the deceleration in manufacturing was sharp: from 12.7 to 2.0 per cent.

The drivers of services growth appear to be more robust than in the other sectors. Transformation of the economy leading to its modernisation has assigned a systemic role for technology, which in turn is raising the demand for services.

There is also the assessment that services have not generated the kind of employment that other sectors have generated. While there has been growth in output, both the quantity and quality of employment that has been generated have not been satisfactory. The fast-growing segment of the services sector required specialised skills, and a smaller proportion of workers benefitted from such growth. A larger proportion of jobs in services was generated in the informal sector, with the consequent implications to the nature of compensation to the work force. The services have indeed provided jobs to the less skilled, but do they hold the promise of better wages?

An important feature of the growth of India's service sector has been the rise of 'modern services' comprising IT software, telecommunication and financial services. In general, 'infrastructure services' that are a critical input to the rest of the economic activities have seen a significant spurt from the growth of the other sectors. Nevertheless, the rise of services in the Indian economy is often seen as an 'exception' to the international experience, in which the growth of manufacturing or industry played a leading role in accelerating economic growth and development before the services became the dominant part of the economy. More detailed analysis has shown that the 'exception' of India's experience has been only in the more recent times and more particularly in the composition of services, its relatively high share of 'modern services'.

The explanations for the rise of services are many. Technological breakthroughs in communication and information technology leading to tradability of these services has been an important part of the explanation. But this explanation finds resonance only when it is supplemented by the availability of suitable labour force and language skills in the country to benefit from the technological breakthroughs. The speed and scale of expansion in the appropriately skilled labour would determine the benefits from technology breakthroughs. The other explanations have included the relative disadvantage the manufacturing sector experienced, whether in terms of the tax regime or the regulatory regime over the service sector that allowed the services to boom. After all, in the first two decades after Independence from Colonial rule, industrial growth exceeded services growth as policies supported industrialisation through state-led industrial enterprises and investments.

While the growth of services has continued in the present decade, there have been questions on its sustainability in the longer term: India aims to sustain its high growth rates of 7 per cent or more, and there are many constraints on this growth, some of which may have been exacerbated by the nature of growth itself, such as the rising income inequality, relative concentration of markets for export of modern services and signs of less liberal trade regime at a global level. Given the important role the services play as input to the other productive sectors of the economy, can productivity improvement in services be the major driver of overall productivity growth in the economy?

Transformation of the economies from agrarian to industrial and domination by the services has been a subject of analysis by many scholars, with an initial articulation of the stylised facts in the classic work of Simon Kuznets. In the recent couple of decades, the rapid growth of services in the developing economies has attracted much attention, even as the East Asian and Southeast Asian experience reflected the classical economic transformation features of moving from an agrarian to industrial and services-dominated economies. It is important to note that even in the consumption needs of the poor, basic or essential services have come to be recognised: whether it is health, education, housing or transportation, the needs are universal.

A comparison of the path of economic growth taken by the two Asian giants, China and India, is inevitable. The services sector has a slightly higher share in India's GDP than in China. But the major contrast is in the shares of manufacturing and agriculture in the two countries. The share of manufacturing in GDP at about 12 per cent is less than half the share seen in China. The share of agriculture in GDP in China is less than half that of India's. China's manufacturing sector grew at a pace that made China the 'global factory'. India's services promised to be a 'global back office'. Nevertheless, the two distinct experiences point to the paths technology development may take in the course of development. Manufacturing in China is 'export-oriented' and the 'ICT services' in India are export-oriented. The transformation from agriculture to industry and then services is more in evidence in China than in India. Is India's path sustainable?

Some of the early analysis of growth of services in the Indian context has been referred to by Gordon and Gupta (2004). What set apart the rise of services in the Indian economy in the decades since the earlier phase was the growth of export of IT services. It was also the growth of telecommunication services. Eichengreen and Gupta (2009, 2011) point to the graded relationship of growth of different groups of services in an economy with references to the levels of per capita income. The promise of accelerated and sustained growth of demand appears to be in the group in which information and communication technologies are integral to its operations. In a major research programme on the trends and patterns of productivity in different sectors of the economy, the differences in the contributions of the 'ICT intensive sector' compared to 'non-ICT intensive sectors' have been highlighted (Krishna et al., 2017). The services revolution was led by technological breakthroughs in the ICT sector and opening a new road to development through the 'knowledge economy'. Is the service revolution a way to cross the 'middle income trap' for the advancing developing economies?

1.2 Focus of the book

A number of studies have helped us understand the issues around the emerging dominance of the services sector in the economy and sustainability of the growth of this sector. Continuation of these efforts is necessary, as sustaining the growth of the services sector is important for sustaining the higher growth of the economy, which in turn is necessary to achieve the many development goals. The income and development gaps between India and the developed world are enormous. The need to create assets and physical and knowledge infrastructure to sustain development momentum is acute given the sharp inequalities of opportunities and income within the economy. There is a wide variation in the spectrum of services and in the range of social and spatial patterns of development of services within the economy. Is the pattern of economic growth, dominated by services, likely to turn the high share of working population into the 'demographic dividend' for India? Will the technological breakthroughs that made rapid expansion of services possible begin to make manufacturing or even some of the services themselves less 'labour-intensive' than before? What should be done, if that indeed were to be the case? Are there challenges to sustaining the high growth of services? The strategies needed to move jobs from 'low' productivity to 'higher' productivity sub-sectors on a significant scale are needed to increase the income levels of the large population employed in the less skilled informal sector services.

The discussion so far has drawn attention to the need for continued efforts to understand the drivers of growth of services in the economy and implications of this growth to employment and income to understand how the transformation that is taking place in the economy would affect the development goals of the nation. At a basic level, it is also necessary to understand how we measure the output of the services, given its largely intangible nature. The present volume addresses issues around the three central concerns relating to the rise of services in the Indian economy: how we measure services output, drivers of high growth of services output and implications of services growth to development. The attempt here is by no means to present a comprehensive analysis but to examine a few questions relating to each of these three central concerns.

1.3 Organisation of the chapters

This volume puts together a set of chapters that address a range of issues relating to the growth of India's service sector, covering measurement of services, heterogeneity of services, factors affecting growth of services exports, employment in services sectors and insights from specific service sectors. The present volume brings to the fore some important concerns in the wake of the prominent role services have played in taking India to be among one of fastest-growing large economies in the world in the recent two decades.

The chapters presented here were first presented in an international conference held in Chennai organised by the Madras Institute of Development Studies, Chennai, and the British Northern Universities India Forum, UK. This volume presents revised versions of selected papers, an additional paper and the Introduction in 11 chapters. The Introduction provides an overview summarising the key messages from the various chapters to an understanding of India's services growth. The chapters following the Introduction are organised under three parts.

1.3.1 Part I: understanding services growth

In **Chapter 2**, V.N. Balasubramanyam and Ahalya Balasubramanyam provide a broad setting for the rise of the services sector in the Indian economy. They note that social and cultural factors have played a significant role in the rapid rise of services in the Indian economy and argue that the high services growth will be sustained because of the 'critical inputs' nature of services.

Chapter 3 is by R. Srinivasan on the rise of service tax revenues in the wake of bringing services into the tax base. It traces the emergence of services as an important tax base, especially when some of the other indirect taxes, such as the customs, began to shrink. It went from a scenario where specific services were identified as taxable to a situation where there was a small negative list of non-taxed services. The chapter argues for simplification of the tax administration by rational division of mutually exclusive powers of tax administration between central and state governments, not permitting cross empowerment. Seamless tax credit and tax refunds for exports as well as interstate trade in goods and services are needed to reduce compliance cost of tax.

Manoranjan Sahoo and M. Suresh Babu draw attention to the links of domestic service sector to the rest of the world and examine the impact of exchange rate policy on services exports in **Chapter 4**. The role of rising services exports is seen to be important for external-sector stability as well as for sustaining the services-led growth in the long run. In this context, the chapter examines the impact of exchange rate movements on services exports from India during 1975 to 2014. They argue that exchange rate policies to maintain price competition need to be complemented by suitable supply-side policies such as encouraging FDI inflows in the service sectors to sustain the rising services exports in the long run.

In **Chapter 5**, A.C. Kulshreshtha briefly reviews the key concepts in the measurement of output as per the System of National Accounts (SNA) 2008 developed by the United Nations. The chapter provides a discussion of the changes in India's National Accounts after the adoption of SNA 2008 framework in 2011–12, with particular reference to the output of the service sectors. Pointing to the amorphous nature of services, the author notes that 'generally speaking, services embrace all economic activities other than those covered under agricultural production, mining, manufacturing and construction activity'. In the Indian national accounts, services comprise the activities of (i) trade, hotels and restaurants; (ii) transport, storage and communication; (iii) financing and insurance; (iv) real estate, renting and business services including the software development activities and legal services; (v) public administration and defence and (vi) community, social and personal services.

1.3.2 Part II: services sector, economic growth and employment

In **Chapter 6** under Part II, Jesim Pais explores the heterogeneity across various subsectors in the services sector in India through the analysis of growth, structure and productivity. The chapter provides detailed analysis at a level of sub-sectors not commonly found in the literature.

The author provides a reclassification of services into four sub-categories based on a combination of end user and ownership. Distributive services accounts for the highest share of services GDP followed by producer services and social services. In terms of labour productivity, the producer services exhibit about three times the labour productivity in social services and in distributive services.

Policies aimed at employment generation and income enhancement should take into consideration the heterogeneity in the services sector. Productivity-enhancing efforts should focus on services that already provide large-scale employment at relatively low wages. A cause for concern is also the low levels of productivity in education and health services.

Chapter 7 is an overview of services growth and implications to employment needs of the economy. K.V. Ramaswamy provides an assessment of the employment scenarios emerging from alternative growth scenarios for the services sector.

The author uses results of the NSSO survey of employment and unemployment for the years 1999–2000 and 2011–12 to make some preliminary projections of employment in the services sector up to the year 2020. The focus is on employment growth among workers in the age group 15 to 59 based on Usual Principal Status. The estimated projections of employment indicate that annual additions to service sector employment falls in the range of 2.4 million to 4.2 million based on the assumption that the services sector annual average output growth rate would be 9 per cent. This will make the share of services sector in the total working-age labour force go up from 30 per cent in 2011–12 to 33 per cent in 2020. Services sector employment is shown to be relatively skill-demanding.

In Chapter 8, Brinda Viswanathan examines diversity in services sector employment in India, using national-level household sample survey data for 2011–12.

The study shows that the services sector is able to absorb low-, medium- and high-skilled workers in different segments within it. However, there is a clear segmentation of lower-end services among the less educated, women, the socially disadvantaged, those in rural areas and those without a working knowledge of English.

A better ecosystem needs to be provided to include the better-skilled women in the work force.

1.3.3 *Part III: insights from sectoral experiences: education, financial services and the IT industry*

We present here three chapters that provide insights into the determinants of growth of specific sectors and implications of growth of specific services to a range of indicators that in turn influence overall growth in a sustainable manner.

In the first of the chapters in Part III, **Chapter 9**, Shika Sarvanabhavan and Meenakshi Rajeev analyse the financial services for the informal economy. The authors focus on the self-employed household enterprises, giving emphasis on the services sector. The authors draw attention to the observation that 'most of the occupations in the services sector in India are "poverty-induced and labour intensive". The productivity is much lower resulting in lesser income which in turn has a negative impact on poverty and growth'. However, in the prevailing conditions of the economy, the services sector does provide employment and help in income generation for a large labour force, and access to credit can enhance the productivity of the sector. The authors note the need for a focus on the small enterprises in services sector and to understand its various impediments to access to finance to improve growth.

Chapter 10 under Part III by P. Duraisamy examines the manner in which the education sector, a producer of a crucial services output, has expanded in the Indian context and whether the manner in which its output is measured reflects the contribution of education to the economy.

This chapter focuses on the issues relating to measurement of output of the education sector, and it examines alternative methodologies in this regard. The chapter points out that the method proposed by Jorgenson-Fraumeni to more accurately capture the impact of education results in 17 to 19 times higher its share in GDP than the current estimates of the educational services in the US. The trends in the share of education sector to GDP in India, its impact on improvements in quality of labour and also as an input in the production process, and returns to education are presented and discussed. The chapter also deals with the challenges and policy issues facing the education sector in India.

The final chapter in Part III by Balaji Parthasarathy presents an assessment of the factors that have helped the rise of the IT industry in the Indian economy and whether these conditions would sustain the growth of the industry in the coming years.

To shed light on the future of Indian ICT services, this chapter examines economist Robert Schware's proposition that 'walking on two legs', that is, the experience gained from a strong domestic market, is critical to entry and export success in the industry. But India's emergence as the world's largest exporter of a range of ICT services, including software, with considerably smaller production for the domestic market, challenges the proposition. Recently, however, the domestic market in India has become significant, that is, much after exports gained prominence. Since Schware does not offer an explanation for this apparent anomaly, this chapter seeks to provide one by emphasising how the socioeconomic value of ICTs comes from abstracting and encoding practices in various domains of human activity.

1.4 The key messages

While the various chapters in the present volume address a wide range of issues relating to India's services sector from different perspectives, they also have a common underlying purpose of exploring the high growth of the sector and its explanations and implications for the economy. In this section, we summarise some of the key messages that emerge from this analysis.

1.4.1 Nature of the services sector and India's advantages

The measurement and scope of the services sector included in India's National Accounts have improved with the adoption of System of National Accounts 2008 starting from 2011–12. However, certain services are embodied in other inputs in a systemic way, and their contribution in the economy is not adequately measured. A case in point is education or, for that matter, health. While the cost of providing these services may be based on direct costs, a healthy person or an educated person earns far more than those who do not possess these characteristics, but this additional value is not attributed directly to education or health. India's education sector has expanded, but its contribution to the economy may be far greater than the cost of providing education.

Historically, services have been a significant part of India's economy. Trading, shipping and financial services to enable these activities were organised along the community lines and the knowledge and expertise accumulated was significant. India's managerial skills appear to be greater in 'managing capital' than 'labour' and this advantage, besides the policies, may have led to preference to 'capital-intensive' sectors of the economy by the organised sector than the 'labour-intensive' sector. However, the 'labour intensity' in such production may not have been captured fully, as the education and skills of labour embodied in the capital-intensive sectors were greater than just the number of labour force employed. The post-Independence initial thrust to industrialisation also led to the need for more skilled and trained workers: scientists and engineers. The establishment of higher education institutions led to creation of a highly skilled labour force which has sustained the development of India's financial sector, information technology industry, communication technology, biotechnology and so on.

India's growth experience has also not been uniform across her states. There are states which have shown rapid growth and modernisation in the last three decades and have benefitted from the growth of services in varying degrees. The southern states of Karnataka, Andhra Pradesh and Tamil Nadu have established significant early presence in the production of 'modern services' such as IT and ITES. While the early development of the modern services in these sectors may have been aided by the presence of higher education institutions, the modern services have made forays into other regions of the country as well where the necessary infrastructure could develop.

The constraints need to be overcome to create new advantages. India now has its growing experience in working in global markets. There has been considerable expansion of educational institutions across the country and expansion of entrepreneurial skills on a wider scale than before. These are the sources of sustained growth for the economy in the medium term, even as the global frontiers of technology are changing the methods of manufacturing and delivering services.

1.4.2 *Services and macroeconomic factors*

An important dimension of modern services in the Indian context has also been the 'external component' driven by the IT services. Macroeconomic policies, such as exchange rate, foreign investment, migration – not only in India but also elsewhere – have an impact on the commercial performance of the sector. Innovations would be critical to make these services reach the domestic market, as the nature and structure of demand in the domestic market would be quite different from the markets in developed economies. It is interesting to note that empirical analysis presented in this volume points to the greater importance of non-price factors, such as FDI inflows, globalisation and the demand conditions, than just the exchange rate.

The overall macroeconomic structure in India has been changing radically. Services have a significant macroeconomic impact as they have become a large contributor to the tax revenues of the government. Transformation of domestic indirect taxes into a unified goods and services tax is affecting business decisions on the choice of sectors for investment and choice of locations for investment in a way that is different from the complex taxation system that preceded.

1.4.3 *Services as inputs*

Infrastructure services – transport, communications, storage – are the inputs in the production and distribution throughout the economy. Manufacturing and moving up the value chain or participation in global value chains require services matching global standards.

The intersectoral linkages have a bearing on sustainability of high growth of the services sector. The present status of modern services as inputs into the manufacturing process are yet to make India a source of globally competitive manufactured products. To offer better employment opportunities to a growing labour force, a growing manufacturing sector would be essential. The manufacturing sector presents a growth opportunity for services that would be mutually reinforcing.

The same is the case with linkages between agriculture and services. The production process is undergoing change because of both introduction of new technologies and changing conditions of production: smaller agricultural land holdings, increasing need to conserve natural resources, rising demand for labour from other sectors and the need to standardise, improve and deliver the products across long distances in short periods of time have placed stiff challenges to the agricultural producers. The onset of changing climate conditions globally presents another set of challenges for agriculture. Addressing these challenges will require innovative services and strengthen the inter-sectoral linkages of services, presenting an opportunity for sustained demand for services.

This perspective emphasises the need for a more balanced approach to policies across sectors. Sustained growth of the economy may require growth of many sectors, although international trade advantages will influence these opportunities. Policies also need to provide opportunities for scaling up of adoption of technologies by incentivising innovations that reduce the cost of services.

1.4.4 Employment and service sector growth

The issue of employment generation through services growth has attracted much debate. Have services provided only high-quality jobs in the economy? The emerging demographic dividend in the form of a large work force will require suitable jobs and suitably skilled workers for the jobs generated.

Disaggregated analysis of services sub-sectors shows that the sub-sectors growing at a fast pace do not generate a commensurate level of employment. A large chunk of employment that has been generated in the recent years has been in the construction sector, which engages less-skilled labour.

A business-as-usual scenario – extrapolating the growth to employment elasticities or trend growth rates – does not suggest that services growth would make a big dent on employment opportunities. The more granular assessment of the household- and individual-level sample survey data shows that education level, knowledge of the English language, gender, caste and regional location matter when it comes to being employed in more remunerative jobs. However, services such as trade, hotels, transport and communication do provide employment to those who are less educated and not familiar with the English language. The services sector may provide increased job opportunities for women, if other factors such as flexible working hours, physical safety and work environment in general would become favourable to women's participation in the work force, a major source of growth for the service sector.

1.4.5 Driving future growth: insights from selected sectors

Financial services are an enabling input to any business. The informal sector, particularly the businesses that are small and employ less-skilled labour, has been underserved traditionally by formal or institutional financial services. Enabling financial inputs to this small segment is necessary to help the small businesses to grow and achieve better commercial performance. A study reported in this volume, focusing on urban self-employed households, points to the need for a number of qualitative changes that may help improve financial services provision to the self-employed in the informal sector.

While there has been very significant policy push to achieve 'financial inclusion', seeking to make access to financial services universal, there is a need to design financial products that are suitable for different segments of the economy.

The contribution of sectors such as education and health may not be captured fully in the national income accounting; as it is measured by the cost of delivering such services, their impact on the economy cannot be underestimated. Embodiment of some of the services in the inputs used in production is reflected in the productivity of those inputs and not in the cost of services themselves.

How can IT services, which made India's presence felt in global business in the recent few decades, develop and exploit its domestic market? The chapter on the strategies for the IT sector to serve the domestic economy, in the present volume, argues for better understanding of the needs of the small and less-served sectors of the economy. Working in partnership with organisations that are assisting the poor, small and informal businesses to grow would provide the understanding needed to bring modern services to this large segment of the economy, especially in the context of the employment it provides to the millions of workers in the country.

The research on India's services growth has been large and growing. While the potential for growth is in evidence from the experience of the advanced economies, the path India has taken – moving to the modern services at an early stage of development – has been unusual. The explanations are several, but the opportunity has had its benefits. The sector's growth has pushed up the growth of the economy as a whole. However, much remains to be done to make modern services play the role of lifting the productivity of the other sectors and making them globally competitive. Modern services also must raise the productivity of the small, informal sectors to make these sectors productive. The role of modern services cannot be overemphasised even in raising the productivity of traditional services sectors such as tourism, a source of opportunities for investments and employment in the local areas.

It is these aspects that will make the high rate of services sector growth sustainable.

References

Eichengreen, B. and P. Gupta (2009, May). 'Two waves of service-sector growth', NBER Working Paper No. w14968, Cambridge.

Eichengreen, B. and P. Gupta (2011). 'The service sector as India's road to economic growth?', *India Policy Forum*, vol. 7, pp. 1–42, Sage India Publications, New Delhi.

Gordon, J. and P. Gupta (2004, September). 'Understanding India's services revolution', IMF Working Paper WP/04/171, Washington, DC. www.imf.org/en/Publications/WP/Issues/2016/12/31/Understanding-Indias-Services-Revolution-17573.

Krishna, K.L., Erumban, A.A., Das, D.K., Aggarwal, S. and P.C. Das (2017). 'Industry origins of economic growth and structural change in India', Working Paper No. 273, Centre for Development Economics, Delhi School of Economics, University of Delhi, New Delhi. www.cdedse.org/pdf/work273.pdf.

Part I

Understanding services growth

2 Can services lead the Indian economy?

V.N. Balasubramanyam and Ahalya Balasubramanyam

2.1 Introduction

'Wonder and dismay': this was the comment of a participant at one of the seminars on India's services sector. Wonder of how services could account for 58 per cent of India's GNP, as high as it is in the developed countries, and dismay that the economy with high levels of unemployment and poverty should harbour a large volume of services not generally known for their contribution to low-income groups and the poor. This chapter argues that whilst these concerns are understandable, they may not be as grave as all that. Most services are essentially inputs: they act as catalysts in the production process, they bridge the distance between the producers and consumers of goods and they promote regional diversification of production. They may not lead the economy, but they can augment and promote the contribution of manufacturing and agriculture to the process of development.

2.2 Extent and nature of services in India

The economic structure of the present-day high-income countries, such as the UK and the USA, can be said to conform to the Kuznets paradigm on growth and structural change. The central thesis of Kuznets is that income inequalities increase with economic growth at first, then reach a plateau as growth continues and decline in the third phase of growth. The thesis is based in the structural change that growth promotes. The process begins with growth in agricultural productivity that promotes manufacturing in more ways than one: income-induced growth in demand for manufactures, low-cost agricultural inputs and low real wage rates for labour released with the growth in agricultural productivity. This then results in the growth of the manufacturing sector and an increase in income inequalities. Further growth results in demand for goods and services with relatively high income elasticities, and the services sector expands. As growth progresses, the spread of demand for goods and services and employment lower income inequalities. This, then, is the Kuznets paradigm with a relationship amongst growth, income inequalities and structural change, beginning with agricultural growth followed by manufactures and then services. These sectoral changes would be accompanied by growth in employment in the manufacturing and service sectors and a reduction in that of agriculture. Such developments are mostly in the developed countries, such as the UK and the USA, where services account for more than 70 per cent of gross value added (GVA). These are countries that have transited from agriculture to services along with a productive manufacturing sector. In the main, it is growth of incomes that generates a demand for services. In contrast, in low-income countries services are lower down the scale, with agriculture contributing to the total output of the economy much more than services. India is an exception. The structure of its economy more nearly resembles that of the high- and middle- income countries than that of the low-income countries (Figure 2.1).

Eichengreen and Gupta (2009) recognise two phases in the growth in demand for services; the first phase occurs at low levels of income and peters out at around a per capita income of $1800, and the second phase of growth in demand for services occurs at around $4800 and decelerates after a time. In India, the first phase seems to have occurred at relatively lower levels of income than those observed in the developed countries. Eichengreen and Gupta's observation that the second wave of growth in demand for services is frequent in countries that are democracies, open to trade and near to financial centres has some relevance to the growth of services in India. A democratic style of government coupled with increasing openness to trade

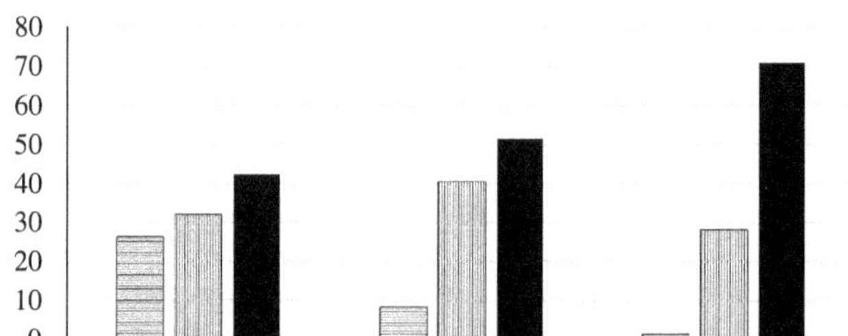

	Low income	Middle income	High income
Agr & allied	26.0	8.2	1.3
Industry	31.7	40.5	28.0
Services	42.3	51.3	70.7

Agr & allied   Industry   Services

Figure 2.1 Share of sectors in value added (%): 2017

Source: Data from the World Development Indicators, World Bank (Undated).

Notes: The figure provides data for only low-, middle- and high-income categories and does not include lower-middle and upper-middle categories; data for high-income category is not available for 2017 and what is shown is for 2016.

since the 1990s and proximity to financial centres complemented by the growth of the software sector are all features of the economy. In addition, the relatively high levels of income inequalities that generate a demand for a variety of producer and consumer services are also factors influencing the growth of India's services sector.

India harbours a varied services sector that accounts for 54 per cent of the GVA, alongside an agriculture sector that is none too efficient and a capital-intensive manufacturing sector that contributes 18 per cent to the national product and employs a bare 10 per cent of the labour force (Table 2.1)

The structure of services in India is varied, ranging from highly human capital–intensive such as business services encompassing information technology–oriented services, to those that are less intensive in human capital, but labour-intensive, such as hotel and restaurant services. Krishna et al. (2017) classify services into market and non-market services and further into 'IT-intensive' and 'non-IT-intensive' services and provide estimates of the contribution of different sub-sectors of services to value added and employment for the year 2011–12. Information and Communications Technology (ICT) oriented – 'IT-intensive' – services, within market services, accounted for 27 per cent of the value added (GVA) in the economy as a whole or nearly half of GVA from services. Those that are not intensive in ICT account for 7.8 per cent of the aggregate value added. The 'non-market services', mostly funded by the government, account for 20 per cent of the aggregate value added, of which education constitutes 4 per cent (Table 2.2).

'Human capital–intensive services', another class of services, including ICT ones and education account for around 31 per cent of services contribution to the value added of the economy. Services as a whole contribute 30 per cent of the total employment in the economy, nearly half of which originates

Table 2.1 Sectoral shares (%) of GVA (in basic prices) and Employment: India

Sector	*Gross Value Added, 2018–19 (%)*	*Employment, 2015 (%)*
Agriculture	14.4	47.2
Industry	31.3	23.0
Of which, Manufacturing	18.0	10.4
Services	54.3	29.8
Total Value	$1.9 trillion	472 million

Source: National Income Data from the RBI Database on the Indian Economy (RBI, Undated) for total GVA and its composition and employment shares derived from the Annual Employment and Unemployment Survey (GOI, 2016) Round 2015–16 and the total number of employed amongst 15 years and older population age group derived based on population projections in GOI (2016) cited earlier and World Bank (Undated).

Table 2.2 Relative contribution of service industries to gross value added and employment: 1980–2011

Sl. No.	*Sector*	*Share in nominal value added (%)*				*Share in employment (%)*			
		1980	*1990*	*2000*	*2011*	*1980*	*1990*	*2000*	*2011*
1	All Services	39.5	44.1	51.0	54.9	16.9	20.0	23.7	29.2
2	Market Services	19.4	23.6	29.9	35.5	9.1	11.9	15.4	18.4
2.1	ICT Intensive	14.8	17.4	22.5	27.7	6.4	8.4	10.8	12.6
2.1.1	Trade	10.7	11.7	13.2	15.9	5.8	7.4	9.2	9.7
2.1.2	Financial Services	3.0	3.9	5.4	5.7	0.3	0.5	0.6	0.9
2.1.3	Post & Telecom	0.6	0.9	1.5	1.1	0.1	0.2	0.3	0.4
2.1.4	Renting of Machinery & Business Services	0.5	0.9	2.4	5.0	0.2	0.3	0.7	1.6
2.2	ICT non-Intensive Services	4.6	6.2	7.4	7.8	2.7	3.5	4.6	5.8
2.2.1	Hotels & Restaurants	0.8	1.0	1.3	1.5	0.8	0.9	1.2	1.7
2.2.2	Transport & Storage	3.8	5.2	6.1	6.3	1.9	2.6	3.4	4.1
3	Non-market Services	20.2	20.5	21.0	19.5	7.9	8.1	8.4	10.9
3.1	Public Admin & Defense etc.	5.0	5.9	6.5	5.9	2.8	2.8	2.5	1.8
3.2	Education	2.5	3.1	4.1	3.9	1.6	1.6	2.2	3.0
3.2	Health & Social Work	0.9	1.2	1.6	1.4	0.6	0.6	0.7	1.0
3.3	Other Services	11.8	10.3	8.8	8.3	2.9	3.1	3.0	5.1

Source: Krishna et al. (2017).

in human capital–intensive services. The IT industry heads the list of human capital–intensive services. It also makes a significant contribution to the exports of the country. Exports of the IT industry as a whole in the fiscal year 2018 accounted for 75 per cent of the output of the industry valued at $167 billion (India Brand Equity Foundation, 2018). It is also a major provider of employment in the services sector, with 3.86 million direct jobs and a hefty 12 million indirect jobs. Its contribution as an input to other services, such as finance and banking, contributes to the human capital intensity of services in general.

In sum, the structure of services in India, given the significant share of ICT intensive sub-sectors, is approximately similar to that in the developed countries.

2.3 What explains the prominence of services in the economy of India?

There are two broad explanations for the observed structure of the economy of India: a historical and sociological one and the Nehru-Mahalanobis design of industrialisation implemented during the mid-1950s. A proximate reason for the prominence of services as opposed to manufacturing in the economy of India lies in India's history and sociology. The sort of education policies put in place during the fifties jelled with the aptitude and background of a select class of people that have for long years occupied positions of power and influence. India has always been an elitist society with its hierarchical caste system, dominated by the Brahmins, the ruling class, and the merchant class, all three commanding power and influence over education, trade and top-level administrative jobs. As Thirthankar Roy observes,

> the historical pattern of demand for education at all levels was biased towards certain castes and communities because these people had an inherited association with literate services. Groups that had contact with scribal professions, medicine, teaching, and priesthood, in the pre-colonial times, entered education, medicine and public administration in the colonial times. These classes and castes eagerly used the new schools and colleges, while other classes and castes entered schools on a smaller scale, and dropped out more readily. The correlation between family history of literate services, preference for service professions, and thus, preference for education, was especially close in the three port cities – Madras, Bombay, and Calcutta.
>
> (Roy, 2011)

Indeed, India's software industry of the present day reflects the sort of caste-oriented education that promoted services in the past. The industry is dominated by members of the middle class, mostly upper castes, especially the Brahmins, who were prominent in civil service jobs in the past (Upadhya, 2004).

Yet another factor allied to education is the predominance of trade and finance in India's economy for long. Business culture or managerial expertise and specialism is to be traced to several unique features of the Indian economy. Foremost of these is the inheritance from history. India has had a long history of business entrepreneurship marked by its caste and community orientation. Foremost amongst these groups are the Banias and the Marwaris, primarily merchants and money lenders, with a prominent role in financing India's foreign trade during the British colonial era. Allied to the caste orientation of the managers was the group or family orientation of firms. These firms produced a diverse range of products, but they all shared risks and drew on a pool of finance and information. They were also traders in their own right. Another group of entrepreneurs were the Parsis, who had no religious affiliation with the Hindu community and were in a class of their own. As Damodaran (2008) notes, the Parsis had special relationship with the British

> being part of neither the Hindu nor Muslim mainstream, nursing no political ambition and exposed to commercial influences because of their proximity to the ports of Bharuch, Surat, and Daman, the Parsis seemed ideal for recruitment as native brokers, agents and shippers.

It is also worth noting the significance of trade and finance in India's economic history through the ages, but especially from the British colonial days. As Roy notes, 'the ratio of trade to domestic product increased from a low of 1 to 2 per cent in 1800 to 20 per cent by 1914' (Roy, 2011). The predominance of trade and finance in India's economy over the years has shaped the managerial class as it exists today. Managers of the day in the private sector are 'market managers' rather than 'man managers'. They are adept at identifying markets for the products their firms produce, locating sources of finance and raising finance and exploring ways and means of acquiring sources of technology and know-how. They are not, however, adept at organising labour and managing engineering technology. In other words, Indian managers are adept at establishing and promoting service-oriented firms rather than manufacturing firms.

The other prominent reason for the growth of services in the economy is the Nehruvian strategy of industrialisation, grounded in ideology. As Nehru put it in his *The Discovery of India*,

> the problems of poverty and unemployment, of national defence and of economic regeneration in general cannot be solved without industrialisation. As a step towards such industrialisation, a comprehensive scheme of national planning should be formulated. This scheme should provide for the development of heavy key industries, medium scale industries and cottage industries.
>
> (Nehru, 1981)

National regeneration was to be achieved through self-sufficiency in investment goods that would in time produce consumer goods. Hence, the strategy, to be driven by the increased production of heavy engineering or capital goods in the short run, required a substantial allocation of investible resources to the capital goods sector. This strategy, though it may lead to a lower growth rate and low levels of consumption in the short run, would yield relatively high growth and consumption in the long run. Thus, there was an assumption of a low social discount rate in the sense that there would be more tomorrow if less was consumed today.

Promotion of capital goods production requires technology and know-how. This too was to be produced indigenously through the promotion of science and engineering education. Towards this end, a number of higher education establishments were founded, and they did yield the sort of human capital that was desired. The Indian Institutes of Management and Institutes of Technology that were initiated during the decade of the fifties now number 19 and 17, respectively. According to the data published in the Statistical Abstract of India, there were a total of 15,703 degree-awarding institutions of higher education in the country at the end of the year 2001–02. These institutions have now provided the sort of human capital required by the service industries.

But why haven't they served the manufacturing sector too? Why is it that the manufacturing sector, and for that matter the agriculture sector too, lags behind services? The proximate answer to these questions is that capital-intensive firms and industries do not require the sort of management and organisation that labour-intensive technologies require. As Hirschman says, 'labour-intensive technologies by their very nature require much more intensive organisation and supervision than capital-intensive technologies' (Hirschman, 1958).

The higher education institutions established to produce skilled technicians and managers required for the operation of state-supported capital-intensive technology industries seemed to have delivered what was required of them. Indeed, the number of graduates with higher education produced by these institutions may have been surplus to requirements. The relaxation of immigration regulations and constraints by the USA, during the decades of the seventies and eighties, appears to have provided a vent for surplus for the graduates the system had produced. These emigrants or the Indian diaspora were a factor of significance in the growth of the software sector in India. Many of them returned back home to establish software firms and several others headed American-owned firms that invested in software in India (Balasubramanyam and Balasubramanyam, 2002).

Other reasons for the failure of India to establish labour-intensive manufacturing firms, such as those in China, include labour laws and regulations that the capitalists were none too happy with and the myriad rules and regulations that business entrepreneurs intending to start up manufacturing firms had to cope with. There was also the reservation of large chunks of manufacturing, much of it with an export potential, for the small-scale industries that for various reasons failed to deliver.

Summing up, the birth and rapid growth of India's services sector and the absence of a large labour-intensive manufacturing sector are to be traced to India's factor endowments: human capital– and services-oriented managerial expertise. These developments are grounded in India's history and culture. It should be added that the growth in services is not due to an increase in the price of services relative to that of manufactures that would escalate their size in value terms, nor is it due to the so-called splintering effect, where services that were performed along with goods production, as in the case of painting of cars, is outsourced to those specialising in services – for example, painting of cars (Nayyar, 2014). It is, though, possible that the firms specialising in the services that are outsourced may experience growth in productivity (Bhagwati, 2004) and experience rapid growth relative to the other states.

2.4 Services – the leading sector of the economy?

Whilst there are several explanations for the growth of services in the Indian economy, the issue of concern is the following: can services lead the economy and provide the badly needed jobs and incomes for the lower-income groups and the ones living in poverty? Could it lead the economy both as a sector on its own and as a complement to other sectors?

One of the well- known definitions of services is this:

> A service may be defined as a change in the condition of a person, or of a good belonging to some economic unit, which is brought about as a result of the activity of some other economic unit, with prior agreement of the former person or economic unit.
>
> (Hill, 1977)

This definition, though it seems to relate to personal services, does emphasise the role of services in changing the condition of a good. Such a change can take several forms, including increased utility of the good, differentiation of the good or product, increased marketability of the good and changes in the production process of the good that increases its productivity. In sum, services act as catalysts in the production process of goods and other services as well. It is in this broad sense that they can be a leading sector in the economy; they facilitate the growth of the other sectors.

What are the features of a leading sector? How does it lead the other sectors? The Ministry of Finance in its Economic Survey 2014–15 (Government of India, 2015) suggests a set of criteria for a sector to be the engine of growth. The five criteria are (i) high level of productivity, (ii) domestic and international convergence of productivity, (iii) expansion, (iv) alignment with comparative advantage and (v) tradability. India's manufacturing sector complies with the first and second criteria but none of the others. The services sector seems to satisfy the growth and convergence criteria, but not the alignment with the comparative advantage criteria, as is commonly interpreted. One of the notable features of the Ministry's report is its acknowledgement that neither sector satisfies all the criteria and the policy makers have to decide whether to embrace the Chinese model or the skills development model.

This is a conclusion that seems obvious, and the Ministry's tilt towards skill intensification seems to be much more appealing than the suggestion of following the Chinese example. For one thing, establishing and organising labour-intensive manufacturing is not the comparative advantage of India, as argued in the previous section, and for another it would be almost impossible to snatch international markets from the long-established Chinese and other Asian exporters of labour-intensive goods. The alternative is to promote services as the leading sector. Again in our view, India's comparative advantage lies in the utilisation of the skills it possesses, the ones that have promoted the services sector.

Components of the services sector, such as business services that includes IT-related activities, seem to be converging both at home and abroad. The only Ministry of Finance criterion that it does not satisfy is that it is not aligned with the comparative advantage of the country in unskilled labour. This is a very broad reading of the comparative advantage of the country. The country has a comparative advantage in unskilled labour only on account of the sheer numbers of labourers, but it possesses neither the organisation nor the managerial skills to effectively exploit the so-called advantage. It would not be amiss to say that India's factor endowments centre on human capital and its comparative advantage is in human capital–intensive services. There are echoes of the Leontief paradox in this interpretation of India's comparative advantage. As is well known, Leontief, based on input-output model-based estimates for the year 1954, argued that contrary to received wisdom, exports of the USA were labour-intensive and imports capital-intensive. The explanation for the result is that US labour is skill-intensive, with each skilled labourer equivalent to four unskilled labourers. It may not be erroneous to apply a similar accounting system to estimate the human capital or skill labour endowments of India. One indicator is the high proportion of India's technology and human capital–intensive exports of manufactures: 61 per cent of total exports of $313 billion in the year 2013–14, of which 49 per cent consisted of chemicals, machinery and gems and jewellery. Add to this $99 billion of software exports (25 per cent of total exports). India's exports do look capital- and human capital–intensive. It is India's endowments of human capital that the country owes to its history and the promotion of human capital–intensive industries in the early years of industrialisation, followed by the breakthrough in the production of software during the decade of the eighties that explains the significant presence of services in the economy.

How best to utilise the endowment of services to promote development? The services sector on its own contributes around 28 per cent to the total employment in the economy, with market-oriented services accounting for 18 per cent of the total. Analyses also show that services contribute much more to the growth of national income than agriculture and manufacturing (Krishna et al., 2016). The issue of significance is how services can be utilised to promote not only income growth but also employment in the economy.

It is essential to keep in mind the obvious fact, emphasised earlier, that most though not all services are inputs and not final products. This is especially so in the case of business services that include finance, insurance and IT services. It is the effective utilisation of the inputs to produce final goods and services that is the central task facing policy makers. The 'Make in India' call should be responded to by utilising the service sector inputs to make final goods and not with attempts to imitate the Chinese model. There are several ways in which this can be done. The first is through the utilisation of services to increase the productivity of agriculture and industry. In other words, utilise services to promote the adoption of modern know-how by labour in agriculture and the unorganised sector of manufacturing. The second is utilisation of services to increase the observed trend in outsourcing the production of components of manufacturing from the firms in the organised sector to those in the unorganised sector. The third is utilisation of services in promoting non-farm production activities in the rural sector that would include migration of manufacturing firms to rural areas. IT services would be central in implementing all of these suggestions. Finance, transport and insurance services could contribute to the marketing of the products produced in the rural sector. In sum, the issue is not one of the role of services vs manufacturing in promoting development but one of utilising the complementarity between the two sectors, exploiting the potential of services in promoting labour skills required in manufacturing and agriculture and in assisting the regional spread of industry. Eichengreen and Gupta (2009) provide a detailed discussion of the debate on services vs manufacturing.

It is encouraging to note that the model we advocate, though in its infancy, is gathering momentum. In states such as Tamil Nadu, the production of components and parts for industries such as motor cars are being moved to rural areas (Ghani, Goswami and Kerr, 2012). The training of rural labour in these cases is organised with the utilisation of computer technology. Demonstration of the production process on a computer screen to the unskilled and semi-skilled labour could be effective in training them for the task. It is of interest that an empirical analysis of urbanisation of industry across states in India finds that there is a significant movement of plants in formal manufacturing to rural areas, whilst informal-sector firms from rural areas are moving into urban areas (Ghani, Goswami and Kerr, 2012). The role of services in both the movement of informal-sector firms to urban areas and vice versa in the case of formal-sector firms could be considerable. The former tend to be labour-intensive activities and the latter are capital-intensive. In both cases, IT services could be of significance in facilitating the cross-regional movement of production. In sum, services in their role as inputs can facilitate growth and development. Their role can be looked upon as a leading sector insofar as they facilitate the growth of employment and incomes for those on the lower rungs of the economic transformation. In this sense, service inputs would be the catalysts in the entire production process in the economy.

2.5 Conclusions

This chapter has argued that the structure of the Indian economy, with services as the major sector contributing to national income, is nothing unexpected or inexplicable. Its origins and growth are to be traced to India's economic history and organisation of the society that has provided the sort of education and managerial know-how that facilitates the growth of services. The chapter also argues that services can be effectively utilised to promote both growth and development in the economy. Eichengreen and Gupta's remark that democracy is a factor in the growth of services seems to be of significance in the world's largest and most diversified democratic country, with its varied spoken languages, millions of Gods the population worships and varied food habits (Eichengreen and Gupta, 2009). The historian Ramachandra Guha's lighthearted remark that this diversified country is held together by the English language, cricket and Lata Mangeshkar in a way underscores the significance of services in India.

References

Balasubramanyam, V.N. and A. Balasubramanyam (2002). 'The software cluster in Bangalore', in J.H. Dunning (ed.) *Regions, Globalization and the Knowledge-Based Economy*, Oxford University Press, Oxford.

Bhagwati, J.N. (2004, June). 'Splintering and disembodiment of services and developing nations', *World Economy*, 7(2), 133–143.

Damodaran, H. (2008). *India's New Capitalists: Caste, Business and Industry in a Modern Nation*, Palgrave Macmillan, London.

Eichengreen, B. and P. Gupta (2009). 'The two waves of service sector growth', NBER Working Paper 14968. www.nber.org/papers/w14968.

Ghani, E., Goswami, A.G. and W.R. Kerr (2012). 'Is India's manufacturing sector moving out of the cities', NBER Working Paper No. 17992.

Government of India (2016). *Report on Fifth Annual Employment: Unemployment Survey (2015–16)*, Ministry of Labour & Employment, Labour Bureau, Chandigarh. http://labourbureaunew.gov.in/UserContent/EUS_5th_1.pdf.

Hill, T.P. (1977). 'On goods and services', *Review of Income and Wealth*, 23(4), 315–338.

Hirschman, A. (1958). *Strategy of Economic Development*, Yale University Press, New Haven.

India Brand Equity Foundation (2018, December). 'Indian IT, ITes & BPM Industry Analysis'. https://www.ibef.org/download/it-ites-dec-2018.pdf.

Krishna, K.L., Das, D.K., Abdul, E., Aggarwal, S. and C.D. Pilu (2016). 'Productivity dynamics in India's service sector: An industry level perspective', Working Paper No. 261, Centre for Development Economics, Delhi School of Economics, New Delhi.

Krishna, K.L., Erumban, A.A., Das, D.K., Aggarwal, S. and P.C. Das (2017). 'Industry origins of economic growth and structural change in India', Working Paper No. 273, Centre for Development Economics, Delhi School of Economics, University of Delhi, New Delhi. www.cdedse.org/pdf/work273.pdf.

Nayyar, G. (2014). *The Services Sector in India's Development*, Cambridge University Press, New York.

Nehru, J.L. (1981). *Discovery of India*, Jawaharlal Nehru Memorial Fund, New Delhi.

RBI (Undated). 'Databank on Indian economy'. https://dbie.rbi.org.in/DBIE/dbie.rbi?site=statistics.

Roy, T. (2011). *The Economic History of India, 1757–2010*, 3rd ed., Oxford University Press, New Delhi.

Upadhya, C. (2004). 'A new transnational capitalist class? Capital flows, business networks, and entrepreneurs in the Indian software industry', *Economic and Political Weekly*, 39(48), 5141–5151.

World Bank (Undated). 'World development indicators', www.wdi.org.

3 Service tax in India

Story of its evolution and amalgamation with goods taxation

R. Srinivasan

3.1 Backdrop

Expanding the tax base, simplifying tax procedures, reducing tax rates and removing tax exemptions were the major aspects of tax reforms in the early 1990s. One of the ways to expand the tax base was to tax the services, which were not taxed until then. Though contribution of the service sector to national income was already high, it did not attract the attention of fiscal managers until the Raja Chelliah Committee report (Government of India, 1993) made a strong case for a service tax.

Though the service tax started with just three services in 1993–94, its importance grew after the customs duty reforms in 1995. As a founder member of the World Trade Organization, India had to lower the tariff barriers on imports and encourage exports through subsidies only in a limited way. This reduced the tax potential of the central government, because customs duty was a major revenue earner until then. Service tax came in handy as a compensating source of tax revenue at this juncture.

The progress of the service tax has been dramatic in terms of expanding its base as well as increasing its contribution to the state exchequer. Now the service tax has entered a yet another stage in its evolution, as it is being subsumed under the goods and services tax (GST). In this chapter, the next two sections deal with the arguments for the levy of tax on services and the conceptual evolution of service tax. In the last two sections, the trend in service tax revenue and the issues to be resolved in the context of subsuming service tax under GST are discussed.

3.2 The case for service tax

The case for service tax in the present form, apart from raising revenue to meet the expanding public expenditure needs, is justified in terms of efficiency and equity principles of taxation. Service tax is not a newfound devise in the early 1990s, as we know that hotel and restaurant services, advertisements, electricity, transport services and entertainment and gambling services were already taxed either as commodities or as specific tax bases by central and state governments (Rao, 2001). But the growth of the service sector's contribution to India's national income was a first trigger to tax this hitherto inadequately taxed and enlarging part of the economy. The service sector, excluding public administration and defence, gradually evolved as the single largest sector in the Indian economy. Its contribution to the net domestic product increased from 29 per cent in 1950–55 to 31 per cent in 1970–75 and then to 37 per cent in 1990–95. In 2011–12, the service sector's contribution to the gross value added (GVA) was 42.8 per cent, which increased to 46.4 per cent in 2014–15. When more than one-half of the economy remains outside the taxation, then it amounts to not only loss of revenue but also efficiency loss due to the wedge between untaxed and taxed sectors of production. The distortion is also due to adding a part of the cost of production on to the cost of services, which is untaxed. The famous example is the greater post-sales service cost of automobiles and consumer durables by the producers than the cost of production of the products. Further, with the aid of modern technology, the characteristics of goods and services remain indistinguishable; hence, some parts of production may escape from taxation under the disguise of non-taxable characteristics of the service (Bagchi, 2004). The equity principle of taxation demands equal taxes on the production of both goods and services. When goods and services are inputs in each other's production system, under the value added tax (VAT) system, a break in the tax chain could be avoided only by taxing both goods and services equally. Zero rating of exports of goods and services also requires this (Rao, 2001).

3.3 Conceptualising service tax

Service tax in its present form has a history of less than 25 years. The framers of the Constitution of India did not visualise the tax on services; hence, it was not listed in the powers of the Union or state governments or even in the concurrent list. The central government, using the residual power vested on it, started the tax on services in July 1994.[1] Previously the Raja Chellaiah Committee on Tax Reforms (1991–93) recommended this tax to increase tax revenue of the central government. The service tax started with three services with a 5 per cent tax rate, and then both the number of services and tax rates were increased. Obviously, the tax revenue collection was also increasing, thus encouraging further tax reforms.

The Report of the Expert Group on Taxation of Services (Government of India, 2001) and the Report of the Task Force on Fiscal Responsibility and Budget Management Act 2004 (Government of India, 2004) recommended substantial changes in the service tax. M.G. Rao, who chaired the Expert Group on Taxation of Services, suggested to bring the service tax under VAT providing input tax credit and ultimately to integrate with Central VAT (CENVAT) for excise on goods (Rao, 2001). He also suggested a dual VAT so that states also could get the authority to tax the services. Consequently,

Service Tax Credit Rules, 2002 (Government of India, 2002), provided input tax credit in a restrictive manner. Credit for tax on input service was provided when both the input and output services were from the same category. This restriction was removed in 2003 and the Service Tax Credit Rules were replaced by CENVAT credit rules in 2004. This provided credit for taxes paid on all inputs – services, intermediate inputs and capital goods. This made service tax a fully non-cascading tax as that of excise duty.

In order to formalise the service tax, The Constitutional (eighty-eighth Amendment) Act, 2003, was enacted to insert article 268A and entry 92C in the List I (Union List).[2] Further, this act also brought the net service tax revenue into the divisible pool so that it could be divided between the centre and state governments as per the recommendations of the Finance Commission.

In 2005, Export of Services Rules were introduced and accordingly a taxable service could be exported without payment of service tax and the central government might also give some tax rebates. In 2006, taxation on import of services was introduced and administered as per Taxation of Services (Provided from Outside India and Received in India) Rules, 2006. Normally, if the service provider is within India, then such a service provider should pay the service tax. If the service provider is from outside India and the receiver of service is in India, then the receiver should pay the service tax.

Rao (2001) placed a compulsive argument for a comprehensive service tax. That is, he argued to give up the selective approach of listing the services under the tax law, which effectively meant that those services not listed would be outside the service tax net. Instead he argued for a negative list, so that only services in the negative list could not be taxed and all other services would be subjected to service tax. This not only gives a comprehensive service tax but also broadens the tax base and makes it more buoyant. The negative list concept was introduced in 2012. A negative list of services has been provided under section 66D of the Finance Act, 1994. This negative list was prepared as per the best practices around the world and including those services that should not be taxed given the Indian peculiarities. Some of the prominent items in the negative list are services of government, department of posts, life insurance, Reserve Bank of India, services relating to agriculture, and transmission of electricity.

Until the concept of a negative list was introduced, there was no need for a comprehensive definition of the term 'service', because only the listed services were subjected to tax. The term 'service' was defined in section 65B (44) of the Finance Act, 1944, to mean any activity for consideration (other than the items excluded therein) carried out by a person for another and to include a declared service. Section 66E of the Finance Act, 1994, lists the declared services. Therefore, a service is taxable if it is a declared service or such a service is not in the negative list. Further, section 93 of the Finance Act, 1994, provides power to grant exemption from service tax for a taxable service or a part of it. After 2012, the service tax became a comprehensive and non-cascading tax; consequently, it became more buoyant.

3.4 Trend in service tax revenue

Until2012, the growth rate in service tax revenue was positive but also quite haphazard (Table 3.1). As the number of services was increasing, so also was the number of tax assesses. The highest growth rate of service tax revenue was 112 per cent in 1995–96 and the lowest growth rate was –4.13 per cent in 2009–10. Most of the high-yielding services were included in the first few years; the growth rates of revenue as well as assesses were lower during 1996–2003. As input tax credit was extended to service tax since 2003 and a greater number of services was brought into the tax net, the growth rate of revenue was high until2007. Thereafter, the growth rate came down.

As pointed out previously, the second major change in the service tax was the introduction of a negative list in 2012. We need to separately discuss the trend in service tax revenue since then.

From Table 3.2 we can infer that the growth of service tax revenue was impressive from 2012. The service tax revenue increased nearly 115 per cent

Table 3.1 Trend in service tax revenue: 1994–2012

Year	*Service Tax Revenue ('crore)*	*% Growth over Previous Year*	*No. of Services in Tax Net*	*No. of Assessees*	*% Growth over Previous Year*	*Tax Rate % (Excluding Cesses)*
1994–95	407	–	3	3943	–	5
1995–96	862	112	6	4866	23.41	5
1996–97	1059	23	6	13982	187.34	5
1997–98	1586	50	18	45991	228.93	5
1998–99	1957	23	26	1,07,479	133.70	5
1999–2000	2128	9	26	1,15,495	7.45	5
2000–01	2613	23	26	1,22,326	5.91	5
2001–02	3302	26	41	1,87,577	53.34	5
2002–03	4122	25	52	2,32,048	23.71	5
2003–04	7891	91	62	4,03,856	74.04	8, 10
2004–05	14,200	80	75	7,74,988	91.89	10
2005–06	23,055	62	84	8,46,155	9.18	10
2006–07	37,598	63	99	9,40,641	11.17	12
2007–08	51,301	36	100	10,73,075	14.08	12
2008–09	60,941	19	106	12,04,570	8.78	12,10
2009–10	58,422	-4.13	109	13,07,286	8.53	10
2010–11	71,016	22	117	13,72,274	4.97	10
2011–12	97,509	37	119	15,35,570	11.90	12
2012–13	1,32,518	36	Negative list	17,12,617	11.53	12

Source: Central Board of Excise and Customs, Government of India (Undated).

Note: Figures for 2012–13 are provisional.

Table 3.2 Trend in service tax revenue: 2011–16

Year	*GVA at Current Prices (Rs Crore)*	*Service Sector Contribution to GVA** (Rs Crore)*	*Service Tax*			*No. of Registrations (lakh)*	*No. of Returns Filed (lakh)*
			(Rs Crore)	*As % Total GVA*	*As % Ser. Contribution to GVA (SSC)*		
2011–12	81,06,656	34,70,634	97,509	1.20	2.81	15.5	1.9
2012–13	92,10,023	40,62,066	1,32,601	1.44	3.26	17.5	7.3
2013–14	1,03,80,813	46,70,505	1,54,778	1.49	3.31	19.8	8.5
2014–15	1,14,72,409	53,25,944	1,67,969	1.46	3.15	22.6	9.8
2015–16*	1,22,98,422	58,16,249	2,10,000 (Revised Estimate)	1.71	3.61	25.1	10.5

Source: Budget Papers (Government of India, Various Years) and CSO (Various Years), Delhi.

Notes: *- estimates of GVA and service sector contribution (SSC) based on estimates published by CSO (Various Years), New Delhi.

** net of value addition by public administration and defence.

in 2015–16 compared to that of 2011–12, whereas during the same period, the rates of increase of GVA and service sector contribution (SSC) were 51 per cent and 68 per cent, respectively. This is reflected in the steady increase in tax-GVA ratio and tax-SSC ratio during this period. The SSC is net of value addition by public administration and defence, as consumption of these two services are excluded from the service tax.

Generally, the growth in service tax revenue is also attributable to the growth in the number of service tax registrations and number of tax returns filed. But on an average only a little over 40 per cent of those who have obtained service tax registrations have been filing tax returns.

Telecommunication is the single largest revenue contributor to the service tax. This is followed by general insurance premium, manpower recruitment, business support services and works contract. Table 3.3 shows the revenue generated from each of these services.

The annual growth rates of revenue from each of the services have been consistently more than 20 per cent in most of the years. The growth rates of revenue from these services could be more than the growth rates of value addition by them.

In spite of the fact that the growth in revenue has been steady and was increasing during 2012–16, yet further improvement in revenue collection is a possibility. The fact that only a little over 40 per cent of the registered service providers file tax returns shows that there should be a substantial tax base that had gone untapped. Further, another reason for the low tax-SSC ratio could be the inadequacies in the tax administration system.

The Comptroller and Auditor General's (CAG) report in 2015 (CAG, 2015) was on levy and collection of service tax on works contract.[3] The

Table 3.3 Service tax from major service categories (Rs crore)

Category	*2011–12*	*2012–13*	*2013–14*	*2014–15*	*2015–16*
Telecommunication	3902	5402 (38)	7538 (40)	12648 (68)	13531 (7)
General Insurance Premium	3877	5234 (35)	6321 (21)	8834 (40)	9263 (5)
Manpower Recruitment	2870	3847 (34)	4432 (15)	7335 (66)	9045 (23)
Business Support Services	2689	4345 (62)	4368 (0.5)	7118 (63)	8415 (18)
Works Contract	3092	4179 (35)	4455 (7)	7434 (67)	8139 (9)

Source: CAG (2016).

Note: Figures in parentheses are growth percentage over previous year.

report was based on the audit of 237 service tax assessees and the following observations were made.

1. On examination of records from data/dump-data relating to works contractors gathered from various sources, we identified 425 works contractors who had executed works contracts and had neither registered with the department nor paid service tax of Rs 447.76 crore.
2. CAG observed 145 cases of non/short-payment of service tax of Rs 44.74 crore.
3. Thirty-four cases of irregular availing/utilisation of CENVAT credit involving an amount of Rs 22.59 crore were found.
4. Fourteen cases of incorrect availing of exemptions involving an amount of Rs 17.81 crore were deducted.
5. Forty-four cases of incorrect application of rate of service tax and non/short-payment of interest of Rs 8.84 crore were also deducted.

These observations clearly show that the tax collection system needs further improvement in order to mobilise more legitimate tax revenue under the service tax.

Another important reason for the under recovery of service tax revenue was the litigations in various courts, appellate authorities and cases pending in the departmental adjudication process. The CAG's report in 2016 (CAG, 2016) says, as per the Finance Ministry's declaration, the amount of service tax revenue to be recovered from cases pending before the department authorities and courts was Rs 1.72 lakh crore in 2013–14 and then it increased to Rs 2.32 lakh crore in 2015–16.

The contribution of the informal sector in the total economy was 55 per cent in 1999–2000 and then reduced to 50 per cent in 2004–05; similarly in the service sector the informal part was 55 per cent and then reduced to 51 per cent during these two years (Kolli and Sinharay, 2011). Hence, when more than 50 per cent of the economy, particularly in the service sector, is non-formal, then to that extent the tax base is reduced correspondingly. This also partially explains the low service tax–SSC ratio of a little more than 3 per cent.

Further, the service tax is zero rated for service exports. On this count, also there could be loss of revenue to the central government. India's net service export in 2012–13 was Rs 3,53,217 crore, which was 8.7 per cent of the SSC. In the previous year, that is, in 2011–12 the net service export was 8.8 per cent of SSC. Thus, higher level of service export also reduces the tax base of service tax.

Though service tax is a newfound instrument to increase revenue of the government on one side, it is also essential to address the issues of equity between taxed and non-taxed sectors of the economy. As expected, the service tax is gaining importance both due to the growth of the service sector and the consequent contribution of tax revenue to the state exchequer.

In spite of the increasing service tax–GVA and service tax–SSC ratios, there is still scope to increase this tax revenue through better tax administration and by bringing a greater part of the service economy into the formal sector.

3.5 Issues in service tax under GST[4]

Service tax has been a VAT under the central government until the launching of GST in 2017. Some of the services like information technology and restaurants were taxed as services by the central government and as goods by the state governments under VAT. This amounted to cascading and double taxation, which the GST is expected to resolve.

But GST is quite likely to create new problems. One, the existing service tax rate is 14 per cent and in addition there are various cesses like Swatch Bharat Cess and Krishi Kalyan Cess. Though these cesses will be done away with in GST, the GST rate in many cases is 18 per cent or more. This will impact the prices of services to the consumer.

Two, the service tax will be divided between the centre and state governments, as GST is a dual tax. Though this gives an additional tax base to the state governments, it reduces the revenue potential of the central government.

Three, with GST being a dual tax, there are conflicting claims to power to administering the GST as far as services are concerned. In the first meeting of the GST Council,[5] the central government wanted to retain the tax administration of the existing service tax registrants and was ready to share administrative powers with the states as far as new service tax registrants are concerned. But states have opposed this proposal. Rather the states suggested a cross-empowerment model (that is, both state and central governments could administer concurrently) for the top service tax assessees. The cross-empowerment model could considerably complicate tax administration and increase the compliance cost of tax.

There are also issues in certain sectors like construction where they should pay GST on both goods and services. In the last GST Council meeting held on December22–23, 2016, the central government proposed a vertical division of assessees; that is, all the assessees irrespective of turnover will be divided between central and state governments. The states have been asking for exclusive administrative power over smaller assessees with an annual turnover of less than Rs 1.5 crore and cross-empowerment over all other assessees. This remains an unresolved issue even today.

Four, the issues of multiple registrations and filing of returns under GST is unavoidable. If a service provider has customers across all the states, until the emergence of GST they had to file returns only to the central government. Now the service provider should file returns for central GST (CGST) to the central government and for state GST (SGST) to the respective state governments. This will be complicated if there is cross-empowerment or concurrent administration by central and state governments.

Five, zero rating for export of services is easier when there is only a service tax. Under GST, the zero rating of service exports would require tax refunds under both CGST and SGST. This is also applicable for export of goods. So we should have a seamless process for tax refunds whenever services are exported, particularly from SGST.

3.6 The way forward

The service sector is a major tax base in India. The service tax system has matured and is ready to transform further under GST. Increasing the tax rate on services under GST is an unavoidable change that would ensure equity in taxation between goods and services. To simplify tax administration, rational division of mutually exclusive powers of tax administration between central and state governments should be preferred to cross-empowerment. Horizontal division of all business establishments engaged in production and/or sale of goods and services between central and state governments would solve this problem. This will also enable seamless tax credit and tax refunds for exports as well as interstate trade in goods and services and reduce compliance cost of tax.

Notes

1 Entry 97 of the Union List states 'any other matter not enumerated in List II (State List) and List III (Concurrent List) including any tax not mentioned in either of the those lists' is treated as a residuary entry.

2 268A. Service tax levied by Union and collected and appropriated by the Union and the States. (1) Taxes on services shall be levied by the Government of India and such tax shall be collected and appropriated by the Government of India and the States in the manner provided in clause (2). (2) The proceeds in any financial year of any such tax levied in accordance with the provisions of clause (1) shall be (a) collected by the Government of India and the States; (b) appropriated by the Government of India and the States, in accordance with such principles of collection and appropriation as may be formulated by Parliament by law.
92C – Taxes on Services.

3 Works contract means a contract wherein transfer of property in goods involved in the execution of such contract is leviable to tax as sale of goods and such contract is for the purpose of carrying out construction, erection, commissioning, installation, completion, fitting out, repair, maintenance, renovation, alteration of any movable or immovable property or for carrying out any other similar activity or a part thereof in relation to such property. However, services provided by way of construction, erection, commissioning, installation, completion, fitting out, repair, maintenance, renovation or alteration of a road, bridge, tunnel or terminal for road transportation for use by the general public were exempted from the service tax.

4 This chapter was written just before the introduction of GST. However, many of the apprehensions expressed here have been addressed. For instance, GST on construction services and restaurants have been well designed. Initially, the registration and tax compliance was complex, and it is being made simpler over time, though we wait for a much easier process to come.

5 The GST Council is a constitutional authority consisting representatives from 29 states and two Union Territories with assemblies and finance minister and deputy finance minister from the central government. This council should decide on the GST laws, systems of GST administration and fixation of GST rates. All the states and the central government should accept the recommendations of the GST Council.

References

Bagchi, A. (2004, May). 'Taxing services: The way forward', *Economic and Political Weekly*, 39(19), 1876–1879.

CAG (2015). *Report on Levy and Collection of Service Tax on Works Contract*, Comptroller and Auditor General of India, Government of India, New Delhi.

CAG (2016). *Report No 1: Report on Central Government Revenue for Year Ending March 2015: Indirect Tax–Service Tax*, Comptroller and Auditor General of India, Government of India, New Delhi.

Central Board of Customs and Indirect Taxes (Undated). 'Analysis of service tax revenue', Department of Revenue, Ministry of Finance, Government of India, New Delhi.www.cbic.gov.in/resources//htdocs-servicetax/ovw/ovw4_analysis-st-rev-ason120913.pdf.

CSO (Various Years). *National Accounts Statistics*, Ministry of Statistics and Programme Implementation, Government of India (GoI), New Delhi.

Government of India (1993). *Report of the Tax Reforms Committee*, Ministry of Finance, New Delhi.

Government of India (2001). *Report of the Expert Group on Taxation of Services*, Ministry of Finance, New Delhi.

Government of India (2002). 'Service tax credit rules', www.ieport.com/service_tax/service_tax_credit_rules_2002.htm (Accessed on 08/09/2018).

Government of India (2004). *Report of the Task Force on Fiscal Responsibility and Budget Management Act*, Ministry of Finance, New Delhi.

Government of India (Various Years). *Budget Papers*, Ministry of Finance, New Delhi.

Kolli, R. and A. Sinharay (2011). 'Share of informal sector and informal employment in GDP and employment', *Journal of Income and Wealth*, 33(2), as cited in National Statistical Commission (2012). Report of the Committee on Unorganised Sector Statistics, Government of India.

Rao, M.G. (2001, October 20–26). 'Taxing services: Issues and strategy', *Economic and Political Weekly*, 36(42), 3999–4006.

4 Exchange rate and India's services exports

Manoranjan Sahoo and M. Suresh Babu

4.1 Introduction

The ever-growing importance of international trade flows in the global economy in recent times has induced emerging and developing economies to follow an export-led growth strategy. Further, it is also argued that higher rates of growth of an economy can be generated not only by the increased participation of labour and capital in production, as proposed in the classical growth models, but also by expanding exports to wider international markets (Pradhan, 2010). Following the success of East Asian countries, India followed the export-led growth strategy in 1990s as a part of its economic reforms programme comprising liberalisation, privatisation and more open economic policies (Sahoo and Dash, 2014). India has also been able to register significant improvements in the quantum of services exports in the last two decades, as illustrated in Figure 4.1. While India's goods export is showing a decreasing trend, its services export is showing an increasing trend over the period, and also the services export is found to increase significantly after the economic reforms of 1991. Services exports have increased from 15.27 per cent of total exports in 1975 to 32.16 per cent of total exports in 2014, a doubling of the share in this time period (World Development Indicators, 2016) and further to 38 per cent in 2017 (Ministry of Finance, 2019). Further, services export also plays an important role in augmenting the current account balance reducing deficits in goods trade.

Given the rising importance of exports in achieving economic growth, many theoretical and empirical models have found an adverse impact of exchange rate movements on the growth of exports. One of the major theoretical formulation is the well-known Mundell-Fleming (M-F) model. The basic argument of M-F model is that in a small open economy, the nominal wage remaining constant, an exchange rate appreciation adversely affects the exports and positively affects the imports of goods and services (Abeysinghe and Yeok, 1998). Given this context, this chapter investigates the impact of exchange rate movements on services exports from India, especially given the growing importance of services exports in the correction of India's balance of payments. Further, past research has also found that, along with

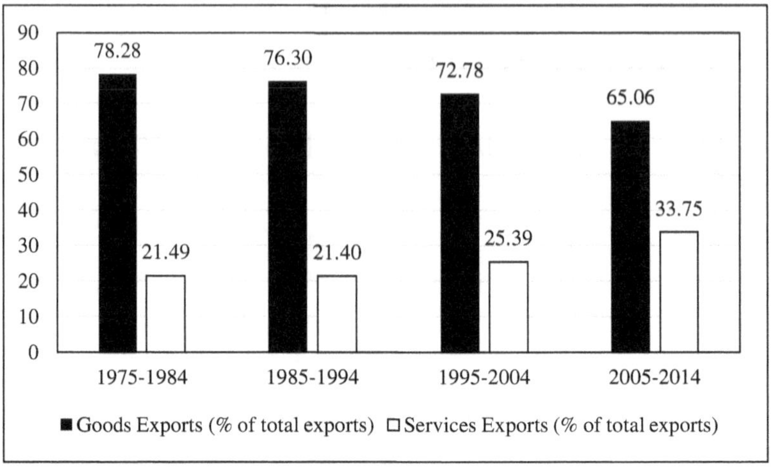

Figure 4.1 Goods exports and services exports (% of total), 1975–2014 (decadal averages)

Source: World Development Indicators (WDI) (The World Bank, Undated).

the price effect, the demand- and supply-side non-price factors also play an important role influencing the goods and services exports (Sahoo and Dash, 2014; Eichengreen and Gupta, 2013). For this reason, we are also investigating the importance of the demand-side factors (world demand for services exports) and the supply-side factors (foreign direct investment inflows, financial development and globalisation) in influencing the services exports from India.

The present study departs from the existing studies on two counts. First, we use a longer time series data, from 1975 to 2014. Second, we investigate the impact of the demand-side as well as supply-side factors that influence services export from India. To the best of our knowledge there is no study, except Sahoo and Dash (2014), which examines the impact of exchange rate movements on services exports in the context of India.

The rest of the chapter is structured as follows. Section 4.2 presents some of the relevant literature related to the effects of exchange rates on trade flows. Section 4.3 describes the data and methods. Section 4.4 presents the findings, and Section 4.5 provides conclusions from the analysis.

4.2 Evidence so far

Evidence on the relationship between services exports and exchange rate is limited, especially in the Indian context, although there are a number of studies focusing on the impact of exchange rate movements on total trade flows. Examining the determinants of the services exports for 15 European countries for the period of 1976–2000, Barcenilla and Molero (2003) found that foreign income, price and exchange rate are the major determinants that influence the services exports in these economies. Kimura and Lee (2006) assessed the factors influencing services trade relative to the goods trade for 10 OECD member countries during 1999–2000. By using the standard gravity model, they found that geographical distance, cost of transport and economic liberalisation are the important factors for the services trade. On similar lines, Shepherd and Van Der Marel (2010) investigated the determinants of the services trade for the Asia Pacific Economic Cooperation (APEC) member countries for the period of 1995–2008. Their results show that market size, membership in a regional trade agreement, distance, restrictive regulations in product markets, and common language are the major determinants of the service trade. Shingal (2010) examined the factors affecting services trade in 25 exporting and 53 importing countries for the period during 1999–2003. The study found that the major factors influencing the services trade are human capital, teledensity and the trade restriction. Further, Van Der Marel (2012) investigated the factors explaining the comparative advantages in the services exports for a sample of 23 OECD economies. This study found that the factor endowments such as skilled labour force and ICT-related capital stock, institutions and better regulatory frameworks are considered as the major sources of comparative advantages in the services exports.

Eichengreen and Gupta (2013), in their study on 60 developing countries including India for the period of 1980–2008, found that per capita income of the exporter country, size of the market, world demand of services exports, infrastructure development, FDI, goods exports and human capital are the major determinants of services exports. Nasir and Kalirajan (2013) examined the factors determining the modern services exports (MSEs) in the economies of South Asian and the East Asian countries during 2002–2008. The study found that the number of graduates and the ICT infrastructure are key determinants of MSEs in the emerging economies. Sahoo and Dash (2014) investigated the determinants of MSEs in India for the period of 1980–2011. The results of the study showed that the endowment of factors of human capital, and physical infrastructure stocks and financial development along with world demand, exchange rate and goods exports are the major determinants of the MSEs in India. They also found that the software and communication exports depend more on the human capital, telecommunication, FDI and quality of institutions than the world demand, infrastructure and real exchange rate.

From this review, it emerges that majority of the studies are 'cross-sectional', focusing on several countries, often with varying heterogeneity in size and patterns of trade. Further, the focus has been on the determinants of services exports with lesser emphasis on exchange rate which is, theoretically, expected to be a major determinant of the exports. We also find a limited number of studies in the Indian context. Our attempt is to fill this gap by emphasising the impact of exchange rate movements on services exports from India.

4.3 Data and analytical approach

The trend in the total services exports (TSE), shown in Figure 4.2, suggests that before the 1990s, the total services export from India has been small in value, dominated by traditional services exports, which exceeded the MSEs. In the period of post-1990s, the TSE increased mainly driven by the growth of MSE. Further, in the post-2005 period, the share of MSE reached 75 per cent of total services exports in 2014 compared to nearly 30 per cent in 1980 (Sahoo et al., 2019). This is mainly because of the far-reaching reforms in the modern services sectors like telecommunications, information technology (IT) and the financial sectors which brought about such spectacular growth (Sahoo and Dash, 2014).

This chapter examines the impact of exchange rate on the services exports using a long time series data set. Data used for the econometric analysis is annual and refers to the period of 1975–2014. The period of study is chosen mainly on the basis of the availability of data, but it does cover the period in which there has been rapid growth of services export. We chose a longer time span mainly for two reasons. First, use of a longer data set is desirable in the empirical statistical analysis. Second, a longer time series also helps in reducing the impact of large year-to-year fluctuations in establishing a long-run relationship among variables. The data is sourced from the World Development Indicators (WDI) of the World Bank and the Handbook of Statistics on Indian Economy, Reserve Bank of India (RBI).

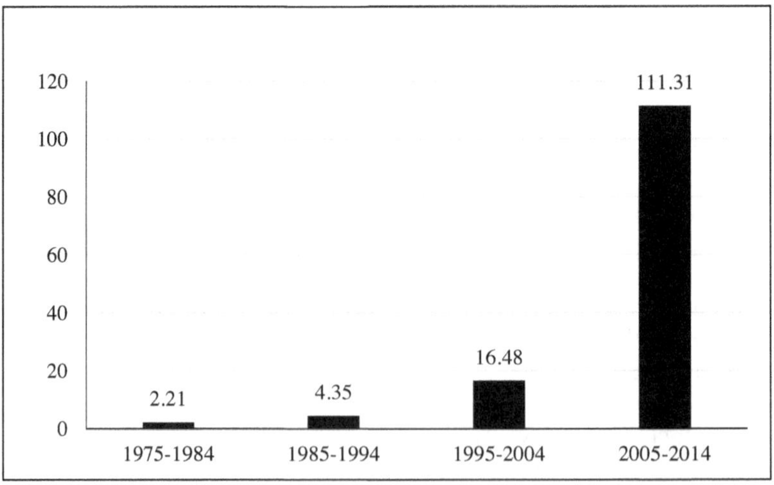

Figure 4.2 Services exports of India (billion US$), 1975–2014 (decadal averages)
Source: World Development Indicators (WDI) (The World Bank, Undated).

The potential relationship between the services export and the other potential explanatory variables on a *ceteris paribus* basis can be briefly explained as follows.

Real effective exchange rate (REER): An appreciation (depreciation) of the domestic currency of an economy with respect to the currency of its trading partners makes the services exports expensive (cheaper) in the international market. This may lead to fall (rise) in the total services exports of an economy.

Goods exports (GEXP): The GEXP is assumed to positively affect the services exports due to the network effect (Egger, Francois and Nelson, 2015). In other words, a country's goods trade networks with other countries can help in increasing the services exports to those countries.

Financial development (FINDEV): Development of the financial sector is important for the production and exports of the services (Sahoo and Dash, 2014). This helps the firms to more easily meet their capital requirements and invest in technical upgrading and new innovative activities, which positively affects their export performances.

Net FDI inflows (FDI): Aggregate FDI inflows are assumed to increase the growth of services exports. Sectoral analysis reveals that this is via increased intra-firm trade by making the firms technologically advanced and competitive in the international market (Mullen and Williams, 2011)

World demand for service exports (SIMP): An economy's services exports may increase (decrease) with the rise (fall) in the demand for its services by the rest of the world. The demand for India's services imports by the rest of the world is measured by world services imports net of India as ratio of world GDP (Sahoo and Dash, 2014).

Globalisation index (GLOBAL): Rising globalisation and economic integration may lead to rising technological advancement, competition and thereby productivity in an economy (Moshirian, 2008). This may lead to rising exports of goods and services to the rest of the world.

Tables 4.1 and 4.2 provide the basic features of the data on a set of variables used in the present analysis. Table 4.1 presents the summary statistics for the variables, along with the definitions and data sources, and Table 4.2 provides estimated pair-wise correlation coefficients between the variables for the period of 1975–2014. TSE and the GEXP are found to be negatively correlated with the real exchange rate. Further, correlation of service exports with financial development, FDI inflows, SIMP and globalisation is found to be high. The initial indication, which shows that the impact of exchange rate on services exports is negative, is what we test in our econometric model.

4.3.1 ARDL bounds testing cointegration approach

Conventional cointegration tests do not control for structural breaks in the model. Given the longer time series and the structural changes that have taken place in the Indian economy during the time period considered,

Table 4.1 Summary statistics for key variables: 1975–2014

Variable	*Definition*	*Mean*	*Standard. Deviation*	*Minimum*	*Maximum*	*Source*
TSE	Total services exports as % GDP	3.336	2.573	0.839	8.664	WDI
REER	Real effective exchange rate (36-currency trade based index)	122.785	28.332	92.750	172.673	RBI
GEXP	Total goods exports as % of GDP	8.485	4.157	4.001	17.127	WDI
FINDEV	Financial development (measured by domestic credit to private sectors as % of GDP)	29.870	11.404	14.676	52.203	WDI
FDI	Net inflows of FDI as % of GDP	0.690	0.859	–0.029	3.546	WDI
SIMP	World services import net of India as % of world GDP	4.670	0.758	3.688	6.295	WDI
GLOBAL	Overall globalisation index	37.853	10.148	25.746	51.642	Dreher (2006)

Source: Authors' calculations.

Table 4.2 Pair-wise correlations among the variables, 1975–2014: correlation coefficients

Variables	*TSE*	*REER*	*GEXP*	*INDEV*	*FDI*	*SIMP*	*GLOBAL*
TSE	1.000						
REER	–0.544	1.000					
GEXP	0.962	–0.658	1.000				
FINDEV	0.971	–0.504	0.932	1.000			
FDI	0.907	–0.546	0.872	0.860	1.000		
SIMP	0.961	–0.537	0.940	0.907	0.879	1.000	
GLOBAL	0.902	–0.802	0.932	0.850	0.843	0.904	1.000

Source: Authors' calculations.

there exists the possibility of structural breaks in the series. Thus, using the conventional tests might yield biased results. Therefore, we use the autoregressive and distributed lag (ARDL) bounds testing approach developed by Pesaran et al. (2001) to test the long-run and short-run impact of exchange rate and the other explanatory variables on services exports. The

ARDL model can give efficient results in the presence of a single structural break in the dependent variable (Shahbaz et al., 2016). This approach has also certain other advantages over the other traditional cointegration tests. First, the ARDL bounds testing approach makes estimation possible even though explanatory variables are found to be endogenous (Pesaran and Shin, 1999; Pesaran, Shin and Smith, 2001) and also eliminates the endogeneity problems which are associated with the Engle-Granger method (Al-Mulali, Saboori and Ozturk, 2015). Second, it can be applied regardless of mixed order of regressors, that is, even if they are of two different orders of integration, whether independent variables are purely I(0), I(1) or mutually integrated (Pesaran, Shin and Smith, 2001). This implies that it is not important to check the integration order of the variables for the ARDL model. Third, it allows one to go for simultaneous analysis of both short-run and long-run effects of the independent variables on the dependent variable. Fourth, it produces superior results in analysing small samples. Because of these advantages, the ARDL bounds testing approach has been applied in the current study to obtain the long-run relationship among the variables considered.

To find the long-run relationship among the variables, the ARDL bounds testing approach takes the following form:

$$\begin{aligned}\Delta TSE_t = {} & a_0 + \sum_{i=1}^{m} a_{1i}\Delta TSE_{t-i} + \sum_{i=0}^{m} a_{2i}\Delta REER_{t-i} + \sum_{i=0}^{m} a_{3i}\Delta GEXP_{t-i} \\ & + \sum_{i=0}^{m} a_{4i}\Delta FINDEV_{t-i} + \sum_{i=0}^{m} a_{5i}\Delta FDI_{t-i} + \sum_{i=0}^{m} a_{6i}\Delta SIMP_{t-i} \\ & + \sum_{i=0}^{m} a_{7i}\Delta GLOBAL_{t-i} + a_8 TSE_{t-1} + a_9 REER_{t-1} \\ & + a_{10} GEXP_{t-1} + a_{11} FINDEV_{t-1} + a_{12} FDI_{t-1} + a_{13} SIMP_{t-1} \\ & + a_{14} GLOBAL_{t-1} + \mu_t \end{aligned} \tag{1}$$

where m is optimal lag length and Δ is first difference of the concerned variables. α_0 is the intercept term and m_t is the error term. The first (first differences as the independent variables) and second (variables in original form) parts of the earlier equation represent error correction dynamics and the long-run relationship among the series, respectively. To test the existence of a long-run relationship, F test is employed. Finally, the computed F statistics are compared with the critical values of Narayan (2005) because alternative lower and upper bounds critical values are more appropriate than that of Pesaran, Shin and Smith (2001) for small-sample-size data sets. A decision can be inferred on the cointegration relationship without knowing the order of integration of the regressors if the computed F statistic falls outside the upper and lower bounds. The optimal lag order is selected on the basis of Akaike information criterion (AIC). The minimum AIC of the model implies optimal lag length.

4.4 Findings

Checking of the stationarity property of the variables is considered as the important precondition for investigating the cointegration among them. For this reason, we use the Zivot-Andrews (ZA) (1992) test, which accommodates information about a single unknown structural break present in the series. The results of ZA test are presented in Table 4.3. All the variables are non-stationary at their levels and stationary at first difference in the presence of a single structural break. No variable is integrated of order two, which allows us to apply the cointegration test.

The ARDL cointegration test results are given in Table 4.4. Here we have estimated two models. Model 1 includes goods exports as an explanatory variable, whereas Model 2 does not include goods exports. This is because goods export is assumed to be correlated to the exchange rate that may cause multicollinearity problems in estimation. Hence, in order to check the consistency of our results we estimated two different models. As it is well known that the ARDL approach is sensitive to the lag length selection in the model, we use the Akaike information criteria (AIC) to select the appropriate lag length. As reported by Lütkepohl (2006), the dynamic link between the series can be well captured with the appropriate selection of the lag length. The optimum lags are given in the column 2 of Table 4.4. For testing the existence of cointegration in different models, we used Narayan's (2005) critical values. The bounds testing results show that the calculated F statistic is found to be greater than the upper bounds critical values when total services export (TSE) is used as dependent variable. The ARDL bounds test, therefore, confirms the long-run relationship between the variables in the Indian economy for the period 1975–2014.

The existence of cointegrating the relationship between the variables leads us to examine the long-run and short-run impact of real exchange rate, goods

Table 4.3 Zivot-Andrews unit root test results

Variables	*Level*			*First Difference*		
	T-Stat.	Break	Decision	T-Stat.	Break	Decision
TSE	−3.147	1994	Unit root	−7.897*	2007	Stationary
REER	−2.757	1993	Unit root	−5.872*	1988	Stationary
GEXP	−2.690	2000	Unit root	−7.278*	1992	Stationary
FINDEV	−3.134	1996	Unit root	−8.054*	2005	Stationary
FDI	−3.210	1990	Unit root	−7.589*	2008	Stationary
SIMP	−4.603	1989	Unit root	−6.138*	1985	Stationary
GLOBAL	−2.440	2008	Unit root	−7.586*	1997	Stationary

Source: Authors' calculations.

Note: * Represents significance at 1 per cent level.

The values −4.93, −4.42 and −4.11 are the tabulated t-statistic values at 1 per cent, 5 per cent and 10 per cent for ZA test with trend.

Table 4.4 The bounds test for cointegrating relationship

Estimated models	*Optimal lag*	*Break*	*F-stat.*
Model 1: TSE=f(REER, GEXP, FINDEV, FDI, SIMP, GLOBAL)	(3,1,2,2,3,3,3)	1994	14.861*
Model 2: TSE=f(REER, FINDEV, FDI, SIMP, GLOBAL)	(3,2,3,1,3,3)	1994	20.791*

Source: Authors' calculations.

Note: We use the ARDL empirical model with unrestricted intercept and unrestricted trend. The upper and lower critical bounds developed by Narayan (2005) are 6.263, 4.527 (4.700, 3.327) and 4.040, 2.831 at 1 per cent (5 per cent) and 10 per cent levels, respectively. The *,** and *** show significance at 1 per cent, 5 per cent and 10 per cent levels, respectively.

Table 4.5 Long-run and short-run estimates

Variables (TSE as dependent variable)	*Model 1 (with GEXP)*	*Model 4 (without GEPXP)*
Long run		
Constant	-6.042*	-6.087*
$REER_t$	-0.009*	-0.007*
$GEXP_t$	-0.031	–
$FINDEV_t$	0.166*	0.160*
FDI_t	0.239*	0.210*
$SIMP_t$	1.034*	0.854*
$GLOBAL_t$	0.065*	0.083*
D_t	0.220**	0.041
Short run		
Constant	-17.755*	-17.185*
$\Delta REER_t$	-0.005	-0.010
$\Delta GEXP_t$	-0.115	–
$\Delta FINDEV_t$	0.149*	0.193*
ΔFDI_t	0.805*	0.832*
$\Delta SIMP_t$	0.675**	0.572
$\Delta GLOBAL_t$	0.013	0.137*
D_t	0.646**	0.116

Source: Authors' calculations.

Note: The *,** and *** indicate significance at 1 per cent, 5 per cent and 10 per cent levels, respectively.

exports, financial development, FDI inflows, world services imports net of India and globalisation on the total services exports of India. Both the long-run and short-run results are reported in Table 4.5.

The results show that the exchange rate movements negatively and significantly affect the TSE, while in the short run also it affects TSE negatively but not significantly. In other words, total services exports are elastic to the exchange rate movements in the long run, whereas in the short run it is inelastic in nature. Our study provides findings similar to Sahoo and Dash (2014), who found that India's MSEs are negatively related to the movements in the exchange rate. Our results also show that FDI inflows, financial development, world demand for services exports and globalisation positively and significantly affect the services exports of India. However, the impact of goods exports is found to be negative but statistically insignificant in both the long run and short run.

Moreover, the results from Table 4.5 show that though the impact of the exchange rate on the total services exports is significant, the coefficient of the exchange rate is very small as compared to the coefficient values of the FDI inflows, financial development, world demand for exports and globalisation. This implies that as compared to the price effect, the supply- and the demand-side factors are more dominant. In other words, the supply- and demand-side factors play a more important role to influence the services exports in India than the exchange rate movements. In addition, the stability of our ARDL models are investigated by employing the cumulative sum of recursive residuals (CUSUM) and the CUSUM of squares (CUSUMsq), suggested by Brown, Durbin and Evans (1975).

4.5 Summing up

In the present analysis, we empirically examine the relationship between services exports and exchange rate movements in India. We use data for the period 1975–2014. The econometric model estimated using the ARDL method incorporates goods exports, financial development, net FDI inflows, world demand for services exports and globalisation as the other potential control variables. The results show that all the variables share a common trend in the long run. Further, we also find that the exchange rate negatively and significantly affects the TSEs from India. However, the supply-augmenting factors, such as FDI inflows, financial development and globalisation, and demand-side factors, such as world demand for services exports, have positive and stronger impact on services exports. This implies that investments, both domestic and FDI, play a positive role in increasing services exports. These investments need to be channelised through an efficient financial system, which requires further financial development. Our results not only point to the significant impact of long-term movements in the exchange rate on services exports but also provide the basis for a broader set of measures to expand services exports, which can assist in meeting the goal of balancing current accounts.

References

Abeysinghe, T. and T.L. Yeok (1998). 'Exchange rate appreciation and export competitiveness: The case of Singapore', *Applied Economics*, 30(1), 51–55.

Al-Mulali, U., Saboori, B. and I. Ozturk (2015). 'Investigating the environmental Kuznets curve hypothesis in Vietnam', *Energy Policy*, 76(1), 123–131.

Barcenilla, S. and J. Molero (2003, May). 'Service export flows: Empirical evidence for European project', *Sustainable Growth, Employment Creation and Technological Integration in the European Knowledge Based Economy (SETI) Project*, Universidad de Zaragoza and Universidad Complutense de Madrid, Madrid.

Brown, R.L., Durbin, J. and J.M. Evans (1975). 'Techniques for testing the constancy of regression relationships over time', *Journal of the Royal Statistical Society*, Series B (Methodological), 149–192.

Egger, P.H., Francois, J. and D.R. Nelson (2015). 'The role of goods-trade networks for services-trade volume', *The World Economy*, 40(3), 532–543.

Eichengreen, B. and P. Gupta (2013). 'Exports of services: Indian experience in perspective', *Indian Growth and Development Review*, 6(1), 35–60.

Kimura, F. and H.H. Lee (2006). 'The gravity equation in international trade in services', *Review of World Economics*, 142(1), 92–121.

Lütkepohl, H. (2006). 'Structural vector autoregressive analysis for cointegrated variables', in O. Hubler and J. Frohn (eds.) *Modern Econometric Analysis*, Springer, Berlin Heidelberg.

Ministry of Finance (2019). *Economic Survey 2018–19*, vol. 2, Government of India, New Delhi.

Moshirian, F. (2008). 'Globalisation, growth and institutions', *Journal of Banking & Finance*, 32(4), 472–479.

Mullen, J.K. and M. Williams (2011). 'Bilateral FDI and Canadian export activity', *The International Trade Journal*, 25(3), 349–371.

Narayan, P.K. (2005). 'The saving and investment nexus for China: Evidence from cointegration tests', *Applied Economics*, 37(17), 1979–1990.

Nasir, S. and K. Kalirajan (2013). 'Export performance of South and East Asia in modern services,' ASARC Working Paper, ANU Canberra.

Pesaran, M.H. and Shin, Y. (1999). 'An autoregressive distributed lag modelling approach to cointegration analysis', in S. Strom (ed.) *Econometrics and Economic Theory in the 20th Century: The Ragnar Frisch Centennial Symposium*, Cambridge University Press, Cambridge.

Pesaran, M.H., Shin, Y. and R.J. Smith (2001). 'Bounds testing approaches to the analysis of level relationships', *Journal of Applied Econometrics*, 16(3), 289–326.

Pradhan, N.C. (2010). 'Exports and economic growth: An examination of ELG hypothesis for India', *Reserve Bank of India Occasional Papers*, 31(3), 35–66.

Sahoo, M., Babu, M.S. and U. Dash (2019). 'Asymmetric effects of exchange rate movements on traditional and modern services exports: Evidence from a large emerging economy', *The Journal of International Trade & Economic Development*, 28(4), 508–531. https://doi.org/10.1080/09638199.2018.1561744.

Sahoo, P. and R.K. Dash (2014). 'India's surge in modern services exports: Empirics for policy', *Journal of Policy Modeling*, 36(6), 1082–1100.

Shahbaz, M., Mallick, H., Mahalik, M.K. and P. Sadorsky (2016). 'The role of globalization on the recent evolution of energy demand in India: Implications for sustainable development', *Energy Economics*, 55, 52–68.

Shepherd, B. and E. Van Der Marel (2010). 'Trade in services in the APEC region: Patterns, determinants and policy implications', APEC Policy Support Unit, Asia-Pacific Economic Cooperation Secretariat, Singapore.

Shingal, A. (2010). 'How much do agreements matter for services trade?', MPRA Paper No. 32815. https://mpra.ub.uni-muenchen.de/32815/.

Van der Marel, E. (2012). 'Determinants of comparative advantage in services', Working Paper No. 87, FIW: Research Centre International Economics, Vienna. http://hdl.handle.net/10419/121086.

The World Bank (Undated). *World Development Indicators*. wdi.worldbank.org.

Zivot, E. and D.W.K. Andrews (1992). 'Further evidence on the great crash, the oil-price shock and the unit-root hypothesis', *Journal of Business and Economic Statistics*, 10(3), 251–270.

5 Measuring services output

Definitional and conceptual issues

A.C. Kulshreshtha

5.1 Introduction

In general terms, 'services' embrace all economic activities other than those covered under agricultural production, mining, manufacturing and construction activity. The terms 'services sector' or 'service-producing economic activities' are used in Indian national accounting to cover all activities included in the tabulation categories of G through S of the National Industrial Classification (NIC) 2008 (consistent with International Standard Industrial Classification (ISIC), Revision 4) (Central Statistical Office, 2008). These comprise the activities of (i) trade, hotels and restaurants, (ii) transport, storage and communication, (iii) financing and insurance, (iv) real estate, renting and business services including software development activities and legal services, (v) public administration and defence and (vi) community, social and personal services.

The service sector, thus, covers a wide range of economic activities. Besides the sectors of trade, hotel and restaurant, transport, storage, communication, real estate and ownership of dwellings, banking and public administration, it also covers the sectors of business services and 'other services', which are by themselves very heterogeneous and more importantly produced substantially in India, requiring special attention for gathering statistics on these economic activities. Business services include business accounting; software development and data processing; information, business and management consultancy; advertisement and other business services. The sector 'other services' comprises education, research and scientific services, medical and health services including veterinary services, sanitary services, religious and other community services, recreation and entertainment services, and personal services like domestic, laundry, dyeing and dry cleaning, and barbers and beauty shops. Emergence of a significant number of service-producing industries leading to rapid expansion of the service sector is a relatively recent phenomenon in the Indian economy. The service sector has grown at a much faster rate than the rest of the economy during the recent years. In India the share of the service sector has increased from 27.0 per cent in 1950–51 to 52.6 per cent in 2014–15 (see Table 5.1).

Table 5.1 Structural changes in the distribution of total GVA during 1950–51 to 2014–15

Industry	*1950–51*	*1970–71*	*1980–81*	*1993–94*	*1999–2000*	*2006–07*	*2011–12*	*2014–15*
1. Primary	**58.2**	**47.3**	**41.3**	**33.5**	**27.3**	**20.5**	**21.6**	**19.3**
2. Secondary	**14.8**	**21.4**	**22.6**	**23.7**	**23**	**24.7**	**29.9**	**28.1**
3. Tertiary or service sector	**27**	**31.3**	**36.1**	**42.8**	**49.3**	**54.8**	**48.5**	**52.6**
3.1 Trade, hotels & restaurant	**8.5**	**10.7**	**12**	**12.7**	**14.2**	**15.4**	**10.8**	**12.0**
3.1.1 Trade	8	10.1	11.3	11.9	13	13.9	9.7	10.9
3.1.2 Hotels & Restaurants	0.5	0.6	0.7	0.8	1.2	1.5	1.1	1.1
3.2 Transport, storage & comm.	**3.1**	**4.3**	**6.1**	**6.5**	**7.5**	**11.4**	**6.5**	**6.9**
3.2.1 Railways	1.2	1.4	1.5	1.2	1.2	1.2	0.7	0.8
3.2.2 Transport by other means	1.4	2.2	3.6	4	4.6	5.3	4.2	4.2
3.2.3 Storage	0.1	0.1	0.1	0.1	0.1	0.1	0.1	0.1
3.2.4 Communication	0.4	0.6	0.9	1.2	1.6	4.9	1.6	1.8
3.3 Financial, real estate and business services	**5.8**	**5.6**	**6.4**	**11.5**	**13.1**	**14.3**	**18.8**	**21.0**
3.3.1 Banking & insurance	1.1	1.7	2.3	5.3	5.9	6.7	5.9	6.1
3.3.2 Real estate, ownership of dwellings & business services	4.7	3.9	4.1	6.2	7.2	7.6	12.9	14.9
3.4 Community, social and personal services	**9.7**	**10.7**	**11.5**	**12**	**14.9**	**13.6**	**12.6**	**12.7**
3.4.1 Public Admin & Defence	2.5	4.1	5.2	5.6	6.9	5.6	6.0	5.8
3.4.2 Other services	7.2	6.6	6.3	6.4	8.1	8	6.5	6.9
4. Total GVA	**100**	**100**	**100**	**100**	**100**	**100**	**100**	**100**

Source: CSO (2016).

Note: Figures for 1950–51 to 1993–94 are based on 1993–94 prices; for 1999–00 to 2006–07 on 1999–00 prices and for 2011–12 onwards on 2011–12 prices.

For most economies, the service sector activities account for a significant portion of their gross domestic product as well as total employment. Data on service sector activities are required by government, business community, analysts, and several others to assess changing structures and examine the growth. Service sector statistics are also required by various regions for understanding the regional distribution in the economy by policy makers and analysts. Such statistics are sought annually and more frequently on the contribution of income and employment of service sector activities.

This chapter provides a discussion on some key concepts in the measurement of output as per the SNA 2008, with particular reference to the output of the service sectors.

5.2 Measurement of macro-economic aggregates

Measurement of macro-economic aggregates like output, input gross value added (GVA), intermediate consumption (IC), final consumption expenditure (FCE) like household FCE (HFCE), FCE of non-profit institutions serving households (NPISH), private FCE (PFCE), government FCE (GFCE), gross fixed capital formation (GFCF), change in inventories (CII), valuables, exports, imports, gross/net national income (GNI/NNI), gross national disposable income (GNDI) and saving are made as per the guidelines of the international standard of the System of National Accounts (SNA) which has been revised over time from SNA 1953 to SNA 1968, then to SNA 1993 and the latest SNA 2008 (see Appendix 5.1 for the basic definitional framework for each of these macro variables). In what follows, we propose to discuss the definitional and conceptual issues relating to the measurement of output of products, focusing on the services produced in the economy as per the latest international standard, the SNA 2008 (United Nations Statistics Division 2008). Measurement of a few typical services are discussed in detail.

5.2.1 Production versus output

Production is an activity carried out by an establishment. It may not always be clear whether an establishment is producing a good or is providing a service. For example, an oil refinery processing crude oil that it owns is producing a good (refined petroleum); if the same refinery processes crude oil belonging to another unit, then it is providing a refinery service to that unit. When the establishments belong to different enterprises (institutional units), the defining principle is that of economic ownership. If an establishment has no discretion about the level of production or the price to be charged for the good, there is evidence that the establishment has not taken economic ownership of the goods being processed and the value of the output should be treated as the processing element only.

When the establishments involved belong to the same enterprise, there is no change of ownership since both establishments have the same owner. However, the principle of transferring risk, which accompanies change of ownership, can still be applied. For example, consider an establishment that receives coal from another establishment in the same enterprise, uses it to generate electricity and then sells the electricity on the open market. The electricity generator has discretion about the amount of coal it demands, the amount of electricity to be generated and the prices to be charged. In such a case, the value of electricity generated should be measured including the cost of the coal consumed in the process, even though there is no legal change in ownership given that both establishments belong to the same enterprise.

Though, in general, all goods and services that are produced and used by the same establishment are excluded from the measure of output, there are exceptions. For example, output is recorded if the goods and services being produced are used for own capital formation of the establishment. Similarly, output is recorded for products entering inventories even if eventually they are withdrawn from inventories for use as intermediate consumption in the same establishment in a later period. Thus, if an establishment develops a plant or original research/software for its own use, it is part of its output of product provided to other units, and then the capital formation created by the establishment needs to be placed as acquisition of assets in the same establishment. If the establishment is a household unincorporated enterprise growing wheat, the value of wheat produced includes wheat kept for household consumption.

As production is related to activities and thus the output of one production process may be a set of products, output is measured for an establishment and may include the output of several production processes undertaken by the establishment.

Output is, thus, defined as the goods and services produced by an establishment, excluding the value of any goods and services used in an activity for which the establishment does not assume the risk of using the products in production and excluding the value of goods and services consumed by the same establishment except for goods and services used for capital formation (fixed capital or changes in inventories) or own final consumption.

5.2.2 Time of recording

Output of most goods or services is usually recorded when their production is completed. However, when it takes a long time to produce a unit of output, it becomes necessary to recognise that output is being produced continuously and to record it as '*work-in-progress*'. For example, the production of certain agricultural products or large durable goods such as ships or buildings may take years to complete. In such cases, it would distort economic reality to treat the output as if it were all produced at the moment of time when the process of production happens to terminate. Whenever a process of production extends over two or more accounting periods, it is necessary to calculate the work-in-progress completed within each of the periods in order to be able to measure how much output is produced in each period.

If the products are completed in an accounting period but not disposed to the user in that period, output is recorded when the work is completed and not when sold. There is thus a significant difference between the value of output in a period and the value of sales, the difference being accounted for by changes in inventories of finished goods and work-in-progress.

5.2.3 Valuation of output

Goods and services produced for sale on the market at economically significant prices are to be valued either at basic prices or at producers' prices. The preferred method of valuation is at basic prices, especially when a system of VAT, or similar deductible tax, is in operation. Producers' prices should be used only when valuation at basic prices is not feasible. It may be clarified that the basic price is the price which the producer gets and it includes taxes *less* subsidies on production, if any. The producers' price is defined as the basic price plus taxes *less* subsidies on products.

Output always has different valuations based on taxes net of subsidies included in the price of the product. Earlier, as per the 1953 and 1968 SNA, factor cost price or factor price was understood as the price without any tax. In the Indian national accounts, the term factor price was in use until 2015 in all the series. However, the term factor price is not encouraged by the 1993 and 2008 SNA, where indirect taxes/subsidies have been distinguished into taxes on products and production. In the new series (base 2011–12), most of the recommendations of the 2008 SNA have been implemented and the output and GVA are valued at basic price. Basic price is the price which includes the value of taxes less subsidies (T–S) on production. Thus, basic price is equal to factor cost price plus T–S on production. Taxes and subsidies on products are *ad valorem*, whereas taxes and subsidies are on the production unit irrespective of the volume produced.

5.2.4 Market and non-market output

Market output in a market economy is that in which case producers make decisions about what and how much to produce. Economically significant price is the factor behind production decisions. Economically significant prices are prices that have a significant effect on the amounts that producers are willing to supply and on the amounts purchasers wish to buy. These prices normally result when the producer has an incentive to adjust supply either with the goal of making a profit in the long run or, at a minimum, covering capital and other costs and consumers have the freedom to purchase or not purchase and make the choice on the basis of the prices charged.

Value of market output is determined as the sum of the following items: (i) value of products sold at economically significant prices, (ii) value of products bartered in exchange for other goods, services or assets, (iii) value of products used for payments in kind, including compensation in kind, (iv) value of products supplied by one establishment to another belonging to the same market enterprise to be used as intermediate inputs where the risk associated with continuing the production process is transferred along with the goods, (v) value of changes in inventories of finished goods and work-in-progress intended for one or other of the earlier uses, and (vi) margins charged on the supply of products, transport margins, margins on the acquisition and disposal of financial assets, and so on.

Output produced by the 'market producers' for own final use is to be valued at the average basic prices of the product sold on the market, provided they are sold in sufficient quantities. If not, the output is to be valued by the total production costs incurred, including consumption of fixed capital (CFC) plus any taxes (less subsidies) on production, plus a net return on the fixed capital and natural resources used in production. The concept of the net return to capital was introduced in 2008 SNA.

Non-market output consists of goods and individual or collective services produced by government units or NPISHs that are supplied free, or at prices that are not economically significant, to other institutional units or the community as a whole, for example, education or health services free or at prices that are not economically significant. Although this output is shown as being acquired by government and NPISHs in the use of income account, it should not be confused with production for own use. The expenditure is made by government and by NPISHs but the use of individual goods and services is by households and the use of collective services by households or other resident institutional units. Any receipts on sales by the government or NPISHs are considered as negative entry in the final uses. If a private-sector unit provides education and/or health service free or at prices not economically significant (non-market kind), the unit needs to be considered as NPISH.

Value of the non-market output provided without charge to households is estimated as the sum of costs of production, as follows: intermediate consumption + compensation of employees + CFC + taxes (less subsidies) on production. No net return to capital is included for non-market production. Similarly, no net return to capital is included in the estimates of production for own final use by non-market producers when these are estimated as the sum of costs.

5.2.5 Recording of sales of services

Sales are recorded when the receivables and payables are created, that is, when the services are provided to the purchaser. Products are valued at the basic prices at which they are sold. The amount payable should be shown in the production account, and the difference between amounts payable and paid should be shown as accounts payable or receivable in the financial account. Subsequent payments of these amounts outstanding are recorded as financial transactions and not as part of the production account. If payments made in advance or in arrears attract interest charges, these should be shown as separate transactions and not included in the value of sales.

5.2.6 *Changes in inventories of work-in-progress*

When the process of production takes a long time to complete, output is being produced continuously as work-in-progress. Such output is recorded whenever the process of production is not completed within a single accounting period so that work-in-progress is carried forward from one period to the next. Work-in-progress may need to be recorded in any industry, including service industries such as the production of movies, research and development, depending upon the length of time it takes to produce a unit of output. The gross fixed capital formation is recorded only when a producer acquires it for use.

5.2.7 *Services of domestic staff*

Paid domestic staff (maids, cooks, chauffeurs, etc.) are formally treated as employees of an unincorporated enterprise that is owned by the household. The services produced are consumed by the same unit that produces them and they constitute a form of own-account production. Value of the output produced is deemed to be equal to the compensation of employees paid.

5.2.8 *Services of owner-occupied dwellings*

Households that own the dwellings they occupy are formally treated as owners of unincorporated enterprises that produce housing services consumed by those same households. Output of the housing services produced by owner occupiers is valued at the estimated rental that a tenant would pay for the similar accommodation.

5.2.9 *Own account construction, gross fixed capital formation*

A wide range of construction activities may be undertaken for the purpose of own gross fixed capital formation in rural areas including community construction activities undertaken by groups of households. Output of own account construction is usually estimated on the basis of costs. However, most of the inputs into community construction projects, including labour inputs, are likely to be provided free, posing valuation problems. As unpaid labour may account for a large part of the inputs, it is important to make some estimate of its value using wage rates paid for similar kinds of work on local labour markets.

In addition, intellectual property products such as R&D and software products may be produced on own account. Such GFCF needs to be estimated again at cost.

5.2.10 Valuation of output for own final use

Output for own final use should be valued at the basic prices at which the goods and services could be sold if offered for sale on the market. The nearest equivalent price is likely to be the so-called 'farm-gate' price. When reliable market prices cannot be obtained, a second best option is to consider sum of their costs of production: as the sum of intermediate consumption + compensation of employees + CFC + a net return to fixed capital + other taxes (less subsidies) on production. By convention, no net return to capital is included when own-account production is undertaken by non-market producers.

For household or unincorporated enterprises, it may not be possible to estimate compensation of employees, CFC and a return to capital separately, in which case an estimate of mixed income, covering all these items, could be made.

5.3 Output of select services

5.3.1 Transportation and storage

The output of *transportation* is measured by the value of the amount receivable for transporting goods or persons. As a concept, a good in one location is recognised as being of a different quality from the same good in another location, so that transporting from one location to another is a process of production in which an economically significant change takes place even if the good remains otherwise unchanged. The volume of transport services may be measured by indicators such as ton-kilometers or passenger-kilometers, which combine both the quantities of goods, or numbers of persons, and the distances over which they are transported. Factors such as speed, frequency or comfort also affect the quality of services provided.

Although the production of *storage* for the market may not be very extensive, the activity of storage is important, as many goods have to be stored in a properly controlled environment where goods are 'transported' from one point of time to another. The same goods available at different times, or locations, may be qualitatively different from each other and command different prices for this reason. Increase in price of a product for being in storage and storage costs incurred are in a production process. An important point to be noted is that the output of storage need to be clearly distinguished from the holding gains/losses, which must be excluded from the value of production of storage since holding gain is considered in the SNA as 'Other changes in price'.

In storage, if the increase in value simply reflects a rise in price with no change in quality, then there is no further production during the period in addition to the costs of storage. However, there are reasons that the increase in value can be construed as further production. One reason is that quality of the good may improve with the passage of time (such as wine or Basmati rice). Another reason could be seasonal factors affecting the supply or the demand for the good that lead to variations in its price over the year, even though its physical qualities may not have changed otherwise. In such circumstances, storage can be regarded as an extension of the production process over time. The storage services become incorporated in the goods, thereby increasing their value while being held in store. Any gain that occurs outside the predetermined period continues to be recorded as a holding gain or loss.

This inclusion of output due to storage applies only to goods that take a long time to complete, those that have an established annual seasonal pattern or those where maturing is part of the regular production process. It does not apply to holding financial assets, valuables or other non-financial assets including land and buildings. Even if anticipated increases in value results in these cases, the motive for holding the items is speculation. The increases in value are treated as holding gains and not as part of the production process.

5.3.2 Wholesale and retail distribution

Wholesalers and retailers, the traders that actually buy and sell goods with only minimal processing such as grading, cleaning, packaging and so on, actually supply services to their customers by storing and displaying a selection of goods in convenient locations and making them available for customers to buy. Their output is measured by the total value of the trade margins realised on the goods they purchase for resale. A trade margin is defined as the difference between the actual or imputed price realised on a good purchased for resale and the price that would have to be paid by the distributor to replace the good at the time it is sold or otherwise disposed of. The margins realised on some goods may be negative if their prices have to be marked down. They would also be negative on goods that are never sold because they go to waste.

The output of trading by a wholesaler or retailer is given by the following identity:

Value of output = (Value of sales)

plus (value of goods purchased for resale and used for intermediate consumption/compensation of employees)

minus (value of goods purchased for resale)

plus (value of additions to inventories of goods for resale) (1)

minus (value of goods withdrawn from inventories of goods for resale)

minus (value of recurrent losses due to normal rates of wastage or accidental damage).

Important points to be noted are the following: (i) goods sold are valued at the prices at which they are actually sold, even if the trader has to mark their prices down. Allowance needs to be made for the effect of reductions in price due to loyalty programmes. (ii) Goods provided to employees as remuneration in kind should be valued at the current purchasers' prices payable by the traders to replace them (zero realised margins). Similarly, goods withdrawn by the owners of unincorporated enterprises for their own final consumption should be valued at the current purchasers' prices payable by the traders to replace them. (iii) Goods purchased for resale should be valued excluding any transport charges invoiced separately by the suppliers or paid to third parties by wholesalers or retailers: these transport services form part of the intermediate consumption of the wholesalers or retailers. (iv) Additions to inventories of goods for resale should be valued at the prices prevailing at the time of entry into inventories, and (v) value of goods withdrawn from inventories of goods for resale depends on whether the goods were acquired with the intention of making a real holding gain over a given period in storage. In the general case, when the goods being resold were not expected to realise a real holding gain while in storage, the value of the goods on withdrawal from inventories should be the cost to the wholesaler or retailer at the time of the withdrawal of acquiring exactly similar replacement goods for later sale. This valuation is necessary to exclude holding gains and losses from the measurement of output, as is the general rule in the SNA. However, when the goods have been stored for reasons of seasonal variation in prices, the expected real holding gain over the anticipated period is deducted from the replacement value of goods withdrawn from inventories. This deduction is fixed in value at the time the goods enter storage and is not altered in the light of actual holding gains, real or nominal. (vi) Value of recurrent losses due to wastage or accidental damage or goods lost are valued in the same way as goods withdrawn from inventories. The costs of storage incurred by traders are treated as part of intermediate consumption.

5.3.3 Output of financial services

Output of financial services is mostly not defined as sales or receipts from the activity. For non-market activities component, the output is obtained conceptually at cost. For financial intermediaries, like banks, the output is obtained as the sum of financial intermediary services indirectly measured (FISIM), which is the major component plus direct charges received for the chargeable services provided. As regards types of financial institutions, the SNA 2008 classifies financial corporations into the following types: central bank; deposit-taking corporations; money market funds (MMF); non-MMF investment funds; other financial intermediaries; financial auxiliaries; and captive financial institutions, each one further categorised into public, national private and foreign controlled units and insurance corporations and pension funds. For financial activities other than the central bank (Reserve Bank of

India [RBI] in the Indian context) mentioned earlier, the classifications could be broadly grouped into three types of agencies: financial intermediation, financial auxiliaries and other financial services. Besides the corporate sector, certain informal-sector financial activities like money lending and chit fund operations do have significant presence in India and other developing countries in Asia and Africa. Such financial services were not recognised in SNA 1993 but are now recognised in SNA 2008 by redefining the FISIM.

5.3.3.1 Output of the central bank (RBI)

The central bank (the RBI in the Indian context), conceptually the bank of banks, has several roles to play in the economy that includes issue of currency, monetary policy services, money supply through fixing currency reserve rates, supervision of banks and financial institutions maintaining financial discipline in the economy, and intermediation through baking division. The issues of currency, monetary policy services, supervisory services, IT services, and so on are collective in nature, serving the community as a whole, and thus represent non-market output. The financial intermediation services are individual in nature, and in the absence of policy intervention in the interest rates charged by the central banks, may be treated as market production. The borderline cases, such as supervisory services, may be classified as non-market services and valued at cost. However, total activities of the central bank are to be placed in the financial corporate sector. The SNA 2008 has clarified that though the central bank is placed in the financial corporate sector, its non-market activities are to be estimated at cost. In the Indian national accounts, until 2015 the earlier series considered activities of RBI as 'market' only for the banking division and 'non-market' for the rest of the activities. In the new series (base year 2011–12) of national accounts, the entire operations of RBI are taken as 'non-market' and thus valued at cost.

As mentioned earlier, as per the SNA 2008, the central bank is in the corporate-financial sector and not in general government. The collective consumption is recorded as expenditure by general government but the government does not incur the costs incurred by the central bank. Therefore, a current transfer of the value of the non-market output is recorded as payable by the central bank and receivable by the general government to cover the purchase of the non-market output of the central bank by government.

The change in the new series of Indian national accounts on treatment of RBI as non-market from the mixed approach adopted in all earlier series was mainly on two counts. One was the fact that the deposit of banks at the RBI is a part of its monetary policy function and RBI does not make any interest payment on these deposits. Two, as per the international practice, now all European countries and almost all the Asian countries are treating their central bank as non-market. Besides, though, RBI can segregate issue and banking department data, but all market and non-market operations of the

RBI cannot be disaggregated. Thus, treating the RBI as a non-market entity was considered. However, this topic remains open for research and review.

5.3.3.2 Financial intermediation

This involves financial risk management and liquidity transformation, activities in which an institutional unit incurs financial liabilities for the purpose of acquiring mainly financial assets. Corporations engaged in these activities obtain funds, not only by taking deposits but also by issuing bills, bonds or other securities. They use these funds as well as own funds to acquire mainly financial assets not only by making advances or loans to others but also by purchasing bills, bonds or other securities.

Financial services provided by means of financial intermediation is a process whereby a financial institution (a bank) accepts deposits from units with 'excess' funds for lending to other units in need of funds. Each of the two parties pays a fee to the bank for the service provided. The unit lending funds accepts a lower rate of interest than that paid by the borrower; the difference is equal to the combined fees implicitly charged by the bank to the depositor and to the borrower. It represents charges for financial intermediation services indirectly measured (FISIM). The bank thus provides a mechanism to allow the first unit to lend to the second. Each of the two parties pays a hidden fee to the bank for the service provided.

It may be mentioned that in the SNA 1993, lending exclusively from own funds was not considered an economic activity and the FISIM was conceptualised only as:

FISIM (on loans (f_L) and deposits (f_D))
= interest receivable (R_L) *less* interest payable (R_D)
= difference between loans stock (Y_L) *and* deposits (Y_D) multiplied by their respective interest rates (r_L and r_D), (2)

$$f_L + f_D = R_L - R_D$$
$$f_L + f_D = r_L Y_L - r_D Y_D$$

However, it is seldom the case that the amount of funds lent by a financial institution exactly matches the amount deposited with them. Some money may have been deposited but not yet loaned; some loans may be financed by the bank's own funds and not from borrowed funds. However, the depositor of funds receives the same amount of interest and service whether or not the funds are then lent by the bank to another customer, and the borrower pays the same rate of interest and receives the same service whether the funds are provided by intermediated funds or the bank's own funds. For this reason, the SNA 2008 recommends an indirect service charge to be imputed in respect of all loans and deposits offered by a financial institution irrespective of the source of the funds. This reference rate applies to both interest paid on loans and interest paid on deposits so that the amounts of interest recorded are calculated as the reference rate times the level of loan or deposit in question. The difference between these amounts and the amounts actually paid to the financial institution are recorded as service charges paid by the borrower or depositor to the financial institution. For clarity, the amounts based on the reference rate recorded in the SNA as interest are described as 'SNA interest' and the total amounts actually paid to or by the financial institution are described as 'bank interest'. The implicit service charge is thus the sum of the bank interest on loans less the SNA interest on the same loans plus the SNA interest on deposits less the bank interest on the same deposits. The service charge is payable by or to the unit in receipt of the loan or owning the deposit as appropriate.

Thus, the implicit service charge is equal to the sum of the bank interest on loans *less* SNA interest on the same loans *plus* SNA interest on deposits *less* the bank interest on the same deposits. The indirect service charge is imputed in respect of all loans and deposits offered by a financial institution irrespective of the source of the funds. In other words, as per the SNA 2008, FISIM on loans (f_L) and deposits (f_D) equals stock of loans multiplied by the difference between interest rate on loans (r_L) and a reference interest rate (rr) plus the stock of deposits multiplied by difference between a reference interest rate and the interest rate on deposits (r_D).

$$\begin{aligned} f_L + f_D &= (r_L - rr)Y_L + (rr - r_D)Y_D \\ f_L + f_D &= rr(Y_D - Y_L) + r_L Y_L - r_D Y_D \end{aligned} \quad (3)$$

The implication is that FISIM derived from the earlier two formulas (2 and 3) are equal when the stock of loans is equal to the stock of deposits. Further, and more importantly, when units are lending exclusively from own funds, FISIM is equivalent to $(r_L - rr)Y_L$.

Advantages of the SNA 2008 FISIM formula (3) are that the services provided to depositors and borrowers are independently estimated irrespective of what the deposits are used for and where funds for providing loans come from, and it facilitates the distribution of indirect service charges to its users in a consistent way by allowing calculations at a detailed level.

The FISIM computation formula (3), however, involves several compilation issues:

- A single reference rate should be used, but (when relevant) a country can use multiple rates.
- Rate prevailing for interbank borrowing and lending may be a suitable as a reference rate.
- For banks within the same economy, there is often little if any service provided in association with banks' lending to and borrowing from other banks.
- A simple way to obtain a reference rate reflecting the maturity structure of financial assets/liabilities is to calculate the average of the sum of

the ratios of interest payable and receivable to the stock of deposits and loans as follows:

$$rr = 0.5(R_D / Y_D + R_L / Y_L)$$

The reference rate to be used in the calculation of SNA interest is a rate between bank interest rates on deposits and loans. The rate prevailing for interbank borrowing and lending may be a choice as a reference rate. In the revised series (base 2011–12) of National Accounts Statistics, reference rate is taken as harmonic average instead of arithmetic average, as the two entities are ratios. However, an appropriate reference rate is still a research area.

MEASUREMENT IN VOLUME TERMS

The measurement of the volume change in the output of financial intermediation should take into account the total output, including the direct charges. In the absence of direct deflators for the output of FISIM, as per the SNA 2008, one of the following approaches could be used:

- Rate of change of the volume indicator can be derived using the rate of change of average stocks of loans and deposits deflated by a general price index (e.g., the GDP deflator) adjusted for quality change in the output of financial services.
- The output indicator method can be used, which involves breaking down the different characteristics linked to financial services (numbers and values of loans and deposits, savings, money transfers, etc.). For each characteristic, an appropriate volume indicator is derived, and volume indicators are then weighted together.

5.3.3.3 Financial auxiliaries and other financial services

Auxiliary financial activities facilitate risk management and liquidity transformation activities. Financial auxiliaries, who are the units primarily engaged in auxiliary financial activities, typically act on behalf of other units and do not put themselves at risk by incurring financial liabilities or by acquiring financial assets as part of an intermediation service.

Financial services associated with the acquisition and disposal of financial assets and liabilities in financial markets: debt securities such as bills and bonds are other forms of financial assets that give rise to interest payments, interest being payable to the owner of the security by the issuer. Some of these interest charges may themselves be imputed from changes in the value of securities as they approach maturity. When a financial institution offers a security for sale, a service charge is levied, the purchase price (or ask price) representing the estimated market value of the security plus a margin. Another charge is levied when a security is sold, the price offered to the seller (the bid price) representing the market value less a margin.

Prices of securities may change rapidly and to avoid including holding gains and losses in the calculation of the service margins; it is important to calculate the margins (the output of the service) on sales and purchases in terms of mid-prices. The mid-price of a security is the average at a given point in time between the bid and ask price. Thus, the margin on the purchase of a security is the difference between the ask price and mid-price at the time of the purchase, and the margin on a sale is the difference between the mid-price and the bid price at the time of the sale.

Equities and investment fund shares or units give rise to property income other than interest but, like debt securities, they are offered for sale and purchase at different prices. The difference between the buying price and mid-price and the mid-price and selling price should be treated as the provision of financial services (output) as in the case of securities.

A large direct fee is likely to be charged by credit card issuers to the units that accept credit cards as a means of payment. The charge is usually calculated as a percentage of the sale; in the case of retailers the sale value corresponds to turnover and not output. Although the percentage is usually small in absolute terms, it is applied to such large figure means that the total value of the charge is very large. The charge represents output of the credit card companies and intermediate consumption of the corporations that accept credit cards as means of payment. Ignoring the role of the credit card company does not affect the measurement of the final consumption or exports on the goods and services concerned but does underestimate the costs of the provider of goods and services and the output of the credit card company. This in turn leads to a misallocation of value added from the credit card company to the provider of the goods and services paid for by credit card. Besides, a card holder may also be charged an explicit fee, usually each year, for holding the card. In addition, if a card holder uses the credit facilities offered by the card, he will pay indirect charges associated with interest payable on the outstanding credit.

5.3.4 Insurance

In non-life insurance only, the risk is covered. Thus, when the event happens for which insurance has been taken, a claim is made. However, in life insurance there is an element of saving besides risk coverage. Thus, besides claims the insurance company pays the insured a sum after completion of a period to the survived person from its actuarial reserve.

Thus, for non-life or term insurance, the gross output (GO) is determined as

$$\text{GO} = \text{premium payable} + \text{supplemental premium} - \text{claims}$$

And for life insurance –

$$\text{GO} = \text{premium payable} + \text{supplemental premium} - \text{claims} - \text{change in actuarial reserve}$$

5.3.5 Research and development (R&D)

R&D is creative work undertaken on a systematic basis to increase the stock of knowledge and use this stock of knowledge for the purpose of discovering or developing new products, including improved versions or qualities of existing products, or discovering or developing new or more efficient processes of production. R&D is not an ancillary activity, and a separate establishment should be distinguished for it when possible. The R&D undertaken by market producers on their own behalf should, in principle, be valued on the basis of the estimated basic prices that would be paid if the research were subcontracted commercially, but in practice is likely to have to be valued on the basis of the total production costs including the costs of fixed assets used in production. R&D undertaken by specialised commercial research laboratories or institutes is valued by receipts from sales, contracts, commissions, fees, and so on in the usual way.

R&D undertaken by government units, universities, non-profit research institutes, and so forth is non-market production and is valued on the basis of the total costs incurred. The activity of R&D is different from teaching. The SNA 2008 recommends expenditure on R&D as fixed capital formation, and the Indian national accounts revised series (base 2011–12) has implemented it.

5.4 Changes in the output of services in the new series

Important changes in the new series of Indian national accounts (base year 2011–12), as a result of the implementation of the recommendations of SNA 2008, in the estimation of output of services sectors are summarised in Table 5.2.

Table 5.2 Key Changes in the Methodology for Estimation of Services Output: Indian National Accounts, Base Year 2011–12

Service Sector	*Changes in the Methodology in 2011–12 in the Estimation of Output*
All Services	Output/GVA valued at basic prices instead of factor cost prices
All Services	Expenditures on Intellectual Property Products (R&D, software, databases) for own use are estimated at cost and included in the output instead of intermediate consumption
Financial Services	For banks, FISIM is estimated using reference rate instead of interest received less interest paid
Financial Services: RBI	Activities of whole RBI considered non-market and output estimated at cost instead of mixed approach, banking department as market and rest as non-market
Financial Services	Lending exclusively from own funds is considered an economic activity. For informal financial services, money lenders, FISIM is estimated using reference rate instead of a proxy of one-third of non-banking financial companies in the old series

Source: Based on Central Statistical Office (2016).

References

Central Statistics Organisation (2008). *National Industrial Classification*, Government of India, Ministry of Statistics and Programme Implementation, New Delhi.

Central Statistical Office (2016). *National Accounts Statistics*, Government of India, Ministry of Statistics and Programme Implementation, New Delhi.

United Nations Statistics Division (2008). *International Standard Industrial Classification (ISIC) of All Economic Activities Rev. 4, Series M, No. 4*, United Nations, New York.

World Bank (1993). *System of National Accounts*. Prepared under the Auspices of the Inter-Secretariat Working Group on National Accounts. Eurostat/IMF/OECD/UN/World Bank Publication.

World Bank (2008). *System of National Accounts*. Prepared under the Auspices of the Inter-Secretariat Working Group on National Accounts. Eurostat/IMF/OECD/UN/World Bank Publication.

Appendix 5.1

National accounts and macro-economic aggregates in SNA 2008

In SNA, measure of production is gross value added (GVA) defined as GVA = GVO – IC, where GVO stands for gross value of output and IC for intermediate consumption. Gross domestic product (GDP) is the sum of GVAs of enterprises in the economy and taxes less subsidies on products. GVA and GVO are at basic prices whereas IC is at purchaser's price. Main identities in SNA, each providing an account are as follows:

Commodity balance: gross value of output of goods and services at market prices (mp)

$$\begin{aligned} GVO_{mp} \equiv\ & IC + PFCE + GFCE + GFCF + CII \\ & + \text{Acquisition less disposal of valuables} + X - M \end{aligned} \tag{1}$$

Where PFCE: private final consumption expenditure (household final consumption expenditure [HFCE] and FCE of non-profit institutions serving households [NPISHs]; GFCE: government final consumption expenditure; GFCF: gross fixed capital formation; CII: change in inventories; X: exports; and M: imports.

Production-side identity

$$GDP_{mp} \equiv GVO_{bp} - IC + \text{product}\ (t - s) + (t - s)\ \text{on imports} \tag{2}$$

Where product (t – s) denotes taxes on products less subsidies on products and (t – s) on imports denotes taxes on imports less subsidies on imports.

Income-side identities

$$\begin{aligned} GDP_{mp} \equiv\ & (CE + OS + MI)\ \text{generated in domestic enterprises} \\ & + \text{Product}\ (t - s) + (t - s)\ \text{on imports} \end{aligned} \tag{3}$$

Where CE denotes compensation of employees, OS denotes operating surplus, and MI denotes mixed income, the mix of CE and OS due to self-employed/own account enterprises.

$$\begin{aligned} \text{GNI} \equiv & (\text{CE} + \text{OS \& MI}) \text{ generated in domestic enterprises} \\ & + \text{Product}(\text{t} - \text{s}) + (\text{t} - \text{s})\text{on imports} \\ & + \text{CE from RoW}(\text{net}) + \text{PI from RoW } (\text{net}) \end{aligned} \tag{4}$$

$$\begin{aligned} \text{GNDI} \equiv & \text{ GNI} + (\text{net})\text{current transfers} \\ & + (\text{Net})\text{taxes on income and wealth from RoW} \end{aligned} \tag{5}$$

Expenditure-side identities

$$\begin{aligned} \text{GDP}_{\text{mp}} \equiv & \text{ PFCE } + \text{GFCE} + \text{GFCF} + \text{CII} + \text{Acquisition less} \\ & \text{disposal of valuables} + \text{X} - \text{M} \end{aligned} \tag{6}$$

$$\text{Gross Savings} \equiv \text{GNDI} - (\text{PFCE} + \text{GFCE}) \tag{7}$$

This implies,

$$\begin{aligned} & \text{Net lending from RoW} \equiv \\ & \text{Gross Savings} + (\text{net}) \text{ Capital transfer receivable} \\ & - (\text{GDCF + acquisition less disposal of valuables}) \\ & - \text{Acquisition less disposal of non-produced non-financial assets} \end{aligned} \tag{8}$$

The SNA framework reflects the economic processes through sequence of accounts that provides an overview of a given economy. Sequence of accounts is structured by institutional sectors (including ROW) in three subsets: current accounts, accumulation accounts and balance sheet accounts. Institutional sectors comprise corporate financial, corporate non-financial, general government, NPISH, and household sector.

Current accounts include production account, identity (2); income accounts comprising generation of income account, identity (3); allocation of primary income account, identity (4); secondary distribution of income account, identity (5); and use of income account, identity (7). Accumulation accounts record all changes in assets and changes in liabilities in the capital and financial account, identity (8). Besides, in the SNA 2008, 'Other changes in assets account' includes 'Other changes in volume of assets account' and 'Revaluation account'. Balance sheets record stocks of assets and liabilities and the difference.

Each account has a balancing item that is significant as a macro-economic aggregate like gross/net domestic product (GDP/NDP), gross/net national income (GNI/NNI), gross/net disposable income (GNDI/NNDI) and gross/net saving and in the capital/financial account as net lending/borrowing.

Source: Author's estimates.

Part II

Services sector, economic growth and employment

6 Services sector in India

An exploration of the heterogeneity across sub-sectors

Jesim Pais

6.1 Introduction

In recent years, there has been an unprecedented growth in services across all countries. While in the advanced industrialised countries this is seen as a continuation of the economic transformation, the above average growth of the services sector as compared with manufacturing and agriculture is also observed in less developed countries like India (GOI, 2012; Eichengreen and Gupta, 2010; Singh, 2006; Papola, 2008). The services sector accounted for about 30 per cent of total gross domestic product (GDP) of India in 1950s; its share in GDP increased to 38 per cent in the 1980s, then to 43 per cent in the 1990s and finally to about 56.5 per cent in 2012–13 (CSO, 2014). Thus, the services sector currently accounts for more than half of India's GDP. This process of tertiarisation (dominance of the tertiary or services sector) of the economy has been accompanied by a decline in the share of the primary sector (agriculture) and a more or less constant share of the secondary (industry) sector over the years.

It has been argued that the disproportionate growth in services, at least in the case of India, is not a recent phenomenon. For example, Mitra (1988) noted the disproportionate growth in services GDP in India in the 1980s. On similar lines, Nagaraj (1991) observed that the large share of the services sector in recent times is due to the relatively higher base in the 1950s and more or less steady growth from early 1950s onwards. While it is true that the share of the services sector was already notable in the 1950s, and there has been steady growth of the sector since, there is no doubt that the nature and quality of growth of services GDP has changed in more recent years. Major changes in the services sector in the recent period is brought about by three important factors: the role of information technology– (IT) and information and communication technology– (ICT) led services, globalisation process and increased reliance on outsourcing (Kotabe, Mol and Murray, 2009).

It has also been pointed out that there is a difference in the nature and type of services between the advanced industrial countries and the countries that are still at lower levels of income. While services sector employment in advanced countries may not imply low-quality employment, in the case of less developed countries a large proportion of the service economy has low-quality employment (Ghosh, 1991). According to one argument, services sector occupations in less developed countries (LDCs) arise out of scarcity of employment opportunities in other sectors. In this context, Ghosh (1991) cited Arthur Lewis (1954) as having 'rightly observed that cheap supply of labour and social prestige consideration of the upper strata of population make possible the employment of a large number of domestic servants in LDCs'. Thus, while labour productivity in the services sector in advanced countries would be on par with or higher than in manufacturing, in less developed countries the labour productivity in services sector is relatively lower. Secondly, accordingly to Ghosh (1991), the distributive services in the tertiary occupations (trade and transport) in LDCs are low-productivity and low-income type as compared with advanced countries, and finally services sector occupations in advanced countries are highly capital-intensive, whereas on the contrary in LDCs there is very little use of capital. Thus, it may be concluded that a part of the services sector growth in LDCs such as India should be treated with caution and should not be taken as an indicator of economic growth.

A study of the services sector at a reasonably disaggregated level is necessary and useful because unlike agriculture (the primary sector) and industry (the secondary sector), the services sector (the tertiary sector) is much more heterogeneous in nature.[1] The heterogeneity of the services sector is to some extent by definition – it comprises all that is not in the primary and secondary sectors. Activities that result in production of services (and not goods) in the agricultural sector and in manufacturing (for example, the work of a worker guarding crops or a factory) are categorised as agricultural activity or manufacturing as the case may be and not as services. In other words, the definition of what constitutes the services sector is not as precise as that of agriculture and manufacturing/industry.

The heterogeneity in the services sector is also technology-driven. Significant technological advancements across the globe, particularly in automation and communication, have led to increase in activities of the 'services' type. Technology-driven fractioning of the production process has led to clear identification of processes that can be categorised as services, especially if they are undertaken by another entity such as in outsourcing. Further, with the process of globalisation and increased reliance of outsourcing as a mode of production organisation, rapid changes have occurred in the economic structures of many economies, including India. And a large part of this change is visible in the form of growth and change in the structure of economies in favour of larger share of the services sector.

In this chapter, we attempt to highlight the heterogeneity within the services sector through the analysis of the growth, structure and contribution of the services sector in India for a period covering three decades: 1980–2010. This analysis is carried out for different sub-sectors within the services sector at a level of disaggregation that has not been adequately attempted so far in the literature. The differences across different sub-sectors in the services sector are also evident from the examination of productivity differences across these subsectors. Finally, we attempt to reclassify various services sector activities into four major sub-categories which are different from the national account sub-categories. This is an attempt to provide a deeper understanding of the differences across the different services sub-sectors.

During the period of 60 years between 1950 and 2010, two important service sub-sectors, viz., trade and public administration, have remained stable with regard to their contribution to services sector GDP in India. In this span of 60 years, banks, road transport, business services and insurance showed notable increase in their share of sectoral GDP, while dwellings, domestic services, recreation and entertainment experienced a secular decline. The two most prominent high-growth services sub-categories were business and private-sector communications. Both these services accounted for a negligible share in total service sector GDP prior to the 1990s, but grew rapidly thereafter. Within business, it was computer-related services that grew most prominently in the more recent period of our study.

The next section has a brief discussion on what constitutes the services sector and the debate on the concept and definitions. In section 6.3, we briefly discuss measurement issues in general and those that are specific to India. In section 6.4, we present a detailed analysis of the growth and structure of service sector GDP, along with their contribution to total GDP growth in India from 1980 until 2009–10, with special focus on the latest period from 2004–05 to 2009–10. In section 6.5, we present a brief discussion on the productivity difference across services sub-sectors. Section 6.6 looks at the different possible reclassifications of services and attempts to understand the prospects of growth and sustainability through this alternative classification.

6.2 What constitutes the services sector?

The term services sector refers to, at the most aggregate level, a large group of activities that include trade, hospitality (hotels, restaurants), transportation, communication, entertainment, health, education, and public services. It can be argued that, even at the aggregate level, the services sector is more heterogeneous than the other two sectors, agriculture (primary sector) and industry (secondary sector). Thus, if the primary sector involves producing goods directly from natural resources (agriculture, fishing, hunting, mining, and so on) and the secondary sector involves modifying material goods into other more useful products and commodities, then the tertiary or the services sector includes all activities that do not produce or modify material goods (Illeris, 2007). In other words, unlike the output of agriculture, mining or manufacturing which are material and tangible, the output of the services sector such as teaching, cleaning, selling, curing and entertaining have no physical form and therefore are immaterial or intangible (Noon, 2003).

Given its nature and heterogeneity, there is a large body of literature in which scholars have debated on the precise definition and identification of the services sector.[2] In this debate, scholars have argued that even in the most advanced countries where the services sector accounts for the largest proportion of all economic activities, it is defined negatively or as a residual comprising all economic activities that do not belong either to the primary or secondary sector (Illeris, 2007).

T.P. Hill wrote a set of influential papers on the concept and definition of the services sector as being distinct from goods (Hill, 1977; 1979). In an early review on what constitutes the production of goods and what would be services, Hill (1977) provides a positive definition of the services sector 'as a change in the condition of a person, or of a good belonging to some economic unit, which is brought about as the result of the activity of some other economic unit, with the prior agreement of the former person or economic unit'.[3] Despite its 'vagueness' in part, the positive definition by Hill was nevertheless influential and contributed to the UN System of National Accounts (Illeris, 2007). The internationally accepted definition of what constitutes services is given by the UN SNA (1993) as follows: 'Services are not separate entities over which ownership rights can be established. They cannot be traded separately from their production. Services are heterogeneous outputs produced to order and typically consist of changes in the conditions of the consuming units realised by the activities of producers at the demand of the consumers'. By the time their production is completed they must have been provided to the consumers.[4] And the production of services must be confined to activities that are capable of being carried out by one unit for the benefit of another. Otherwise, service industries could not develop and there could be no markets for services. It is also possible for a unit to produce a service for its own consumption provided that the type of activity is such that it could have been carried out by another unit.[5]

6.3 Services sector measurement issues

The problem of measurement of the services sector has engaged governments and scholars for several years.[6] There are mainly three major problems with regard to measurement of services sector value added. The first relates to the inability to measure the value of the output itself. For example, there are services that are not marketed or do not have an explicit 'market value' such as services that are provided by public administration, health services, education services, ownership of dwellings, defence services and banking and financial services. Here the general method of measuring value added is the value of wages given to workers in the sector. Thus, an increase in either employment or in wages both lead to a corresponding increase in value added. In case of services such as health and education, Hill and McGibbon (1966) argued that the demand for such services 'is likely to be highly income elastic so that their relatively slow measured rate of growth in real terms must be viewed with some scepticism'. The second problem relates to obtaining the real value of services as opposed to the nominal value. The absence of appropriate price deflators for many different types of services makes it difficult to arrive at the value added in services in real terms. There have been a number of attempts to overcome this problem by using different methods of deflation. The most popular method is the method of double deflation. In the method of double deflation, the value of output and value of inputs are deflated separately by their appropriate price indices, and the value added for the service is then estimated as the difference between the output and inputs (CSO, 2007). The third set of issues is to do with the inability to actually make measurements on the ground and hence the use of indicators as proxies for the existence and growth of some services. For example, in the case of a number of services, employment (that is, the total number of persons employed in providing that service to rest of the economy) is used as an indicator to arrive at the size and growth of the service. Thus, the total value added in the services sector is arrived at using different methods and measures for different services.[7]

In addition to the earlier three general issues, India also faces some specific issues of services sector measurement. According to Shetty (2007), the main problem with regard to estimating services GDP in India emanates from the fact that the estimates for GDP are arrived at in seven main categories, each being subdivided into subcategories and each of the subcategories in turn being classified further into three institutional sectors viz., private sector, public corporate sector and the unorganised sector. Each of these three institutional sectors has its own characteristics, making collection of data and estimates complicated and complex (Shetty, 2007). Due to the lack of availability of appropriate data, the method used in arriving at the estimate of GDP in case of a number of services, especially in the unorganised sector and in a few cases in the private corporate sector, a method is evolved where by GDP is obtained as a product of estimates of value added per worker and estimates of total number of workers. In this method, first a measure of the average gross value added (GVA) per worker in the particular sector or sub-sector is obtained through specialised surveys that are conducted for this purpose. The estimates for the total employment in the sector are then obtained from another source. The estimated GVA and total employment are then multiplied to obtain estimates of the GDP of that sector. The problem with this method is that not only could there be a regular mismatch between obtaining estimates for GVA and employment but also resource and other constraints imply that the GVA estimates or even employment estimates in the inter-survey period which can be five to six years in case of National Sample Survey (NSS) and ten years in case of the Census are based on extrapolations. In the case of the services sector, which has been identified as a fast-changing and growing sector of the economy, such extrapolations on thin past data do not lead to robust estimates. This is obvious from the difference in estimates for the same year and in current prices of various services when the series are revised from time to time.[8] Not surprisingly, the differences are higher at higher levels of disaggregation.

Another limitation with regard to the measurement and estimation of services GDP in India is that estimates are not obtained at a sufficiently disaggregated level. While there is an improvement on this front with every new release of GDP series, the latest being the series with base year 2004–05, when compared with the manufacturing sector, the services are far behind.[9] In this exercise of improving the coverage in every new GDP services, the Central Statistical Organisation (CSO) also regroups economic activities according to a new classification scheme. In a detailed critique of this classification scheme, Banerjee, Baksi and Roy (2007) conclude that data from the NSS enterprises surveys subsequent to the changes made in the 1999–2000 series support the regrouping of service sector activities.

Thus, any empirical analysis of the services sector has the limitations of the earlier shortcomings pertaining to the complexities of measuring the services sector. In India, the Central Statistical Organisation (CSO) estimates GDP figures for all sectors of the economy including the services sector. Notwithstanding the issues highlighted earlier, the services sector GDP estimates of CSO are the only source for understanding the performance of the services sector for various sub-categories of services in India.

6.4 Analysis of the services sector GDP in India (1980–2010)[10]

In this section, we undertake a detailed analysis of the growth and structure of the services sector in India using data on GDP from the latest series released in 2011 by the CSO. The new series is with the base year 2004–05 and the CSO has released data with this new base year from 1950–51 onwards until 2009–10.[11] These data are available at a level of disaggregation that includes about 40 services activities/sub-sectors. In addition, for data from 2004–05 onwards there are four additional categories within business services, which is also a sub-sector within services that has relatively high growth in recent years.

We compute the growth rate of various constituents of the services sector and their sub-categories. We also evaluate the structure of the services sector in terms of how various sub-sectors contribute to its GDP and analyse whether there is any change in the structure during the span of our study period. We further assess the contribution of various services sub-sectors to total GDP growth for the period 1980–2010.

6.4.1 Growth

In Table 6.1, we present the growth rate the service sector GDP from 1980 until 2010, divided into three sub-periods, viz., 1980–81 to 1996–97, 1996–97 to 2004–05 and 2004–05 to 2009–10. The growth of the services sector

Table 6.1 Growth rate of GDP by service sector sub-sectors: 1979–80 to 2009–10 (% per annum)

Sl. No.	*Description of category*	*1979–80 to 1995–96*	*1995–96 to 2004–05*	*2004–05 to 2009–10*
1	**Trade, hotels & restaurants**	**6.4**	7.8	9.1
1.1	Trade	6.4	10.7	9.1
1.2	Hotel and restaurant	7.0	12.8	8.5
2	**All transport**	**6.3**	**7.6**	8.0
2.1	Railways	3.7	5.1	9.1
2.1.1	Passenger related	4.0	6.1	11.5
2.1.2	Goods transport related	3.9	4.4	7.9
2.2	Other transport	7.1	8.1	7.8
2.2.1	Road transport	7.3	8.6	7.7
2.2.2	Water transport	4.6	6.1	7.8
2.2.3	Air transport	5.5	4.1	14.8
2.2.4	Service incidental to transport	8.3	6.3	5.5
3	**Storage**	2.8	2.1	8.0
4	**Communications**	8.1	20.7	26.7
4.1	Public-sector communications	7.3	17.0	16.4
4.1.1	Public-sector postal services	0.5	–3.4	–1.6
4.1.2	Telephones	9.2	20.8	17.3
4.2	Private-sector communications		36.4	41.1
5	**Banking and insurance**	9.5	8.5	15.6
5.1	Banking	10.6	7.8	15.2
5.1.1	Banks	8.8	13.0	20.1
5.1.2	Banking department of RBI	8.4	–190.5	–183.4
5.1.3	Post office saving bank	2.6	7.6	2.7
5.1.4	Non-banking financial institutions	22.8	4.7	3.8
5.1.5	Co-operative credit societies	6.7	5.7	3.3
5.1.6	Employees' provident fund org.	6.1	7.9	13.0
6	**Insurance**	5.0	12.5	17.5
6.1	Life (other than postal life)	8.7	16.0	19.4
6.2	Postal life	10.6	7.0	7.0
6.3	Non-life	2.9	8.6	14.7
7	**Real estate, dwellings business services**	7.4	7.0	9.4
7.1	Dwellings	7.1	2.6	3.6
7.1.1	Rural	7.7	1.9	5.3
7.1.2	Urban	6.7	3.1	1.2
7.2	Real estate	3.8	5.0	26.0

(*Continued*)

Table 6.1 (Continued)

Sl. No.	*Description of category*	*1979–80 to 1995–96*	*1995–96 to 2004–05*	*2004–05 to 2009–10*
7.3	Business services	10.7	21.3	17.2
7.4	Legal services	7.9	3.7	7.9
8	**Community services**	6.0	8.5	7.9
8.1	Education (and research & scientific)	6.4	8.6	8.6
8.1.1	Education			7.4
8.1.2	Research & scientific			18.4
8.3	Medical & health	7.1	9.9	4.4
8.4	Religious & other community membership organisations	3.1	4.1	14.2
9	**Recreation & entertainment services**	3.0	3.0	8.9
10	**Radio & TV broadcasting**	6.0	-15.9	-1.5
11	**Personal services**	3.8	6.4	5.7
11.1	Domestic	1.0	7.3	9.6
11.2	Laundry, dyeing & dry cleaning	3.9	6.0	3.8
11.3	Barber & beauty shops	0.6	6.1	3.9
11.4	Tailoring	5.2	6.8	12.9
11.5	Other services, n.e.c.	6.6	6.3	1.1
12	**Sanitary services services/activities n.e.c.**	5.0	3.4	7.8
13	**International & other extra territorial bodies**	-0.8	4.9	4.9
14	**Public administration & defence**	5.4	6.3	9.2
	Total services sector	6.5	7.7	10.3

Source: Author's computations using data from NAS (CSO, various annual issues).

Note: n.e.c. = not elsewhere classified.

accelerated from the early 1980s onwards. The average annual growth rate of the services sector from 1980–81 to 1995–96 was about 6.5 per cent. The services sector growth further increased to 7.7 per cent in the period from 1996–97 to 2004–05 and finally to 10.3 per cent in the most recent period from 2004–05 to 2009–10 (Table 6.1).

In the period from 1980 to 1995–96, among the relatively larger service activities, road transport (7.3 per cent), banks (8.8 per cent) and hotels and restaurants (7.0 per cent) had growth rates of sectoral GDP higher than the average for services (6.9 per cent). Among the services that were relatively of smaller size but that experienced notable high growth in this period were business services (10.7 per cent), public-sector communications (7.3 per cent), life insurance (8.7 per cent) and public-sector telephones (10.7 per cent). All other services such as trade, public administration, education services and railways that accounted for a major part of the growth in services in the earlier period from 1950 to 1980 appear to have lower-than-average growth from 1980–81 to 1995–96.

The pattern of services growth appears to have changed from 1996–97 onwards. From 1996–97 until 2004–05, the total services GDP grew at 7.7 per cent. The highlights of services growth in this period are high growth of banking and insurance services, communication services and business services. The growth rate of trade that had declined in the previous two time periods appears to have picked up between 1995–96 and 2004–05. The annual average growth rate of trade in this period was 10.7 per cent. Road transport continued with its previous growth performance, achieving about 8.6 per cent per annum. The most spectacular growth performance is however from communication services. In this, public-sector telephones (20.8 per cent) and private-sector communication (36 per cent) both emerge as rising services, albeit from a low base.[12] In this period, there was also high growth in the banking and insurance sector: banks (13 per cent), non-life insurance (8.6 per cent) and life insurance (16 per cent). The services that remained relatively large but experienced lower-than-average growth rates between 1996–97 and 2004–05 were dwellings (2.6 per cent), public administration (6.3 per cent) and railways (5.1 per cent).

6.4.2 *Structure and change in the structure of services from 1980–2004*

In the 1980s, the services sector was in a way dominated by the public sector. Of the top 10 services which together accounted for about 79 per cent of services GDP, services dominated by the public sector accounted for over 30 per cent. These are public administration (14.5 per cent of services GDP), railways (3.4 per cent), medical and health services (2.6 per cent) and banks (2.4 per cent). The other services that were partially in the public sector domain are road transport (7.9 per cent) and education (6.9 per cent). The non-public-sector-related services that accounted for major share of services GDP in the 1980s were trade (22.2 per cent), dwellings (14.6 per cent), personal services (3.7 per cent) and recreation services (2.1 per cent) (Table 6.2).

By 1995–96, a few years into the regime of new economic policies that favoured privatisation and reduced role of the state, the services that were previously in the public sector continued to grow. However, this growth could be due to the presence and growth in the private sector activities in these services. Public administration and railways, the two services fully in the public domain, had lower shares in services GDP in 1995–96 as compared to that in the 1980s. Data at this level of disaggregation do not permit

Table 6.2 Share of sub-sectors in total services sector GDP: 1979–80 to 2009–10 (%)

Sl. No.	*Description of category*	*1980–81*	*1991–92*	*1995–96*	*1999–00*	*2004–05*	*2009–10*
1	Trade, hotels & restaurants	30.7	27.5	29.9	28.9	30.2	28.5
1.1	Trade	22.2	19.8	21.5	20.5	27.5	26.0
1.2	Hotel and restaurant	1.7	1.6	1.8	2.0	2.7	2.5
2	All transport	13.4	12.8	12.7	11.6	12.6	11.3
2.1	Railways	3.4	2.9	2.3	1.9	1.8	1.7
2.1.1	Passenger related	0.9	0.7	0.6	0.6	0.5	0.6
2.1.2	Goods transport related	2.3	2.0	1.6	1.3	1.2	1.1
2.2	Other transport	10.0	9.9	10.4	9.7	10.8	9.6
2.2.1	Road transport	7.9	8.0	8.4	8.0	9.1	8.1
2.2.2	Water transport	0.6	0.4	0.5	0.4	0.4	0.4
2.2.3	Air transport	0.6	0.5	0.5	0.3	0.4	0.4
2.2.4	Service incidental to transport	0.7	1.0	1.0	1.0	0.9	0.7
3	Storage	0.3	0.2	0.2	0.1	0.1	0.1
4	Communications	0.9	0.9	1.1	1.6	3.1	6.2
4.1	Public-sector communications	0.9	0.8	1.0	1.4	2.1	2.7
4.1.1	Public-sector postal services	0.9	0.5	0.3	0.3	0.1	0.1
4.1.2	Telephones	0.5	0.5	0.7	1.0	1.9	2.6
4.2	Private-sector communications	0.0	0.1	0.1	0.2	1.0	3.5
5	Banking and insurance	6.2	9.9	10.1	11.6	10.8	13.7
5.1	Banking	4.7	7.8	8.8	10.2	8.9	11.1
5.1.1	Banks	2.4	3.6	3.6	3.9	5.5	8.3
5.1.2	Banking department of RBI	0.7	1.0	1.0	1.0	-0.2	0.0
5.1.3	Post office saving bank	0.1	0.1	0.1	0.1	0.1	0.1
5.1.4	Non-banking financial institutions	0.3	2.2	3.4	4.1	2.6	1.9
5.1.5	Co-operative credit societies	1.0	1.0	1.1	1.1	0.9	0.7
5.1.6	Employees' provident fund org.	0.0	0.0	0.0	0.0	0.0	0.0
6	Insurance	1.6	2.1	1.3	1.4	1.9	2.7
6.1	Life (other than postal life)	0.4	0.5	0.6	0.7	1.1	1.7

6.2	Postal life	0.0	0.0	0.0	0.0	0.0	0.0
6.3	Non-life	1.2	1.6	0.7	0.7	0.8	1.0
7	Real estate, dwellings business services	15.3	18.3	17.8	17.3	16.9	16.2
7.1	Dwellings	14.6	17.3	16.2	13.0	10.5	7.6
7.1.1	Rural	8.2	10.5	9.7	7.5	5.9	4.7
7.1.2	Urban	6.4	7.1	6.8	5.6	4.6	3.0
7.2	Real estate	0.6	0.4	0.4	0.3	0.3	0.6
7.3	Business services	1.0	1.5	1.9	3.2	5.5	7.4
7.4	Legal services	0.7	0.8	0.8	0.7	0.6	0.5
8	Community services	11.6	11.3	10.9	11.7	11.7	10.4
8.1	Education (and research & scientific)	6.9	7.1	6.9	7.7	7.4	6.9
8.1.1	Education	–	–	–	–	–	5.9
8.1.2	Research & scientific	–	–	–	–	–	1.0
8.3	Medical & health	2.6	2.8	2.8	3.0	3.4	2.6
8.4	Religious & other community membership organisations	1.9	1.3	1.1	1.0	0.8	1.0
9	Recreation & entertainment services	2.1	1.4	1.2	1.0	0.8	0.8
10	Radio & TV broadcasting	0.4	0.4	0.4	0.1	0.0	0.0
11	Personal services	3.7	2.5	2.5	2.2	2.3	1.8
11.1	Domestic	0.7	0.3	0.3	0.3	0.3	0.3
11.2	Laundry, dyeing & dry cleaning	0.5	0.5	0.4	0.3	0.3	0.2
11.3	Barber & beauty shops	1.0	0.5	0.4	0.3	0.3	0.3
11.4	Tailoring	0.5	0.5	0.5	0.4	0.4	0.5
11.5	Other services, n.e.c.	0.9	0.7	1.0	0.9	0.9	0.6
12	Sanitary services services/activities n.e.c.	0.5	0.5	0.4	0.4	0.3	0.3
13	International & other extra territorial bodies	0.3	0.2	0.1	0.1	0.1	0.1
14	Public administration & defence	14.5	14.1	12.4	13.3	11.1	10.5
	Total services sector	100.0	100.0	100.0	100.0	100.0	100.0

Source: Author's computations using data from NAS (CSO, various annual issues).

Note: n.e.c. = not elsewhere classified.

the separation of the public- and the private-sector activities, and a separate analysis is required which is not being undertaken here.

In the year 1995–96, the top 10 services in terms of GDP remain the same as in the 1980s, except for a few changes. Recreation and entertainment, with a lower share in 1995–96 than in 1980, exits from the list of top 10 services, while the fast-growing non-banking financial institutions accounting for about 3.4 per cent of the services GDP are in. Business services GDP, which has experienced significant growth over this period, appears to be in the 11th position in terms of GDP shares in 1995–96. Trade, whose growth rate was below the services sector average for several years, begins to revive, and its share in 1995–96, though lower than in 1980, is still higher than in 1991–92. On the other hand, public administration, which also had lower-than-average growth rates in the period from 1980 to 1995–96, has a lower share in 1995–96.

Major changes occurred in the structure of services GDP in the period between 1995–96 and 2004–05. Trade continued to lead as the largest contributor to services GDP by accounting for about 27.5 per cent of services GDP. This is the highest share trade has ever had since the 1950s. In 2004–05, public administration (11.1 per cent), dwellings (10.5 per cent), road transport (9 per cent), education (7.4 per cent), banks (5.5 per cent) and business services (5.5 per cent) are the major contributors to services GDP. Other important services accounting for over 2 per cent of the services GDP are hotels and restaurants (2.7 per cent), non-banking financial institutions (2.7 per cent) and public-sector communications (2.1 per cent).

6.4.3 Contribution to growth 1980 to 2004–05

A few services continued as major contributors to growth of services GDP (Table 6.3). The top five contributors to services growth in the period from 1980 to 1996 were trade (which accounted for about 21.5 per cent of total services growth), followed by dwellings (16.2 per cent), public administration and defence (12.2 per cent), road transport (8.4 per cent) and education services (6.9 per cent). Together, these top five services contributed to about 65 per cent of the services growth in the period from 1980 to 1996.

As seen from Table 6.3, in the next time period from 1996 to 2004–05, the contribution of trade to services GDP growth further increased, along with the contribution of road transport, education, banks, business services and Hotels and restaurants. In the period from 1996 to 2004–05, the contribution to services GDP growth of two important services declined, and they are dwellings (which had a sharp decline contributing only to about 5.2 per cent of services GDP growth) and public administration, which contributed to about 10.2 per cent of GDP growth, down from the earlier period of about 12.2 per cent.

Table 6.3 Contribution to GDP growth by service sub-sectors: 1979–80 to 2009–10 (%)

Sl No.	*Description of category*	*1979–80 to 1995–96*	*1995–96 to 2004–05*	*2004–05 to 2009–10*
1	Trade, hotels & restaurants	29.9	30.4	26.5
1.1	Trade	21.5	29.8	24.3
1.2	Hotel and restaurant	1.8	3.0	2.3
2	All transport	12.7	12.6	9.8
2.1	Railways	2.0	1.5	1.6
2.1.1	Passenger related	0.6	0.5	0.6
2.1.2	Goods transport related	1.4	0.9	0.9
2.2	Other transport	10.4	11.0	8.1
2.2.1	Road transport	8.4	9.4	6.8
2.2.2	Water transport	0.4	0.4	0.3
2.2.3	Air transport	0.5	0.3	0.5
2.2.4	Service incidental to transport	1.0	0.8	0.5
3	Storage	0.2	0.1	0.1
4	Communications	1.1	3.0	8.1
4.1	Public-sector communications	1.0	2.2	3.3
4.1.1	Public-sector postal services	0.1	-0.1	0.0
4.1.2	Telephones	0.7	1.9	3.3
4.2	Private-sector communications	0.0	0.6	4.1
5	Banking and insurance	9.5	11.2	16.4
5.1	Banking	7.9	8.9	13.1
5.1.1	Banks	3.4	6.0	10.6
5.1.2	Banking department of RBI	0.9	-23.7	3.5
5.1.3	Post office saving bank	0.1	0.1	0.0
5.1.4	Non-banking financial institutions	1.2	2.1	1.0
5.1.5	Co-operative credit societies	1.1	0.8	0.3
5.1.6	Employees' provident fund org.	0.0	0.0	0.0
6	Insurance	1.3	2.1	3.3
6.1	Life (other than postal life)	0.6	1.2	2.1
6.2	Postal life	0.0	0.0	0.0
6.3	Non-life	0.6	0.8	1.1
7	Real estate, dwellings business services	17.7	16.3	15.4
7.1	Dwellings	16.2	5.4	3.6
7.1.1	Rural	9.6	2.4	3.0
7.1.2	Urban	6.8	2.7	0.5

(*Continued*)

Table 6.3 (Continued)

Sl No.	*Description of category*	*1979–80 to 1995–96*	*1995–96 to 2004–05*	*2004–05 to 2009–10*
7.2	Real estate	0.3	0.2	0.8
7.3	Business services	1.7	5.2	9.2
7.4	Legal services	0.8	0.4	0.4
8	Community services	10.9	12.0	8.9
8.1	Education (and research & scientific)	6.9	7.7	6.2
8.1.1	Education			4.8
8.1.2	Research & scientific			1.2
8.3	Medical & health	2.8	3.6	1.4
8.4	Religious & other community membership organisations	0.9	0.6	1.2
9	Recreation & entertainment services	1.0	0.5	0.7
10	Radio & TV broadcasting	0.4	–0.9	0.0
11	Personal services	2.2	2.1	1.2
11.1	Domestic	0.1	0.3	0.3
11.2	Laundry, dyeing & dry cleaning	0.3	0.3	0.1
11.3	Barber & beauty shops	0.1	0.3	0.1
11.4	Tailoring	0.5	0.4	0.5
11.5	Other services, n.e.c.	1.0	0.8	0.1
12	Sanitary services services/ activities n.e.c.	0.4	0.2	0.2
13	International & other extra territorial bodies	0.0	0.1	0.0
14	Public administration & defence	12.2	10.2	9.8
	Total services sector	100.0	100.0	100.0

Source: Author's computations using data from NAS (CSO, various annual issues).

Note: n.e.c. = not elsewhere classified.

6.4.4 *Growth and structure in the most recent period of 2004–05 to 2009–10*

The most recent period for which we attempt to analyse services sector GDP growth and structure, 2004–05 to 2009–10, is also the most vibrant and high-growth period for the economy as a whole, but more for the services sector. Of all the periods discussed earlier, the growth rate of services GDP was the highest (at 10.3 per cent per annum) in this period. As in the previous periods, several individual service activities outperformed the average in terms of GDP growth. New and emerging services that appeared in the previous years as having potential for growth now proved that point by exhibiting remarkably high rates of GDP growth.

Relatively large service activities that outperformed the average annual growth rate of services in this period were banks (20.1 per cent), business services (17.2 per cent), private-sector communications (41.1 per cent), public-sector communications (16.4 per cent) and non-life insurance services (14.7 per cent). Other services that accounted for a relatively smaller proportion of total services GDP and nevertheless had very high growth rates of GDP in this period were real estate (26.0 per cent), life insurance (19.4 per cent) and air transport (14.8 per cent).

The services that continued to be important in terms of their share in GDP but that grew significantly slowly in this period are dwellings (3.6 per cent), road transport (7.7 per cent) and non-banking financial institutions (3.8 per cent).

6.4.5 The structure of the services sector from 2004–05 to 2009–10

In 2009–10, as in the previous years, trade was the largest of all service subsectors, accounting for about 26 per cent of services GDP. This was marginally lower than its share in 2004–05, which was about 27.5 per cent. Public administration came second, accounting for about 10.5 per cent of services GDP in 2009–10. This was followed by banks (8.3 per cent), road transport (8.1 per cent), dwellings (7.6 per cent), business services (7.4 per cent) and education (6.9 per cent) (Table 6.2).

The top 10 contributors to services GDP growth in this period are presented in Table 6.3. Trade contributed to about a fourth of the total services growth. The services that contributed to growth in services GDP growth at a rate higher than in the previous time period were banks (10.6 per cent), business services (9.2 per cent), private-sector communications (4.1 per cent) and public-sector telephones (3.3 per cent). Other services that were in the top 10 in terms of their contribution to services GDP growth were public administration (9.8 per cent), road transport (6.8 per cent), education services (6.2 per cent), dwellings (3.6 per cent) and hotels and restaurants (2.3 per cent).

Business services have emerged as a major contributor to services sector GDP growth between 2004–05 and 2009–10. Business services accounted for about 7.4 per cent of services GDP in 2009–10. These services in turn are made up of computer-related services (5.4 per cent), accounting services (0.2 per cent), research and development (1.5 per cent) and legal services (0.5 per cent). In terms of growth of GDP, high double-digit growth by business services is essentially led by computer-related services (17.34 per cent) and research and development (19.04 per cent). The nature and type of business services show that these have relatively higher exposure to the external sector. Given their size, business services could have important contributions to the services GDP growth itself. As seen from Table 6.3, business services contributed to about 9.2 per cent of the total services sector growth and, of this, computer-related services contributed as much as 6.9 per cent.

To summarise this discussion on the growth and structure of the services sector in India, the largest sub-sector in the services sector is trade – retail and wholesale taken together. Besides retail and wholesale trade in fruits, vegetables, milk, meat, grocery and so on, this is also motor vehicle sales and service, machinery and so on. Trade accounted for 26 per cent of total services GDP in 2009–10. This is followed by banking and financial services (11.1 per cent in 2009–10) – banks, postal savings, pension funds and so on. Public administration comes third, accounting for about 10.5 per cent in 2009–10, followed by road transport (8 per cent) and dwellings (7.6 per cent).

6.4.6 *A brief discussion of the services sector between 1950 and 2010*[13]

In the period from 1950 to 2009–10, two important service sub-sectors, trade and public administration, appear to remain stable with regard to their contribution to services sector GDP. The share of trade changed from 25 per cent to about 26 per cent. Similarly, the share of public administration changed from 9 per cent to 10 per cent. A closer look at the interim period of about 60 years shows that trade displays a U-shaped pattern with regard to its share in total services GDP – its share first declined to about 20 per cent in 1991–92 before increasing to 27 per cent in 2009–10. Similarly, public administration displays an inverse U-shaped pattern with regard to its share in total services GDP. Public administration peaked with a share in services GDP of about 14.7 per cent before declining to 10 per cent in 2009–10.

The services that have notable increases in shares through the period from 1950 until 2009–10 are banks (whose GDP increased from about 1.2 per cent in 1950–51 to 8.3 per cent in 2009–10), road transport (from 4.5 per cent to 8 per cent), business services (from 0.8 per cent to 7.4 per cent) and insurance (0.8 to 2.7 per cent). Of these, the share of business services increased sharply starting from the mid-1990s.

Services that experienced a secular decline in the period from 1950s until 2009–10 are dwellings (23.8 per cent to 7.6 per cent), domestic services (8.4 per cent to 1.8 per cent), recreation and entertainment services (5.4 per cent to 0.8 per cent) and radio and TV (1.0 to 0.015 per cent). Of these, the last three experienced a decline in share only after 1995–96.

Services that exhibited an inverse U-shaped pattern in their change of their shares in GDP are public administration, education and health. Their respective shares in services GDP increased until about the 1980s before beginning to decline. Hotels and restaurants, on the other hand, showed a U-shaped pattern, with their share declining until about the late 1980s and then increasing.

Finally, there are two services that stand out prominently in terms of high growth in recent years. The first is business services and the second is private-sector communications. Both these services accounted for negligible shares in the 1950s and 1960s, right up to the 1980s. Their share began to increase only after, and major increases happened only in the 1990s and after. Private-sector communications, which did not exist in any significant way until 1990–91 (0.1 per cent), grew to account for about 3.5 per cent of services GDP in 2009–10. Similarly, business services, of which computer-related services is a major component, accounted for only about 1.3 per cent of the services GDP in 1989–90, and this share increased to 7.4 per cent in 2009–10.

6.5 Analysis of services sector productivity (2004–05 and 2009–10)

Productivity or labour productivity gives an estimate of the average economic value generated by an average worker. Labour productivity levels in a way determine the quality of employment. High levels of labour productivity by themselves do not ensure high wage levels and better conditions of work. However, high levels of labour productivity are one of the necessary conditions to achieve high wage levels and better conditions of work. In other words, it can be said that high-productivity sectors are likely to provide better-quality employment. It can be also said, with a few caveats, that high productivity employment is also likely to be more sustainable and stable. Productivity difference across different service activities also has implications for equity.[14]

The concept of productivity as used in this discussion does not have technological connotation, as in manufacturing productivity. This is both because of the lack of technology-led innovation in a number of service activities and also because of the diverse mix of criteria that have been used in forming subsectors within the services sector. Of course, in recent years there are a number of services where there is an actual enhancing of labour productivity due to the use of computers and communications technologies. Our data, however, do not provide us an indication of the productivity growth, and hence do not allow us to identify productivity gains due to technology or otherwise.

As we have discussed in section 6.4, GDP data over a fairly long period of time are available by about 40 categories at the most disaggregated level. Employment data are available at an even more disaggregated level, that is, five-digit level of industrial classification for the years 2004–05 and 2009–10 from the national sample surveys on employment and unemployment.[15] Combining the GDP data at the maximum possible level of disaggregation and matching the same with employment data, we have estimated productivity per worker in the services sector for about 36 service activities for the years 2004–05 and 2009–10. In the discussion following, we describe the productivity levels across these 36 service activities.

We identify high-productivity services as well as low-productivity services and estimate employment in both. Through this exercise, we attempt to identify service activities that are likely to be more sustainable and stable and provide good quality employment. We also examine whether within the services sector there is a mismatch between some services that provide the bulk of the employment (low productivity) and others that account for the bulk of the income (high productivity). Finally, we study the changes in productivity in the period between 2004–05 and 2009–10, the period of relatively high growth in services in India.

During 2009–10, the average productivity for the Indian economy (combining all the three sectors – agriculture, manufacturing and services) as a whole was estimated at Rs 95,478 per worker per year at 2004–05 prices. The average productivity figures for agriculture, manufacturing and services sectors in the same period were Rs 26,537, Rs 1,39,054 and Rs 2,09,391 per worker per year, respectively. Thus, while average labour productivity in agriculture was far below the national average, that of the manufacturing and services sectors were way above the national average, the average labour productivity of the services sector being the highest.

6.5.1 Labour productivity within the services sector

In the year 2009–10, the labour productivity across different services ranged from as low as Rs 19,600 per worker per year in private households with employed persons to as high as Rs 67,94,000 in the non-life insurance sector (Table 6.4).[16] Growth in productivity between 2004–05 and 2009–10 was highest in the non-life insurance sector (29.3 per cent), followed by the communications sector (25.4 per cent per annum), renting of machinery and research and development (both 17 per cent). The labour productivity in banks grew by 14.7 per cent. The labour productivity in households with employed persons grew at a rate of 14.4 per cent, albeit from a very low base.

The services in which the labour productivity grew the least or was negative in the period from 2004–05 to 2009–10 were storage activities (–4.2 per cent), radio and TV (–4.1 per cent) and computer-related activities (–0.4 per cent). Two important public or state-run services also exhibit negative productivity growth; they are the banking department of RBI (–175.6 per cent) and employees' provident fund (–5.2 per cent) (Table 6.4).

High-productivity services

For the purposes of this analysis, high-productivity services are defined as having productivity levels that were five times the average for the services sector in 2004–05 or 2009–10. The top five services with highest labour productivity in 2009–10 were non-life insurance (Rs 67,94,000 per worker per year) followed by banks (Rs 14,59,000 per worker per year), air transport (Rs 11,48,000 per worker per year), communications (Rs 10,53,000

Table 6.4 Productivity in the services sector, disaggregated level: 2004–05 and 2009–10

Sl No.	*Description of category*	*Labour productivity (Rs 1000 per worker)*		*Growth in productivity*
		2004–05	*2009–10*	*(% per year)*
1	GDP Trade, Hotels & Restaurants	98.2	146.4	8.3
1.1	Trade	101.4	152.2	8.5
1.2	Hotel and restaurant	74.8	105.2	7.0
2	All transport (railway + others)	127.7	163.0	5.0
2.1	Railways	272.7	416.8	8.9
2.2	Other transport	117.0	146.7	4.6
2.2.1	Road transport	102.4	129.2	4.8
2.2.2	Water transport	507.5	552.4	1.7
2.2.3	Air transport	665.1	1148.0	11.5
2.2.4	Service incidental to transport	493.1	385.0	–4.8
3	Storage	211.4	170.3	–4.2
4	Communications GDP (public and private sector)	263.7	885.3	27.4
4.1	Public-sector postal services	41.5	59.7	7.6
4.2	Communications other than post (public + private)	339.9	1052.6	25.4
	Banking and insurance	585.7	883.8	8.6
5	Banking	600.0	934.6	9.3
5.1	Banks (including postal savings)	733.9	1458.9	14.7
5.2	Banking department of RBI	–130.7	32.2	–175.6
5.3	Non-banking financial institutions, including co-operative societies	660.0	653.2	–0.2
5.4	Employees' provident fund org.	44.6	34.2	–5.2
6	Insurance	527.9	720.6	6.4
6.1	Life insurance (including postal life insurance)	351.6	476.9	6.3
6.3	Non-life insurance	1883.6	6794.1	29.3
7	Real estate, dwellings business services	632.2	741.5	3.2
7.1	Dwellings (urban + rural)	4905.2	5538.6	2.5
7.2	Real estate	406.0	424.5	0.9
7.3	Business services	255.8	418.0	10.3
7.3.1	Renting of machinery	36.1	81.1	17.6
7.3.2	Computer-related services	802.2	786.9	–0.4
7.3.3	Legal services	168.5	223.9	5.8

(*Continued*)

Table 6.4 (Continued)

Sl No.	*Description of category*	*Labour productivity (Rs 1000 per worker)*		*Growth in productivity*
		2004–05	*2009–10*	*(% per year)*
7.3.4	Accounting	108.4	160.9	8.2
7.3.5	Research development	107.3	235.0	17.0
8	Education	105.9	148.0	6.9
9	Medical & health	150.8	182.7	3.9
10	Religious and other community membership organisations	81.1	153.3	13.6
11	Recreation & entertainment	140.0	250.0	12.3
12	Radio & TV broadcasting	83.5	67.6	-4.1
13	Personal and other services	17.5	24.6	7.0
13.1	Private household with employed person	10.0	19.6	14.4
13.2	Washing & cleaning of textiles	24.6	40.4	10.4
13.3	Hair dressing and other beauty treatment	24.3	27.0	2.1
13.4	Custom tailoring	18.6	22.5	3.9
14	Sanitary services	121.5	127.8	1.0
15	Funeral-related activities & other services	325.4	250.1	-5.1
16	International & other extra territorial bodies	3739.2	5891.6	9.5
17	Public administration & defence	212.8	288.0	6.2
	Total services	140.1	209.4	8.4

Source: Author's estimations using data from NAS (CSO, 2014) and NSS (68th round).

Note: Gross value added data are from the NAS (CSO, 2014), while employment estimates are obtained from unit-level data from the 68th round NSS surveys on employment and unemployment.

per worker per year) and computer-related services (Rs 7,87,000 per worker per year) (Table 6.5).

In comparison with the average productivity in the services sector, the productivity levels in the high-productivity services in 2009–10 was as much as 32.4 times in case of non-life insurance, 7 times in the case of banks and 3.8 times in the case of computer-related services (Table 6.5). In comparison with the national average productivity levels, the productivity levels in the high-productivity services were even larger. For example, in 2009–10, non-life insurance had 71 times the national average productivity, while banks had 15 times the national productivity and computer-related services had 8.2 times the national productivity.

Table 6.5 High-productivity services, 2004–05 and 2009–10

Sl No.	*Description of category*	*Labour productivity (Rs 1000 per worker)*		*Comparison with average productivity of services sector*		*Comparison with national average productivity*	
		2004–05	*2009–10*	*2004–05*	*2009–10*	*2004–05*	*2009–10*
1	Air transport	665	1148	4.7	5.5	10.4	12.0
2	Communications other than post (public + private)	340	1053	2.4	5.0	5.3	11.0
3	Banks (including postal savings)	734	1459	5.2	7.0	11.5	15.3
4	Non-banking financial institutions, including co-operative societies	660	653	4.7	3.1	10.3	6.8
5	Non-life insurance	1884	6794	13.4	32.4	29.5	71.2
6	Computer-related services	802	787	5.7	3.8	12.5	8.2
7	International & other extra territorial bodies	3739	5892	26.7	28.1	58.5	61.7

Source: Same as in Table 6.4.

Note: High-productivity services are defined as those having five times the average productivity for the services sector in either year.

A point to be noted here is that despite their high levels of productivity, these services provide very little employment. For example, the high-productivity services discussed earlier together accounted for about 16.8 per cent of the national GDP in 2009–10. They, however, accounted for only about 1.14 per cent of the total employment.

Low-productivity services

Similar to the definition of the high-productivity services, low-productivity services are defined as having productivity levels that are equal to or less than half the average for the services sector either in 2004–05 or in 2009–10 or in both years. In the year 2009–10, the latest year for which we have made estimations of labour productivity, the service activity with the lowest labour productivity is in private households with employed persons (Rs 19,600 per worker per year); this is followed by custom tailoring (Rs 22,500 per worker per year), hair dressing and other beauty treatment (Rs 27,000 per worker per year), washing and cleaning of textiles (Rs 40,400 per worker per year), public-sector postal services (Rs 59,700 per worker per year) and hotel and restaurants (Rs 1,05,200 per worker per year) (Table 6.6).

It would be appropriate at this stage to compare high-productivity services with the average productivity levels in the manufacturing sector (Table 6.7). Non-life insurance had a productivity of about 49 times that in manufacturing in 2009–10, while banks and air transport had productivity levels that were 10 times and 8 times the average in manufacturing, respectively. Though the results are mixed, the levels of productivity in high-productivity services grew at faster rates than in manufacture in case of air transport, communications, banks and non-life insurance (Table 6.7). Computer services and non-banking financial institutions are the only sectors where the productivity growth was negative in the period from 2004–05 to 2009–10.

As is evident from the estimates of average-productivity and high-productivity services provided earlier, low-productivity services are at levels that appear to be the lowest in the economy. In order to examine this, we compare the productivity levels in these low-productivity services with productivity levels in agriculture. Two of these low-productivity services – private households with employed persons and custom tailoring – had productivity levels in 2009–20 that were lower than in agriculture. Further, another low-productivity service – hair dressing and other beauty treatment – had productivity levels more or less similar to that of agriculture (Table 6.8). The remaining low-productivity services had productivity levels marginally higher than in agriculture.

Table 6.6 Comparison of high-productivity services with manufacturing: 2004–05 and 2009–10

Sl No.	*Description of category*	*Comparison with manufacturing productivity*	
		2004–05	*2009–10*
1	Air transport	7.9	8.3
2	Communications other than post (public + private)	4.0	7.6
3	Banks (including postal savings)	8.7	10.5
4	Non-banking financial institutions, including co-operative societies	7.9	4.7
5	Non-life insurance	22.4	48.9
6	Computer-related services	9.5	5.7
7	International & other extra territorial bodies	44.5	42.4

Source: Same as in Table 6.4.

Table 6.7 Low-productivity services: 2004–05 and 2009–10

Sl No.	*Description of category*	*Labour productivity (Rs 1000 per worker)*		*Comparison with average productivity of services sector*		*Comparison with national average productivity*	
		2004–05	*2009–10*	*2004–05*	*2009–10*	*2004–05*	*2009–10*
1	Private household with employed person	9.97	20	0.07	0.09	0.16	0.20
2	Washing & cleaning of textiles	24.58	40	0.18	0.19	0.38	0.42
3	Hair dressing and other beauty treatment	24.28	27	0.17	0.13	0.38	0.28
4	Custom tailoring	18.57	23	0.13	0.11	0.29	0.24
5	Public-sector postal services	41.47	60	0.30	0.28	0.65	0.63
6	Employees' provident fund org.	44.61	34	0.32	0.16	0.70	0.36
7	Hotel and restaurant	74.82	105	0.53	0.50	1.17	1.10

Source: Same as in Table 6.4.

Note: Low-productivity services are defined as those having at half the average productivity for the services sector in either year.

Table 6.8 Comparison of low-productivity services with agriculture and manufacturing: 2004–05 and 2009–10

Sl No.	*Description of category*	*Comparison with manufacturing productivity*		*Comparison with agriculture productivity*	
		2004–05	*2009–10*	*2004–05*	*2009–10*
1	Private household with employed person	0.12	0.14	0.47	0.74
2	Washing & cleaning of textiles	0.29	0.29	1.17	1.52
3	Hair dressing and other beauty treatment	0.29	0.19	1.15	1.02
4	Custom tailoring	0.22	0.16	0.88	0.85
5	Public-sector postal services	0.49	0.43	1.97	2.25
6	Employees' provident fund org.	0.53	0.25	2.12	1.29
7	Hotel and restaurant	0.89	0.76	3.56	3.96

Source: Same as in Table 6.4.

At this stage, it would also be appropriate to compare the low productivity with average productivity levels in the manufacturing sector. All the low-productivity services had levels of labour productivity that were lower than in manufacturing. The final point to be noted about low-productivity services is that in 2009–10, together these services accounted for 2.2 per cent of the national GDP. Their share in national employment was, however, nearly double, at 4.28 per cent. In other words, low-productivity services provide for proportionately larger avenues of employment within the services sector relative to high-productivity services.

Thus, within the services sector, there is one set of activities that are high-productivity and employing relatively smaller number of workers, while there is another set of activities with very low levels of productivity employing relatively large number of workers. This mismatch between productivity and employment has long-term implications for the policy of poverty and equity in the country.

6.6 Alternate classification of the services sector: an analysis

In the debate on the growth and prominence of services, some scholars have argued that part of what is called services is actually manufacturing. There could be a blurring of the distinction between manufacturing and services in many instances. Firstly, there are services that exhibit features of production; secondly, there are services that directly lead to production; thirdly, embedded services are those where final products have components of goods and services; and finally, repair services also have features that are very similar to that of production.[17]

Services that exhibit some features of production are, for example, restaurants and butchers. In restaurants, processing of food is undertaken and served to customers. Since it is not possible to separate the activity in the kitchen from that in the dining hall of the restaurant, the entire business of a restaurant is classified as a service. However, on closer examination, not only does a restaurant ‘produce’ processed food, in case of restaurants that act mainly as takeaways, the semblance with the process of production of processed food is even larger. Another such activity is that of a butcher. In less developed countries, the activity of a butcher would be classified as a service activity. However, as the economy gets more and more complex, slaughterhouses are involved, meat processing plants are set up and meat packaging and storing facilities are also set up. The meat is then sold either in super markets or in specialised shops. Thus, as the economy gets more and more advanced, the activity of the butcher is subdivided with one part classified under manufacturing and the other part involving sale of meat as service.

Then there are services that directly lead to production (as intermediate goods) or productive services. Some examples are computing services, accounting services and some types of legal services. All these services are directly related to the ensuing production process or, in other words, large-scale production cannot be undertaken without the use of these services.

Embedded services are those in which the final products have components of both goods and services. For example, in recent years most equipment and machinery are produced to run on some kind or software and at the time of the purchase of such equipment, the software is already installed in it. Another example of embedded services is all kinds of repair and refurbishing of old machinery and motor vehicles that render these 'as good as new' and ready for resale.

Repair and maintenance of equipment and machinery that are used in the process of manufacturing could very well be classified as part of manufacturing. In the National Industrial Classification and the System of National Accounts adopted in India, all kinds of repair services except for repair and maintenance of motor vehicles are classified under industry/manufacture and not under services.

The blurring between goods and services or a goods–services continuum has led to a debate on what constitutes services. Some scholars have argued that with regard to some services, the strict dichotomy made between services and manufacturing is 'overdrawn' as these services are organised on ways that are similar to manufacturing (Hill, 1977; Singh, 2006). This has also led scholars to propose alternate schemes of classification of services by their similarity to or distinction from the process of manufacture.

Based on end user or beneficiary of services, services have been classified into two types, viz., producer services/household services and intermediate services/consumer services. This scheme of classification has, however, proved to be not useful as the two categories are not mutually exclusive, with a large overlap between them. A second classification, based on the method of financing of the services, has been attempted, viz., state-funded or tax-funded services and private services. This classification is also not useful, as the tax and state policy both may and do vary from state to state and over time. A third type of classification is based on the marketability of the service. Thus, services are classified as marketed services (assumed to be mainly provided by private enterprises) or non-marketed services (assumed to be provided by the state). But in the present times where a number of services are provided both by the market and by the state, this classification also does not appear to be useful in providing a better understanding of the services sector.

Based on a combination of end user and ownership, Browning and Singelmann (1975) have proposed a four-way classification of services. By this classification, distributive services are those involving transportation, communication, retail and wholesale trade. Producer services include banking, insurance, other financial activities and business services – accounting, computer services, legal services and so on. Social services include health, education, welfare services and other government services, and personal services include domestic and personal services, hotels, restaurants and entertainment.

Table 6.9 Classification of services based on user and ownership

Sl. No.	*Description of category*	*GDP (% share in total)*		*Employment (% share in total)*		*Comparison with average productivity of services sector*	
		2004–05	*2009–10*	*2004–05*	*2009–10*	*2004–05*	*2009–10*
1	Distributive services	43.3	43.7	53.6	52.0	0.81	0.84
2	Personal services	5.0	4.6	17.2	16.6	0.29	0.28
3	Producer services	17.4	22.4	6.1	7.7	2.84	2.92
4	Social services	23.9	21.8	22.5	22.6	1.06	0.96
5	Total services	100.0	100.0	100.0	100.0	1.00	1.00

Source: Author's calculations.

Note: The categories in this table are adapted from Browning and Singelmann (1975).

The classification of Browning and Singelmann (1975) places all services into one category or another and these are mutually exclusive. Apart from this, services that can be linked to production such as producer services and distributive services are clearly identified.

In this chapter we adopt the Browning and Singelmann classification with some minor changes to suit the Indian data to understand the structure of the services sector in India for the most recent period from 2004–05 to 2009–10 (Table 6.9). Our estimates show that distributive services account for the largest share in employment and GDP followed by social services. The share of both distributive services and social services in GDP also more or less corresponds to their share in total employment (Table 6.9). Producer services are as large as social services in terms of GDP (in 2009–10), but account for a relatively smaller share of employment. On the contrary, personal services that account for the least in terms of GDP share account for a substantial share in employment.

In terms of labour productivity, producer services have the highest productivity, which was about 2.92 times the average labour productivity in services for 2009–10. Personal services, on the other hand, had the lowest labour productivity, accounting for less than a third of the average productivity for services. In the Indian services growth story, the dominance of producer services and distributive services in the Indian economy is perhaps good news. The low productivity and relatively high employment in personal services is perhaps bad news.

6.7 Summary and conclusion

In this chapter, we have explored the heterogeneity across various subsectors in the services sector in India through the analysis of growth, structure and productivity of the services sub-sector. The level of disaggregation at which we present estimates is not found often in the literature on services sector in India.

Business services and private-sector communications stand out prominently in terms of high growth in recent years. Both these services, however, accounted for negligible shares in the 1950s and 1960s, right up to the 1980s. Their share began to increase only after the 1980s, and major increases happened only in the 1990s and after.

This chapter discusses in some detail the contribution of different services sub-sectors to GDP growth. In this way, the top 10 contributors to GDP growth in the most recent period of study (2004–09) are also identified. There is a wide variation in the growth path of different sub-sectors. While trade, public administration and defence, road transport and education continue to remain in the top 10 contributors to GDP growth, their contribution between 2004 and 2010 is lower than in the period from 1995–96 to 2004. On the other hand, banks, business services and private-sector telecommunications are the sub-sectors with increasing contribution to GDP growth.

There is a wide variation in the productivity levels among service sub-sectors. In order to demonstrate the difference across services sub-sectors and their heterogeneity, this chapter also discusses labour productivity differences across different sub-sectors. Six services sub-sectors with productivity levels that are five times the average services sector productivity are identified along with six others that had productivity levels that were half that of the average productivity levels. The average labour productivity in some services are found to be lower than even productivity in agriculture. High-productivity services account for a negligible share in total employment, while low-productivity services account for the bulk of employment.

The last section of this chapter is an attempt to reclassify services into four sub-categories based on a combination of end use and ownership. Distributive services accounts for the highest share of services GDP, followed by producer services and social services. In terms of labour productivity, though, producer services has about three times the labour productivity in social services and in distributive services. While demonstrating high levels of productivity differences across sub-sectors of the services economy, we also find that a major part of the employment in the services sector is in the relatively low-productivity services. Services that are desirable for a growing economy such as producer services account for only a small share of employment. Distributive services such as trade and transport are important for the economy and account for over half of the services sector employment. The labour productivity in the distributive services is, however, very low.

Policies aimed at the employment generation and income enhancement should take into consideration the heterogeneity in the services sector. Productivity enhancing efforts should focus on services that already provide large-scale employment at relatively low wages. A cause for concern is also the low levels of productivity in education and health services.

Notes

1 The heterogeneity discussed here is different from the concept of differences in 'quality of service' discussed by Noon (2003).
2 For a summary of historical definitions of services, see Walters and Bergiel (1982), cited in Joshi (2008).
3 For a very brief and concise discussion of the distinction between goods-producing operations and service operations, see Noon (2003).
4 Section 6.8, UN SNA (1993) page 148.
5 Section 6.9, UN SNA (1993) page 148.
6 See, for example, a detailed discussion on the measures and methods in the OECD countries by Hill and McGibbon (1966).
7 For a fuller understanding of the more recent measure and methods used to arrive at the services sector GDP in India, see CSO (2007).
8 According to Sharma, Hazra and Chitkara (2007), for years subsequent to the base year (once the new series are released) in respect to various industry groups, the estimates of value added are based on different procedures, depending upon the availability of data.
9 For a comparison of the level of disaggregation between the previous series (base year: 1999–2000) and the series before that (base year: 1993–94) and the improvements therein, see Table 6.3 and discussion in Sharma, Hazra and Chitkara (2007).
10 For a similar discussion for the extended period from 1950 to 1980, see Pais (2014).
11 The system of national accounts was revised again in 2015 with base year 2011–12. The estimates after this revision are very different from before. The debates of the new methodology are still on, and estimates are not comparable with previous estimates.
12 During this study, it has been brought to my notice that measurement issues plague the estimates of GDP in the telecommunications sector. The estimates on the number of mobile connections used in the estimation of GDP are apparently highly inflated. Nevertheless, even after discounting for the inflated number of mobile connections in an appropriate manner, in comparison with other services, the growth performance of the communications sector continues to be remarkable.
13 For a more detailed discussion, see Pais (2014).
14 Level of education and skills are linked to quality of employment obtained, in general, and this holds for the different sub-sectors in services too. For more and the links between education and quality of employment in the services sector in India, see Nayyar (2012).
15 Estimates from unit level data of the NSS 61st and 66th rounds.
16 According to the NAS, 'The economic activities covered in services sector include ownership of dwellings (occupied residential houses) *including imputed value of owner occupied dwellings* also'. Thus in a large number of cases, the value added is derived due to the existence and use of residential premises. And in a large number of cases, this may involve insignificant amounts of employment. Hence in the discussion of productivity of the services sector, we exclude the sub-sector under the heading 'dwellings'.
17 See Singh (2006) for a discussion of the important of productive services for the growth of the manufacturing sector. In another context, Kumar, Kar and Sanjay (2007) make a somewhat different argument with regard to the manufacturing sector. Their argument is, however, that several firms in unorganised manufacturing that outsource work from other firms should be placed in a category called 'manufacturing services' as they in fact only provide (manufacturing) services. This has implications for calculating sectoral GDP: 'these activities are treated as "manufacturing" while estimating domestic product or supply side aggregates, but as "services" while estimating expenditure or use side aggregates'.

References

Banerjee, P.K. Baksi, A. and N. Roy (2007). 'Regrouping of economic activities: A feasibility study', *Economic and Political Weekly*, 42(37), 3745–3749.

Browning, H.L. and J. Singelmann (1975). *The Emergence of a Service Society: Demographic and Sociological Aspects of the Sectoral Transformation of the Labor Force in the U.S.A.*, National Technical Information Service, Springfield.

CSO (2007). *National Accounts Statistics: Sources and Methods 2007*, Central Statistics Office, Ministry of statistics and programme implementation, Government of India, New Delhi.

CSO (2014). *National Accounts Statistics*, Central Statistics Office, Ministry of statistics and programme implementation, Government of India, New Delhi.

CSO (Various Years). *National Accounts Statistics*, Central Statistics Office, Ministry of statistics and programme implementation, Government of India, New Delhi.

Eichengreen, B. and P. Gupta (2010). 'The service sector as India's road to economic growth?', Working Paper No. 249, Indian Council for Research on International Economic Relations, New Delhi.

Ghosh, B.N. (1991). 'Development of tertiary sector', *Economic and Political Weekly*, 26(8), 452.

GOI (2012). *Economic Survey 2011–12*, Ministry of Finance, Government of India, New Delhi.

GOI (2014, December). *Data Book*, Planning Commission of India, Government of India, New Delhi. https://niti.gov.in/planningcommission.gov.in/docs/data/datatable/data_2312/DatabookDec2014%202.pdf.

Hill, T.P. (1977). 'On goods and services', *Review of Income and Wealth*, 23(4), 315–338.

Hill, T.P. (1979). 'Do It Yourself and GDP,' *Review of Income and Wealth*, 25(1), 31–39.

Hill, T.P. and J. McGibbon (1966). 'Growth of sector real product: Measures and methods in selected OECD countries', *Review of Income and Wealth*, 12(1), 35–55.

Illeris, S. (2007). 'The nature of services', in J.R. Bryson and P.W. Daniels (eds.) *The Handbook of Services Industries*, Edward Elgar Publishing Inc, Cheltenham, UK.

Joshi, S. (2008). *Growth and Structure of Tertiary Sector in Developing Economies*, Academic Foundation, New Delhi.

Kotabe, M., Mol, M.J. and J.Y. Murray (2009). 'Global sourcing strategy', in *The SAGE Handbook of International Marketing*, SAGE Publications. 14 May, 2010. www.sage-ereference.com/hdbk_intlmarket/Article_n14.html.

Kumar, V., Kar, A. and Sanjay (2007). 'Service producing manufacturing units and their impact on sectoral GDP', *Economic and Political Weekly*, 42(37), 3776–3780.

Lewis, A. (1954). 'Economic development with unlimited supplies of labour', *The Manchester School*, 22(2): 139–191.

Mitra, A. (1988). 'Disproportionality and the services sector: A note', *Social Scientist*, 16(4), Four Decades of Economic Development II, 3–8.

Nagaraj, R. (1991). 'Excess growth of tertiary sector?', *Economic and Political Weekly*, 26(5), 247–248.

Nayyar, G. (2012). 'The quality of employment in India's services sector: Exploring the heterogeneity', *Applied Economics*, 44, 4701–4719.

Noon, C.E. (2003). 'Service operations', in *Encyclopaedia of Health Care Management 2003*, SAGE Publications. www.sage-ereference.com/healthcaremanagement/Article_n723.html (downloaded 14/05/2010).

Pais, J. (2014). 'Growth and structure of the services sector in India', Working Paper 160, Institute for Studies in Industrial Development, New Delhi.

Papola, T.S. (2008). 'Industry and employment: Dissecting recent Indian experience', in S.R. Hashim, K.S.C. Rao, K.V.K. Ranganathan and M.R. Murthy (eds.) *Indian Industrial Development and Globalisation*, Academic Foundation, New Delhi.

Sharma, R., Hazra, S. and S. Chitkara (2007). 'Measurement of GDP of services sector in the new series of national accounts statistics', *Economic and Political Weekly*, 42(37), 3727–3731.

Shetty, S.L. (2007). 'Status paper on database issues of the services sector', *Economic and Political Weekly*, 42(37), 3723–3726.

Singh, N. (2006). 'Services-led industrialization in India: Assessment and lessons', Working Paper No. 290, Stanford Center for International Development, Stanford University, Stanford.

UN SNA (1993). *System of National Accounts 1993*, United Nations, New York.

Walters, C.G. and B.J. Bergiel (1982). *Marketing Channels*, 2nd ed., Scott, Foresman, London.

7 Employment potential in the services sector in India

An overview

K.V. Ramaswamy

7.1 Introduction

Will India's services-led growth since the 1980s soak up people looking for jobs and who are entering the labour force? A simple answer would be no, and an elaborate answer would say 'It depends on many factors'. This challenging question has taken a much more serious dimension with the media reports of introduction of 'automation' and 'digitisation' and other new technologies in information technology (IT) taking away the routine jobs outsourced to labour-abundant economies like India.[1] This chapter looks at the employment potential in the services sector in India using recent available data and makes some preliminary projections. Analysts who have emphasised the changing role of the services sector from follower to leading sector of economic development because of the 'services revolution' have often paid insufficient attention to the dimension of employment potential. It has been argued that services-led growth in South Asia suggests the availability of a new boat that latecomers to development could take (Ghani, 2010).

In this scenario, labour shifting out of agriculture will get directly absorbed in services rather than in manufacturing. This is obviously contentious and others have raised doubts over this proposition, pointing out the absence of similarity between output shares and employment shares of the services sector in India's economy. This difference in services sector contribution to output and employment has been a significant component of the recent discourse on economic growth, employment and the need for strategic policy shift to achieve manufacturing-led growth. Even though recent data and studies have dispelled the popular notion of 'job-less' growth, the larger task is one of understanding potential employment creation prospects and orders of magnitude.

In this sense, apprehension continues regarding the possibility of services-employment-led structural change in India. One of the studies, after examining services sector growth and employment in South Asia in the 1990s, cautiously concluded that the services sector in India could continue to be the main source of employment despite its lower employment elasticity of output (0.36) relative to the world (0.57) (Bosworth and Maertens, 2010).[2] The higher share of the services sector in terms of contribution to total employment in the 1990s is the basis for this expectation. Whether this holds well in the future is an empirical matter and provides the motivation for this chapter.

Following this short introduction, section 7.2 presents a brief discussion of growth and structural change in India and the facts regarding services-led growth. Sub-section 7.2.1 points out the challenge of employment creation in terms of growth of the working-age population and labour force. Section 7.3 contains the projections of employment growth in the services sector up to the year 2020 based on certain rules of thumb. Concluding remarks are given in section 7.4.

7.2 Growth and structural change

The gross domestic product (GDP) per capita grew annually by an average of 1.2 per cent in the 1960s and 1970s, but this growth rate changed to an average of 3.5 per cent in the 1980s, to 3.7 per cent in the 1990s and to 5.5 per cent in the 2000s. India has transformed itself to be counted among the fastest-growing economies in the world, with an average GDP per capita growth rate of 3.7 per cent in the years 1980 to 2004. In terms of GDP growth performance (GDP at factor cost at constant 2004–05 prices) alone, one finds that the Indian economy's average annual growth rate was 3.5 per cent during 1951–82 and increased to 5.4 per cent in the next two decades (1983–1999), followed by a growth rate of above 7 per cent in the 2000s. In particular, the growth rate was 6.1 per cent during 2001–02 to 2004–05, 7.4 per cent during 2005–06 to 2007–08 and 7.7 per cent during 2008–09 to 2011–12. The economic policy reform of 1991 has played an important role in driving this growth, but other preexisting factors have also influenced the pattern of development (Kochhar et al., 2006).

The first and perhaps foremost feature of India's recent growth experience is that it is led by the services sector, unlike in other countries of East Asia and China. In the broader context of economic development and structural change, the observed sequence was that manufacturing followed agriculture, while the service sector became prominent only at a later stage. India's experience appeared to be different, with the share of services sector in GDP sharply going up in the 1990s, beginning with a share of 43 per cent in 1990–91, to reach a high share of 57 per cent in 2009–10. The changes in GDP shares of agriculture, manufacturing and services over the period 1950–51 to 2012–13 is shown in Figure 7.1.[3] This rapid rise in the share of services has taken place at lower levels of per capita income when compared to presently advanced countries and other Asian economies.

In 1895, the share of services in the UK was about 53 per cent, comparable to India in 2004, but the level of GDP per capita was 4,100 international dollars (at 1990 prices)[4] compared to 2,278 dollars in India in 2004. Similarly, in Germany the share of services was 53 per cent during 1890–1899, with an average per capita GDP of 6,000 dollars and came

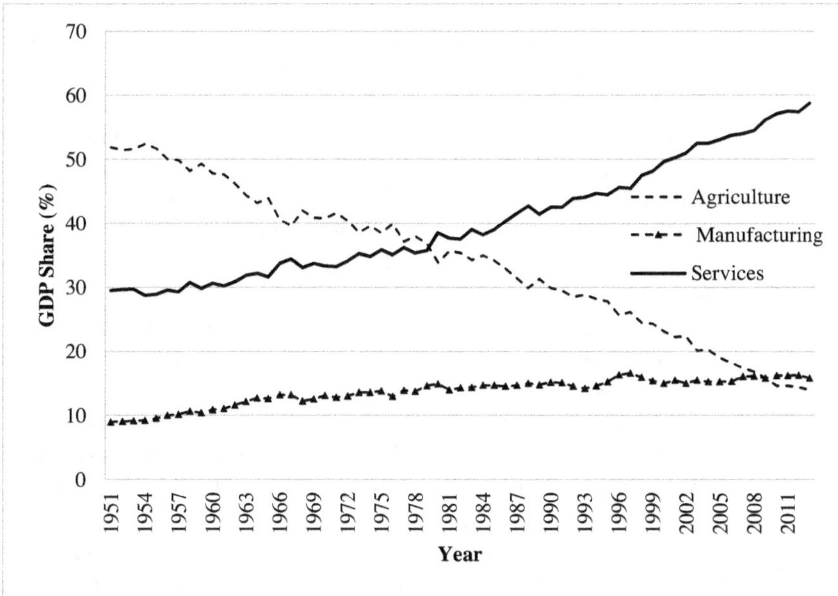

Figure 7.1 Share in GDP by sector in India, 1950–51 to 2012–13

Source: Handbook of Statistics on the Indian Economy 2015–16 (Reserve Bank of India, 2016).

down to 38 per cent by the end of the period. In the case of Japan, services accounted for 48 per cent during 1933–37 and declined to 42 per cent by 1942. The GDP per capita of Japan increased to 2,700 dollars in 1942 from 2,200 dollars in 1937. The upshot is that at similar stages of development, India had a larger share of services in GDP. If we take another fast-growing comparable developing country like Malaysia, we find that the share of services was 49 per cent in 2005 with a per capita GDP level of 9,000 dollars. By 2005, India's per capita GDP was about 2,400 dollars but with a services share of 54 per cent, the flip side of this structural development is that of premature deindustrialisation, to borrow the term used by Rodrik (2013). In presently developed countries like the US (in 1953), Britain (in 1961), Germany (1970) and Sweden (in 1961), the manufacturing share of employment peaked (more than 30 per cent) when their per capita GDP levels were 9,000–11,000 dollars, and then deindustrialisation began with the decline of the manufacturing sector. The developing countries like Brazil, China and India seem to exhibit a contrasting experience. In these countries, manufacturing employment shares have been observed to shrink while per capita GDP levels have been in the range of 2,000–5,000 dollars at 1990 prices (Rodrik, 2013). Whether this process of skipping stages of development or bypassing industrialisation could keep India on the high growth path or whether it is sustainable is a moot question.

In what sense could the recent growth in India be called services-led growth? To answer this question, Ghose (2015) looks at the contribution of three sectors – agriculture, manufacturing and services – to GDP growth since 1982. The contribution of the services sector is found to be higher than the contribution of all other sectors put together in the years since 1982. In the period 1983–99, the services sector contributed 53.7 per cent of GDP growth (5.4 per cent), but it went up to 63.3 per cent in the period 2000–10. In short, the growth is services-led in India in the sense that the proportional contribution of services to GDP growth is higher relative to all other sectors. The changes in structure of GDP at two points in time (1999–2000 and 2011–12) are presented in Table 7.1.[5]

The service sector output has grown rapidly since 1990, and by 2005 the share of services in GDP had reached well above the international norm that corresponds to the average share of services in countries with similar per capita GDP (Eichengreen and Gupta, 2011). National Accounts Statistics (NAS) data indicate that the service sector has clocked an average annual compound growth rate of 8.7 per cent per annum between 1999–2000 and 2009–10 as against 7.7 per cent achieved by manufacturing during the same period. Within the service sector, the group transport, storage and communications has grown the fastest at 11.8 per cent. It is followed by trade and hotels at 8.5 per cent and other business services at 7.9 per cent. The distribution of total employment for two selected years by industry is presented in Table 7.2. The services sector contributes about 27 per cent of total employment in the Indian economy.

Both demand-side and supply-side factors have been shown to have played important roles in this 'services revolution' (Rakshit, 2007). Two types of

Table 7.1 Distribution of GDP at factor cost by industry of origin (2004–05 prices)

Industry/Sector	*GDP Share 1999–2000*	*GDP Share 2011–12*
1. Agriculture	23.2	14.4
2. Mining & Quarrying	3.0	2.1
3. Manufacturing	15.0	16.3
4. Electricity, water, etc.	2.5	1.9
5. Construction	6.5	7.9
6. Trade (Retail+ Wholesale), Hotel and Restaurant, Transport, Storage and Communications	21.1	26.7
7. Other Services Like Financial, Business, Public Administration, Education	28.5	30.7
8. Services (6+7)	49.6	57.4
9. All Sectors	100	100

Source: Handbook of Statistics on Indian Economy 2015–16 (Reserve Bank of India, 2016).

Table 7.2 Distribution of employment by industry (%)*

Sector	*1999–2000*	*2011–12*
Agriculture	60.4	47.5
Mining, Electricity & Water Supply	0.8	1.1
Manufacturing	11.0	12.9
Construction	4.4	10.6
Services	23.4	27.0
Economy	100.0	99.1**

Source: Author's estimates based on NSSO Survey results of respective years.

Note:

* Total employment by UPSS.

** Figures do not add up to 100 because some National Industrial Classification (NIC) categories are not estimated.

demand for services are final demand from consumers (both domestic and exports) and intermediate demand services from other two sectors of the economy, namely, industry and agriculture. Faster growth of final demand for service sector output is indicated by the growth in private household consumption expenditure and a rapid growth of export of services.[6] During the time period 1995–2005, private consumption of services grew at an average of 8.6 per cent and export of services grew at 19.1 per cent, much higher than the growth rate of services GDP at 8 per cent (Rakshit, 2007). Based on the NAS, it is estimated that the household income elasticity of demand for services averaged 1.5 for the period 1998–2005 (Rakshit, 2007). In another study, it is reported to be significantly greater than unity based on data on consumer expenditure in National Sample Surveys (NSS) (Nayyar, 2012).

A supply-related factor of importance has been technological change or total factor productivity growth (TFPG) in the services sector. Indirect evidence in support of this factor is the declining incremental capital-output ratio and increasing labour productivity growth in the service-sector since 1995. A study by Bosworth and Maertens (2010) estimated that the average growth rate of output per worker was 4.9 per cent during 1990–2000 and that of TFPG was 3.1 per cent per annum, much higher than that of industry and economy during the same period. During 2000–06, the growth rates of output per worker and TFPG were found to be lower, at 4.6 and 1.9 per cent per annum, similar to that of the total economy. Another detailed study of productivity growth in India which covers different sectors of the Indian economy including the services sector is by Das et al. (2016). They have reported an average TFPG rate of 1.1 per cent during 1978–1993, which increased to 2.4 per cent during 1993–2004 (Das et al., 2016). This is consistent with the argument of acceleration of services sector productivity growth in the 1990s.

7.2.1 *India's working-age population, labour force and the employment challenge*

India's population was estimated to be 1.31 billion in 2015 and was projected to reach 1.38 billion in 2020 and 1.43 billion in 2025 as per the United Nations revised 2015 projections (UN, 2015). Focusing on the period 2015–20, the years of immediate concern to us, the share of the working-age population (15–64 years) was estimated to be 66.6 per cent in 2020, up from 65.6 per cent in 2015. The growth rate of working age population in this period (1.48 per cent per annum) will be higher than the growth rate of the population (1.16 per cent per annum). This is an indicator of potential demographic dividend, and the challenge is to create jobs and make the dividend a reality. We can understand this challenge better if we focus on the growth of the working-age labour force. Following Ghose (2016), the working-age labour force can be defined as those falling in the age bracket 15–59 years. Notice that the labour force consists of those who are employed and those who are not employed but seeking employment in the age bracket of 15–59 years. The annual addition to the working-age labour force is estimated to be in the range of 5.8 million for the period 2015 to 2030. This may be regarded as the core labour force, and it is part of the overall labour force that includes all those in ages 5 and older. Recently, Ghose (2019) has estimated that 7.1 million to 8 million persons will be joining the labour force (age 15+) annually between 2018 and 2035. This would be the minimum number of jobs per year that need to be created over the next 17 years. More detailed calculations in Ghose (2019) that included estimates of surplus labour and those currently unemployed in the labour force indicated that India is required to absorb around 12.5 million persons in new jobs every year between 2018 and 2035. Given this challenge of job creation, let us turn to the services sector and its performance in terms of employment generation in the recent past and attempt some rule of thumb projections to gauge the employment potential.

7.3 Services sector employment: some projections

7.3.1 *UPSS versus UPS employment*

In NSS surveys, two major types of economic activity status of persons are distinguished. A person may be engaged in an economic activity for major part of the reference year and he will be considered as employed and his activity/work status is called usual principal status (UPS). Other persons who are either unemployed or out of the labour force may have engaged in an activity for at least 30 days in the reference year, and such persons' activity status is called subsidiary status. When we add together all persons who are in the labour force either based on the UPS or on the basis of subsidiary activity status, we get an estimate of total employment by UPSS (usual principal and subsidiary status). When we count only those persons who are employed for a major part of the reference year, we get an estimate of total employment in terms of UPS. The total number of workers in the economy in terms of UPSS will be obviously larger than UPS employment. The UPSS employment number is the most widely used, even though UPS employment is relatively well defined. First, consider the data on UPSS employment to be followed by analysis of UPS employment data in greater detail.

The absolute levels in UPSS employment in two selected years 1999–2000 and 2011–12 and the corresponding average growth rate are presented in Table 7.3. The services sector employment growth rate (2.7 per cent) is faster than total employment (1.4 per cent) in the period under consideration. The services sector contributed 45 per cent of the total employment growth. The business services sector that includes real estate, IT and

Table 7.3 Employment growth by sector (UPSS*): 1999–2000 to 2011–12

Sector	*1999–2000 (Million)*	*2011–12 (Million)*	*Annual Growth Rate (%)*	*Share (%) in Total Employment (2011–12)*
Agriculture	240.3	224.4	-0.6	47.5
Mining & quarrying	2.3	2.6	1.2	0.6
Manufacturing	43.8	61.3	2.8	13.0
Electricity, water, etc.	1.0	2.6	7.9	0.5
Construction	17.5	49.9	9.1	10.6
Trade	36.3	45.6	1.9	9.6
Hotels	4.6	8.1	4.9	1.7
Transport, storage & communications	14.6	21.4	3.2	4.5
Banking & insurance	2.2	4.5	6.4	1.0
Real estate-IT-ITES-business services**	2.7	9.3	10.9	2.0
Public administration and defence	10.5	8.3	-1.9	1.8
Education	8.5	14.5	4.6	3.1
Health	2.9	4.6	3.8	1.0
Other	10.9	15.5	3.0	3.3
Total services	93.0	127.6	2.7	27.0
Total employment	397.9	472.5	1.4	100

Source: Author's estimates based on NSS Survey Reports 55th and 68th Rounds.

Note:

* All ages.

** In 2011–12 the estimated employment in call centres was 0.24 million.

ITES (information technology enabled services) has the fastest employment growth rate (10.9 per cent) starting with a small base of 2.7 million persons in 1999–2000.

This is followed by banking and insurance, hotels and education services. In terms of UPSS employment, the services sector added 2.9 million workers per year over the period under consideration.

The earlier analysis of UPSS employment gives a broad and somewhat crude picture of employment creation. It is important to consider differences between organised and unorganised sectors and focus on UPS employment. Working conditions are substantially different between organised and unorganised segments of the labour force in terms of wage payments, productivity, compliance of labour regulations, and so on. It is important to examine the employment potential of the organised segment in the services sector. The organised segment constituted about 31 per cent of total services sector UPS employment in 2011–12. The economic policy objective is certainly not to promote unorganised sector jobs with low wages and low productivity. Interestingly, UPS employment in organised services has grown faster than aggregate economy employment, and it has higher employment elasticity relative to other groups (Table 7.4).

The question of UPS employment performance in the key sub-sectors of the organised services is equally important. The relevant data are shown in Table 7.5. The real estate and business services segment has the highest growth (20.3 per cent) in employment followed by communication, banking and finance (5.3 per cent). Employment growth in trade, hotels and transport (4.7 per cent) is similar to the growth rate in aggregate organised services. The segments with the highest employment elasticity (1.3) are real estate and business services. The most important point to keep in mind is that its share in organised services employment was just 1 per cent in 2011–12. Even if we consider communication, banking, real estate and business services together, their combined share is just 2 per cent in organised services. The segment with the highest share is community, social

Table 7.4 Services sector employment growth (UPS*): 2000–2012

Sector	*Employment Growth Rate*	*Employment Elasticity***
Organised Services	4.4	0.51
Unorganised Services	2.4	0.28
Total Services	2.9	0.34
Total Economy	1.5	0.22

Note:
* Working age 15–59.
** Author's estimate based on Table 2.13 in Ghose (2016).

Table 7.5 Organised services sector (UPS*): growth of output and employment: 1999–2000 to 2011–12

Sector	*Output Growth (% per Annum**)*	*Employment Growth (% per Annum)*	*Employment Elasticity*	*Share in Employment (%) in 2011–12*
Organised Services	9.4	4.4	0.468***	9.4
1. Trade, Hotels and Transport	9.6	4.7	0.49	1.8
2. Communication, Finance-Real Estate, Business Services	13.3	9.9	0.744	2.0
2.1 Communication and Finance	12.8	5.3	0.414	1.0
2.2 Real Estate and Business Services	15.7	20.3	1.293	1.0
3. Community, Social and Personal Services	5.5	2.4	0.436	5.5

Note:
* Working age 15–59.
** Year-on-year average.
*** Author's estimate based on Table 2.13 and Table 6.6 in Ghose (2016).

and personal services (5.5 per cent), which includes education and health services, and it turned out to be the sector with the slowest growth rate in employment (2.4 per cent).

We now consider projections of employment in the services sector as a whole. First consider the UPS employment projections and then projections of UPSS employment.

Consider two alternative rules of thumb to make the projections. Rule 1 assumes that observed past growth rates of employment in the recent period (1999–2000 to 2011–12) hold good in the future. Rule 2 states that assumed elasticity of employment based on past data will remain the same in the period for which projections are made. Using rule 1 is straightforward but use of rule 2 involves two steps. First, one needs to estimate the employment growth rate based on the assumed output growth rate and the employment elasticity. In the second step, use the estimate of the employment growth rate to make the projections. Regarding the output growth rate, it is assumed that services sector growth will be 9 per cent annum. This is apparently realistic considering the fact that average growth rate of GVA at basic prices for the services sector during 2011–12 to 2015–16 is estimated to be 8.9 per cent and the growth rate between 2011–12 and 2017–18 has turned out to be a shade lower, at 8.6 per cent (Table 7.6).

Table 7.6 GVA at basic prices (2011–12 prices): structure and growth rates

Year	*Agriculture*	*Industry*	*Construction*	*Services*	*Trade and Hotels Transport, Communication*	*Financial, Real Estate and Services*	*Public Administration and Defence*	*GVA at Basic Price*
Share in Total GVA (Per Cent)								
2011–12	18.5	22.9	9.6	49.0	17.4	18.9	12.7	100
2012–13	17.8	22.8	9.2	50.2	18.2	19.6	12.5	100
2013–14	17.5	22.5	9.0	51.0	18.4	20.3	12.3	100
2014–15	16.3	22.4	8.8	52.5	18.9	21.0	12.7	100
2015–16	15.4	22.7	8.5	53.4	19.6	21.6	12.6	100
2016–17	15.2	23.4	8.1	53.3	19.0	22.0	12.3	100
2017–18	14.9	23.2	8.0	53.9	19.1	21.9	12.9	100
Growth Rate: Year-on-Year (Per Cent)								
2012–13	1.5	4.8	0.6	8.1	9.7	9.5	4.1	5.4
2013–14	4.2	5.2	4.6	7.8	6.5	10.1	4.5	6.3
2014–15	–0.2	6.5	4.4	10.3	9.4	10.6	10.7	7.1
2015–16	1.2	8.8	3.9	8.9	10.2	10.3	6.6	7.2
2016–17	6.3	8.3	6.1	8.4	7.7	8.7	9.2	6.9
2017–18	5.0	6.1	5.6	8.1	7.7	6.2	11.9	6.6
Average	3.1	7.2	3.8	8.6	8.6	10.1	6.5	6.9

Source: Reserve Bank of India (2019).

Table 7.7 Employment (UPS) in the services sector: projected growth (million workers) under different assumptions

Sl. No	*Year*	*Projection 1**	*Projection 2**	*Projection 3**	*Projection 4**
1	2011–12	118.9	118.9	118.9	118.9
2	2012–13	122.3	122.6	124.4	121.2
3	2013–14	125.9	126.5	130.1	123.5
4	2014–15	129.5	130.5	136.1	125.8
5	2015–16	133.3	134.7	142.3	128.2
6	2016–17	137.1	139.0	148.9	130.6
7	2017–18	141.1	143.4	155.7	133.1
8	2018–19	145.1	148.0	162.9	135.6
9	2019–20	149.3	152.8	170.4	138.2
Absolute increase in employment over the period 2012–20 Working age (15–59)		30.4	33.9	51.5	19.3

Source: Author's calculations.

Note:

* Projection 1: assumption: average employment growth rate will be 2.89 per cent based on past growth in output (8.5 per cent in 2000–12) and employment elasticity of 0.34.

* Projection 2: assumption: employment growth rate in organised services at 4.6 per cent and unorganised services will grow at 2.51 per cent per annum based on observed employment elasticity of 0.51 and 0.28, respectively, and output growth of 9 per cent per annum.

* Projection 3: assumption: average employment growth rate at 4.6 per cent assuming services sector elasticity of 0.51 and output growth at 9 per cent.

* Projection 4: assumption: average employment growth rate at 1.9 per cent assuming employment elasticity of 0.21 observed in 2005–12 and output growth at 9 per cent.

The results of the exercise on projection of employment as per UPS and UPSS measures under different scenarios are presented in Tables 7.7 and 7.8, respectively, and implications are as follows:

1 Projection 3 based on employment elasticity of 0.51 yields the most optimistic projection, with an annual addition of 6.4 million. The underlying assumption of employment elasticity is taken from that observed for organised services in 1999–2000 to 2011–12. As we noted earlier, the organised services share in total services sector employment is only 31 per cent in 2011–12.
2 Projection 4 may be considered as the pessimistic scenario, as it suggests an annual addition of 2.4 million. It is based on the total services sector employment elasticity of 0.21 in the period 1999–2000 to 2011–12.
3 Projection 1 and projection 2 have yielded moderate increases in annual additions that range from 3.8 to 4.2 million. Projection 2 in particular

is appealing, as it is based on separate elasticity estimates and employment growth rates for organised and unorganised services.

4 In short, these projections of employment suggest that annual addition ranges from 2.4 million to 4.2 million, leaving out the optimistic estimate. This apparently looks reasonable in light of the fact that observed average addition to services employment was 2.9 million per year during 1999–2000 to 2011–12.

5 What would be the share of the services sector in total projected employment in the year 2020? The projections here indicate that it will fall in the range of 30 per cent to 33 per cent depending on which projection holds in the future. The projected level of total UPS labour force in 2020 is 463 million (Ghose, 2016). In 2011–12, the services sector share in total UPS labour force was 30 per cent.[7]

6 A similar exercise for UPSS employment is carried out and presented in Table 7.8. The estimates of annual additions are in the same ballpark as in the case of UPS estimates.

Table 7.8 Employment in the services sector (UPSS): projected employment growth (million workers) under different assumptions

Sl. No	*Year*	*Projection 1**	*Projection 2***	*Projection 3****	*Projection 4*****
1	2011–12	127.4	127.4	127.4	127.4
2	2012–13	130.8	130.9	134.3	129.8
3	2013–14	134.3	134.5	141.5	132.3
4	2014–15	137.8	138.2	149.2	134.8
5	2015–16	141.5	142.0	157.2	137.4
6	2016–17	145.3	145.9	165.7	140.0
7	2017–18	149.1	149.9	174.7	142.6
8	2018–19	153.1	154.0	184.1	145.3
9	2019–20	157.2	158.3	194.0	148.1
Absolute increase in employment over the period 2012–20		29.8	30.9	66.6	20.7

Source: Author's calculations.

Note:

* Projection 1: assumption: average employment growth rate will be 2.66 per cent based on past growth in total services employment.

** Projection 2: assumption: average employment growth rate is 2.75 per cent assuming services sector employment elasticity of 0.31 (2000–12) and output growth will be 9 per cent.

*** Projection 3: assumption: average employment growth rate is 5.4 per cent assuming services sector elasticity of 0.6 (2010–12 in business services) and output growth will be 9 per cent.

**** Projection 4: assumption: average employment growth rate is 1.9 per cent assuming services sector elasticity of 0.21 (2005–12) and output growth will be 9 per cent.

UPSS is usual principal and subsidiary status.

7.3.2 Services employment based on PLFS data 2017–18

In May 2019, the National Statistical Office (NSO) of the Government of India released the first annual report on 'employment and unemployment' based on the Periodic Labour Force Survey (PLFS) conducted by NSSO from July 2017 to June 2018 (NSO, 2019). The indicators of employment and unemployment that are presented in this PLFS report are based on the usual status (PS+SS) approach and current weekly status approach. This is in contrast to the earlier NSSO surveys that were conducted once in five years, also called the quinquennial 'Employment Unemployment Survey' (EUS). The question of comparability of PLFS survey results with that of earlier EUS estimates is not yet resolved. We will not go into the details of the comparability issue here. It is important to note that the estimates of the labour force indicators in the PLFS report are based on the usual status (PS+SS) approach and current weekly status approach.[8] More importantly, the selection of sample units in the second stage is based on the number of members in the household having level of general education as secondary (10th standard) or higher.[9] In the earlier NSSO surveys, the second stage stratum is used to be based on monthly per capita consumer expenditure (MPCE) of the sample household. Whether differences in sample weights and other differences between the two employment surveys will render them non-comparable or not is not yet clear. Fortunately, estimates of employment in different sectors based on the PLFS are available in a recent study (Mehrotra and Parida, 2019), and we will present estimates of employment in the services sector to bring the discussion up to date and make some relevant observations in the present context. The estimates of employment in absolute numbers and the corresponding share in total employment and the sub-sectors of the services sector in 2017–18 are presented in Table 7.9.

Table 7.9 Employment by sector and selected services sub-sectors: 2017–18

Sectors	*Absolute Numbers*	*Share (%)*
Agriculture	205.3	44.1
Manufacturing	56.4	12.1
Construction	54.3	11.7
Services	144.4	31.0
Total Employment	465.1	100.0
Hotels & Restaurants	8.7	6.0
Transport Services	22.4	15.5
Post Telecommunications	5.3	3.7
Finance & Insurance & Auxiliary Financial Services	4.9	3.4
Computer & Related Activities	2.6	1.8
Services	144.4	100.0

Source: Author's estimate based on Table 1 and Table 5 in Mehrotra and Parida (2019).

Note: Employment in mining, electricity, water and gas are not presented.

The employment estimates for the year 2017–18 lead to the following broad observations. First, the overall structure or the distribution of employment has not changed much in recent years. Second, the share of services sector in total UPSS employment is 31 per cent (144.4 million in absolute numbers). This is broadly consistent with the projected estimates (see the last column in Table 7.8, for instance). Third, the segment transport services (mainly land transport) has emerged as significant sub-sector of services. Fourth, the new technology-based services like telecommunication, finance and computer (IT and IT enabled services) services have remained relatively smaller sub-sectors of the services sector in India in terms of employment. This leads me to ask the next question: whether the services sector is relatively skill-demanding and how that is likely to affect employment in the services sector as a whole.

7.4 Is the services sector relatively skill-demanding?

The skill profile of the jobs that the services sector could potentially create in the next decade are another significant dimension that is overlooked in the earlier analysis. It has been pointed out that services-led growth in the recent past has generated slower growth of unskilled jobs relative to jobs that could have been created if growth was led by the manufacturing sector (Ghose, 2016: 97). This argument is based on the implicit assumption that regular-formal employees may be regarded as highly skilled labour, regular-informal employees as skilled labour and casual employees as unskilled labour. The data show significant changes in the workforce composition in terms of types of employees (regular-formal, regular-informal and casual) in organised services and in organised services. Regular-formal workers are found to constitute 66 per cent of organised services and only 31.6 per cent of manufacturing employees in 2011–12. In the category organised services-II (communication, financial, real estate and business services) it is reported to be much higher, at 68.6 per cent in 2011–12 (Ghose, 2016). A higher share of regular-formal employees in services is argued to suggest a higher skill level of employees. Skill is measured by the level of education of employees.

It is important to observe that there exists a large difference in the level of education between household types (casual, self-employed, regular wage-salary) in rural and urban areas of India. In the NSS survey reports, literates with a general educational level of secondary and above including diploma/certificate course have been considered as educated (NSSO, 2015). In 2011–12 the NSSO survey (NSSO, 2015) results show that the proportion of the educated persons was the highest for the household type 'regular wage/salary earning' (46.8 per cent) and the lowest for household type 'casual labour' (13.2 per cent) in rural areas. In urban areas, the proportion of the educated persons was the highest among the household type 'others' (65.3 per cent) and it was the lowest for 'casual labour' (19.3 per cent).

Therefore, one would like to see more evidence in terms of changes in the educational composition of the workforce over time in the services sector relative to manufacturing in order substantiate the argument that the services sector is relatively skill-demanding. Some evidence in support of this proposition is provided in Table 7.10, in the form of the distribution by educational levels over time in these two sectors in urban India. Only three levels of education levels are distinguished, namely, those with below primary education that includes not literate, those with middle school education and those with above secondary school that includes those with diploma and those with above graduate education. The distribution is presented separately for males and females. The change over time in the service sector is uneven compared to manufacturing. The proportion of male workers with 'secondary education and above' is significantly higher (61 per cent) in services compared to manufacturing (46 per cent) in 2009–10. Among females, the difference is found to be much more substantial, with a 56 per cent share of those with secondary education and above in services against 23 per cent in manufacturing. Further, it has been found that the share of workers with a graduate education and above among males is almost twice as that of manufacturing in 2009–10 (Ramaswamy and Agrawal, 2013). The upshot of this analysis suggests that if current education-skill distribution is taken as the underlying skill-demand structure, then the services sector has much less potential capacity to absorb labour with lower levels of education relative to manufacturing.

Table 7.10 Distribution of workers by level of education in urban India (%)

Education Level	*Males*			
	Manufacturing		*Services*	
	1999–2000	*2009–10*	*1999–2000*	*2009–10*
Below Primary	39.2	32.5	31.8	22.6
Middle	19.8	21.2	18.9	16.2
Secondary & Above	41.0	46.3	49.3	61.2
Education Level	*Females*			
	Manufacturing		*Services*	
	1999–2000	*2009–10*	*1999–2000*	*2009–10*
Below Primary	68.8	55.8	46.2	34.5
Middle	15.2	20.8	8.8	9.6
Secondary & Above	15.9	23.4	45.0	55.9

Source: Based on NSS Unit Level Records of 55th and 66th Rounds.

7.5 Concluding observations

This chapter has examined the employment potential of services sector in India, focusing on employment growth of workers in the age group 15 to 59 years based on UPS status. Growth rates in employment based on the other widely used criteria of employment status, namely UPSS, were also estimated. The base year for the projection was taken as 2011–12 the survey year of the NSS 68th Round of EUS and the terminal year is taken as 2020. The projections of employment suggest that annual additions to service sector employment falls in the range of 2.4 million to 4.2 million based on the assumption that services sector annual average output growth rate would be 9 per cent. This will make the share of the services sector in the total working-age labour force go up from 30 per cent in 2011–12 to 33 per cent in 2020. Analysis of more recent data for the year 2017–18 based on the PLFS surveys is found to be along the lines of the analysis of NSSO survey data and confirms the apprehension that increases in the employment opportunities for the growing labour force is likely to be modest. This is certainly not a very optimistic scenario.

Notes

1 *The Economic Times*, IT sector to lose 6.4 lakh 'low-skilled' jobs to automation by 2021: HfS Research, Dated June 05, 2016, internet edition, accessed on November 10, 2016.
2 This study admits incremental higher contribution of the services sector to employment in South Asia but does not say anything about the future (Bosworth and Maerten, 2010).
3 This is based on national income accounts statistics taken from the *Handbook of Statistics on Indian Economy 2015–16*, published by Reserve Bank of India (2016).
4 These figures are taken from Verma (2012) and measured in terms of 1990 Geary-Khemis (GK) dollars. Refer to the original for more comparisons with other countries. Also see Ramaswamy (2015).
5 The GDP shares are based on GDP in current prices.
6 See Rakshit (2007), Nayyar (2012), and Ghose (2015, 2016) for detailed discussion of services-led growth and related issues.
7 Estimates based on the data in Ghose (2016).
8 The activity status determined on the basis of the reference period of last 365 days preceding the date of survey is known as the usual activity status of the person, and the activity status determined on the basis of a reference period of last 7 days preceding the date of survey is known as the current weekly status (CWS) of the person.
9 For details on the stages of sample selection see NSO (2019).

References

Bosworth, B. and A. Maertens (2010). 'Economic growth and employment generation: The role of the service sector', in E. Ghani (ed.) *The Service Revolution in South Asia*, Oxford University Press, New Delhi.

Das, D.K., Erumban, A.A., Aggarwal, S. and S. Sengupta (2016). 'Productivity growth in India under different policy regimes', in D. Jorgenson, K. Fukao and M.P. Timmer (eds.) *The World Economy: Growth or Stagnation*, Cambridge University Press, Cambridge, UK.

Eichengreen, B. and P. Gupta (2011). 'The service sector as India's road to economic growth in India', in *India Policy Forum: 2010–11*, vol. 7, Sage Publications, New Delhi.

Ghani, E. (ed.) (2010). *The Service Revolution in South Asia*, Oxford University Press, New Delhi.

Ghose, A. (2015). 'Services-led growth and employment in India', in K.V. Ramaswamy (ed.) *Labour, Employment and Economic Growth in India*, Cambridge University Press, New Delhi.

Ghose, A. (2016). *India Employment Report 2016*, Institute of Human Development and Oxford University Press, New Delhi.

Ghose, A. (2019). *Employment in India*, Oxford University Press, New Delhi.

Kochhar, K., Kumar, U., Rajan, R., Subramanian, A. and I. Tokatlidis (2006). 'India's pattern of development: What happened, what follows?', *Journal of Monetary Economics*, 53(5), 981–1019.

Mehrotra, S. and J.K. Parida (2019). 'India's employment crisis: Rising education levels and falling non-agricultural job growth', CSE Working Paper No. 2019-04. https://cse.azimpremjiuniversity.edu.in/wp-content/uploads/2019/10/Mehrotra_Parida_India_Employment Crisis.pdf (Accessed on 25/12/2019).

Nayyar, G. (2012). *The Service Sector in India's Development*, Cambridge University Press, Cambridge.

NSO (2019). *Annual Report, Periodic Labour Force Survey (July 2017–June 2018)*, National Statistical Office, Ministry of Statistics and Programme Implementation, Government of India, New Delhi.

NSSO (2001). *Employment and Unemployment Situation in India 1999–2000, Parts I & II, Fifty Fifth Round (July 1999–June 2000)*, Report No. 458, National Sample Survey Organization, Ministry of Statistics and Programme Implementation, Government of India, New Delhi.

NSSO (2011). *Employment and Unemployment Situation in India 2009–10, Report No. 537(66/10/1)*, National Sample Survey Organisation, Ministry of Statistics and Programme Implementation, Government of India, New Delhi.

NSSO (2013). *Key Indicators of Employment and Unemployment in India 2011–12, Sixty Eighth Round (July 2011–June 2012)*, Report No. KI/68/10, National Sample Survey Organization, Ministry of Statistics and Programme Implementation, Government of India, New Delhi.

NSSO (2015). *Status of Education and Vocational Training in India, Sixty Eighth Round (July 2011–June 2012)*, Report No. 566 (68/10/6), National Sample Survey Organization, Ministry of Statistics and Programme Implementation, Government of India, New Delhi.

Rakshit, M. (2007). 'Services-led growth: The Indian experience', *ICRA Bulletin Money & Finance*, 3(1), 91–126.

Ramaswamy, K.V. (2015). 'Introduction', in K.V. Ramaswamy (ed.) *Labour, Employment and Economic Growth in India*, Cambridge University Press, New Delhi.

Ramaswamy, K.V. and T. Agrawal (2013). 'Services-led growth, employment, and skill and job quality: A study of manufacturing and service sectors in urban India', in S. Mahendra Dev (ed.) *India Development Report 2012–13*, Oxford University Press, New Delhi.

Reserve Bank of India (2016). *Handbook of Statistics on Indian Economy 2015–16*, Reserve Bank of India, Mumbai.

Reserve Bank of India (2019). *Handbook of Statistics on Indian Economy 2018–19*, Reserve Bank of India, Mumbai.

Rodrik, D. (2013). 'Perils of premature deindustrialization', www.project-syndicate.org/commentary/dani-rodrikdeveloping-economies-missing-manufacturing#K9kffEZoSPSVT3xT.99 (Accessed on 10/11/2016).

Verma, R. (2012). 'Structural transformation and jobless growth in the Indian economy', in C. Ghate (ed.) *The Oxford Handbook of the Indian Economy*, pp. 276–310, Oxford University Press, New York.

UN (2015). *World Population Prospects: The 2015 Revision*, United Nations Department of Economic and Social Affairs/Population Division, New York.

8 Diversity in services sector employment in India

Evidence from India Human Development Survey, 2011–12

Brinda Viswanathan

8.1 Introduction

India's employment grew from 459.4 million in 2004–05 to 474.2 million in 2011–12 but declined to 465.1 million in 2017–18 (ILO, 2016; Mehrotra and Parida, 2019). The period between 2005 and 2011 saw a slow growth in employment, while the GDP growth rate of the country was between 7 and 8 per cent per annum. The slow growth in employment was attributed to increase in school enrolment, withdrawal of rural women from the workforce and low growth in agriculture (Thomas, 2013; Mehrotra and Parida, 2019). Since 2012, the GDP growth rate per annum has remained at about 7 per cent or below, while employment has fallen along with a substantial increase in unemployed from 10.6 million to 30 million during this period.

The female workforce participation rate (FWPR) has declined from 32.7 per cent in 2004–05 to 24.6 per cent in 2011–12 and further to 17.6 per cent in 2017–18 in rural areas, in comparison to the stable workforce participation rate of 54 per cent for males which declined to 51.7 per cent in 2017–18. In urban areas, the FWPR shows a further decline from 16.6 per cent in 2004–05 to 14.2 per cent in 2017–18, while for men it declined marginally from 54.9 per cent to 53 per cent during this period. All these rates are based on the usual (principal and subsidiary) activity status.[1] The subsidiary status employment for women (compared to men) is higher by 3 to 4 percentage points in rural areas and about 1 to 2 percentage points in urban areas[2] (GoI, 2014). Another feature that has changed recently among women in the labour market is that casual labour share in urban and self-employment share in rural areas have decreased with an increase in regular wage/salaried employment share in both these sectors (GoI, 2014). This could be considered as an improvement in the quality of employment for them, as there is more job security in wage/salaried employment given that self-employment for women was largely in unpaid work. This gender gap in both quantity and quality of employment is comparable to only a few countries in the world like Turkey and countries of the Middle East and North Africa (Chaudhary and Verick, 2014).

Two other worrisome features of the Indian labour market are informality and unemployment rates, and here again women face more adverse outcomes than men. A whopping 92 per cent of the total employed (male + female) are in the informal sector, and this has increased in the last decade (ILO, 2016); the services sector accounts for 75 per cent of the informal sector employment (Joshi, 2004). The youth (15–29 years) unemployment rates range from 5 per cent to 19 per cent with variations between rural and urban, males and females and age segments (15–19, 20–24 and 25–29 years) as shown in ILO (2016) and Mehrotra and Parida (2019). In both these aspects – informality of employment and unemployment – women's share dominates substantially compared to men. Female unemployment rates were higher than males until 2011–12, but in 2017–18 the male unemployment rate increased substantially compared to females in both rural and urban areas (GoI, 2019).[3] Alongside the underrepresentation of women in the labour market, there is also underrepresentation of rural areas and socially disadvantaged groups in jobs that provide secure contracts (Nayyar, 2012).

Given these broad patterns of employment, the sectoral shares are the major determinants of poverty and regional development (Mazumdar and Sarkar, 2007; Unni and Naik, 2011). This is because the quality of employment in terms of labour productivity and security of job contracts depend on the sub-sectoral component of employment. For instance, service sector employment is shown to be prone to 'dualism', wherein some sectors like trade and hotels, transportation and communication are at the lower end while financial services and community and public services are at the top end of quality as measured by either per capita income accruing to such households or in terms of value added per worker (Mazumdar and Sarkar, 2007). Nayyar (2012) shows that service sector employment is heterogenous in skills and has both low and high education. Further, the employers in the subdivisions of the service sector are both of 'good' and 'poor' quality in terms of the job contracts and social security benefits that they offer to their employees. He also finds that between 1993–94 and 2004–05 the expansion of employment has happened in the subdivisions of the services sector with low education skills. Banga and Bansal (2009) find that women accounted for about 16 per cent of the services employment in 2004–05, while Mazumdar and Sarkar (2007) find that women constituted only 10 per cent of the formal sector tertiary employment in 1999–2000. This not only reflects a weak representation of women in the services sector but also that the employment quality is poor, albeit the information pertains to different time points.

One of the advantages of the services sector is that it liaises with both industry and agriculture, thereby building forward and backward linkages, and hence provides a larger scope for employment.

This chapter presents an assessment of the diversity in employment within the services sector focusing on female employment and also tries to explore the proximate factors that explain the choice of sub-sector-level employment within the services in comparison to other sectors of agriculture, manufacturing and construction. The factors include both labour supply variables like individual profile and household characteristics, and the demand-side variables are knowledge of English language, quality of job contract and location of the job.

8.2 Employment patterns in services sector vis-à-vis other sectors

The services sector has shown more dynamism both in terms of absorbing labour and increases in labour productivity compared to the industrial sector (Mazumdar and Sarkar, 2007; Basu and Das, 2016). However, the labour absorption out of agriculture has happened only in a limited manner, and service growth was associated with urban sector employment more than the rural sector (Unni and Naik, 2011). India's services sector has a high share in income and relatively low share in employment, while in China, the shares of both income and employment in services are low (GoI, 2015). But in both these countries, the shares of services in both GDP and employment have increased in the last decade and a half. Employment elasticity has increased for both services and industry in 2009–10 to 2011–12 compared to 2004–05 to 2009–10, though industry had relatively higher employment elasticity (GoI, 2015). Among the different sub-sectors of services, there was continuous increase in employment share in trade, hotels, and restaurants; transport, storage, and communication; and financial, insurance, real estate and business services, from 1993–94 to 2017–18. Other services have a very high share among urban women close to 45 per cent in 2017–18, increasing from 36 per cent in 2004–05.

Eichengreen and Gupta (2010) classify the services sector into three groups: *traditional*, comprising retail and wholesale trade, transport and storage, public administration and defence; *hybrid* of modern and traditional services comprising education, healthcare and social work, hotels and restaurants and other community, social, and personal services; and *modern*, comprising financial intermediation, computer services, business services, communications and legal and technical services. The last type within the services sector was the one that showed maximum productivity growth arising from some of the segments like banking, communications and business services contributing to large export growth. Mukherjee (2013) finds that TFP growth in India was highest in the service sector at 1.58 per cent per annum, followed by agriculture at 1.06 per cent and manufacturing at 0.3 per cent during 1980–2008. In comparison to this, the growth rates in labour productivity have been the highest for manufacturing at 5.5 per cent, followed by that for services at 3.5 per cent and the least for agriculture for 1.9 per cent during the same period.

8.3 Trends in sectoral share of employment

In this section, the trends in workforce participation rates are presented across the broad industrial sectors among men and women in rural and urban areas separately. This is based on the data from National Sample Survey Organisation (NSSO), which is the only source that provides such data at the national level.

Figure 8.1 shows the share of primary, secondary and tertiary sectors in employment (usual status) for rural and urban areas and males and females. The primary sector consists only of agriculture and allied activities; the tertiary sector consists of construction, trade, hotels and restaurants and so on, transport storage and communications, and community, public and other services.[4] The remaining sectors of mining and manufacturing are taken as the secondary sector. For males, the share of agriculture declines significantly

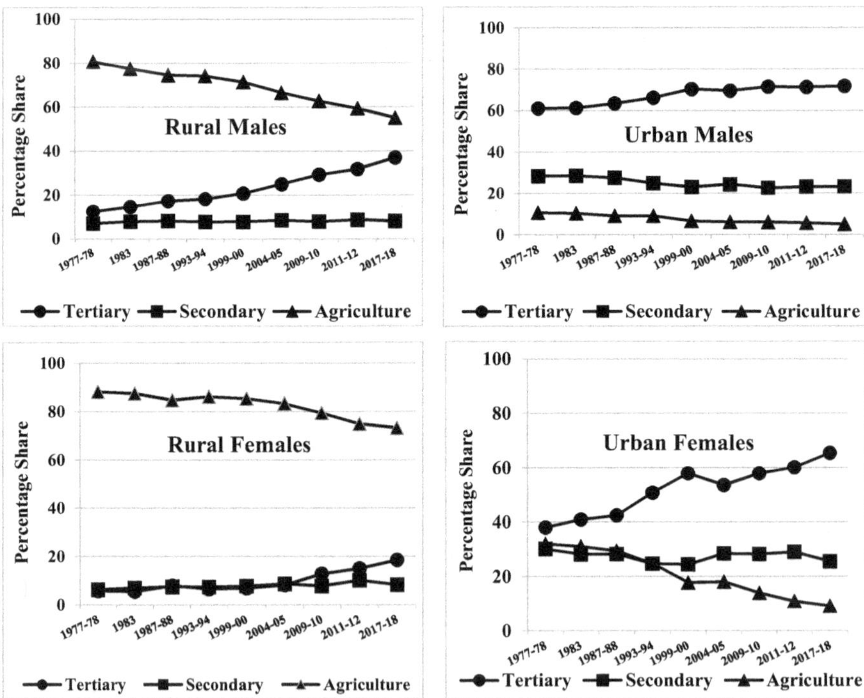

Figure 8.1 Trends in broad sectoral shares in employment: rural and urban males and females

Source: GoI (2019).

by 10 percentage points in the 2000s taken over by services, while in urban areas the shares across sectors seem to have stabilised since 1999. The secondary sector continues to have the lowest share among the three in rural and services the highest in urban areas. Rural employment for women shows far less sectoral diversity, with agriculture having the dominant share in employment. This has to be viewed alongside the fact that there has been overall withdrawal of women from the labour market. The urban labour market for women shows that the share of agriculture is being replaced by the tertiary sector share since 1999.

Within the services sector, the trends from Figure 8.2 show that that the only sub-sector that is dominating for rural males is construction and thereby contributing to the rise in the services sector share. The construction sector did not show changes in shares for urban males and trade, transport, retail trade

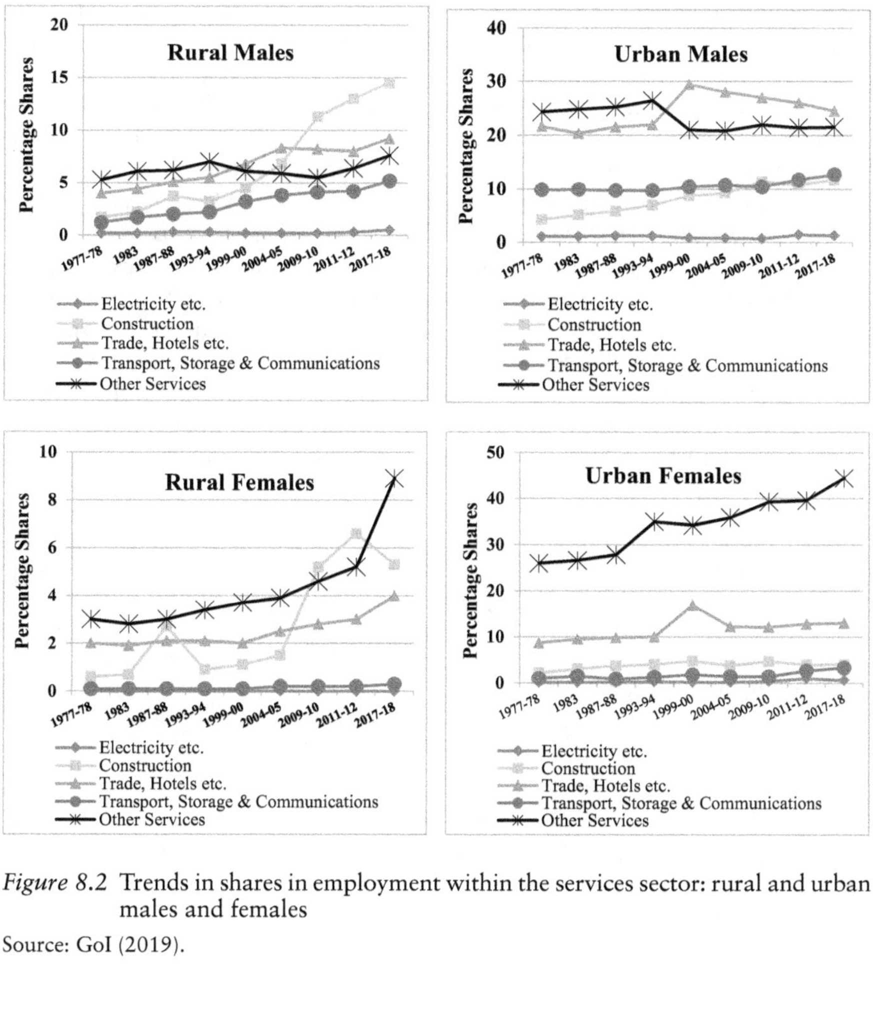

Figure 8.2 Trends in shares in employment within the services sector: rural and urban males and females

Source: GoI (2019).

and so on has gained dominance in the 2000s over 'other services'. This latter type of change in composition is also noted for rural males. For females, 'other services' dominate, with some diversity in rural areas though their shares are all below 10 per cent. In the following sections India Human Development Survey Data is analysed to understand the individual, household and regional factors associated with employment choice across different sectors of the economy.

8.4 Explaining distribution of employment across sectors

8.4.1 Methodology and data

The econometric specification adopted in the present analysis explains the probability of an individual employed in a particular sector in terms of individual, household and regional characteristics. The sectors are classified into eight sectors on the basis of primary employment. The eight sectors are listed in Appendix Table A.1 and is based on the eight groups of the one-digit classification of NIC, 1987.[5] The multinomial logit model is a preferred specification which explains the probability of an individual to be associated with one of the eight sectors (equations 1 and 2).[6] The model specification is such that the coefficient estimates are obtained only for seven sectors, leaving out one of the sectors as a reference (omitted) sector which is agriculture in this specification. This econometric specification is similar to that estimated by Nayyar (2012) using the NSS data for 1993–94 and 2004–05 wherein the industrial sector is used as the reference category in the multinomial logit model. In this study, the agricultural sector is preferred for comparison as it has low labour productivity and one could understand the factors that influence the employment in other sectors vis-à-vis this sector. Further, the analysis here is carried out using India Human Development Survey Data for 2011–12 which has a richer set of information on individual characteristics compared to the NSS data.

For the *ith* individual, the probability of each outcome (j), that is, being employed in jth particular sector of the economy is written as follows:

$$\text{Prob}\left(Y_i = j\right) = \frac{e^{\beta_j' x_i}}{1 + \sum_{k=1}^{7} e^{\beta_k' x_i}} \quad \text{for } j = 1, \ldots 7 \tag{1}$$

$$\text{and Prob}\left(Y_i = 0\right) = \frac{1}{1 + \sum_{k=1}^{7} e^{\beta_k' x_i}} \tag{2}$$

Though the model is estimated using equations (1) and (2), the specification as in (3) gives estimates of log odds ratios or relative risk ratios (RRR) for each of the seven sectors with respect to the reference (agricultural with $Y_i = 0$) sector is often preferred.

$$\ln\left[\frac{P_{ij}}{P_{i0}}\right] = \beta_j' \mathbf{X}_{ij} \qquad \text{for j} = 1, \ldots 7 \tag{3}$$

$\boldsymbol{\beta}_j$ is the set of coefficients associated with the *jth* outcome for the set of regressors $\mathbf{X}_{ij}$, corresponding to the *ith* individual choosing the *jth* sector of employment. The analysis focuses on men and women aged 15–65 years employed in the labour market either as self-employed or as wage and salaried earners. The set of regressors representing individual characteristics are age; sex; own education classified into six mutually exclusive groups; knowledge of English classified as 'none', 'little' and 'fluent'; and types of contract they have for their jobs.

It is well known that some jobs in the services sector need a fairly good knowledge of English and some need limited knowledge, while in many other sectors this language skill is not very essential. Kapur and Chakraborty (2008) find that lack of English knowledge significantly lowers the wages in West Bengal, thereby increasing the inequality in wages. More importantly, this wage gap arises through the more remunerative occupations which pay a premium for the knowledge of English over and above the educational attainment. Azam, Chin and Prakash (2013) find that the average (unadjusted) wages for males in 2005 is Rs 42 per hour for those who speak fluent English, while for those who cannot speak English at all it is Rs 10. After controlling for various other factors including education, they find that relative to workers who speak no English, hourly wages are on average 34 per cent (13 per cent) higher for workers who speak fluent (little) English for men. Even though women workers who are fluent (little) in English get an additional 22 per cent (10 per cent) of their average hourly wages compared to the non-English-speaking women, the gender wage gap persists. Given these earlier findings, in this study knowledge of English language is included among the set of regressors. Further, as in Nayyar (2012), who classifies the jobs into 'good' and 'bad' contracts, the present study also uses relevant information from this database and the work is classified as weak, medium and strong based on the security of the contract. This is discussed in more detail in section 8.4. Both English knowledge and type of security in employment though are reported for an individual, and they should be considered as demand-side variables as they are determined by the nature of work carried in that sector and the formal and informal institutions that govern the activity in that sector.

Household-level variables included in the regressors are caste, religion and parent's education classified into six education groups similar to the categories for one's own education. Father's education is included to control for the unobserved ability of the individual that could be correlated with English language skills or one's own education. Parental education would impact the intergenerational transmission of access to resources that would enhance acquisition of better skills and consequently the choice of location of the employment. Two types of regional variables are included to account for any omitted variable bias, as jobs are created either based on geographical features of a region or other infrastructure and institutional factors that may be necessary for a particular sector. The two examples in this context are agriculture (soil quality, weather and temperature and irrigation facilities) and financial services (metropolitan cities). The first type of regional variable has four categories based on the location of residence in terms of rural – classified further into less developed and more developed villages (as available in the database) – and urban – classified into metro cities and other urban areas comprising smaller cities and towns. The second type of regional variable pertains to the state of residence but grouped as zones on the basis of their geographical locations and explained in section 8.4.3.

This analysis is carried out using the second wave of India Human Development Survey Data for the year 2011–12 (Desai and Vanneman, 2015). This data set provides details of employment for agriculture, non-farm business and wages and salaried individuals. The industrial classification is based on National Industrial Classification (NIC, 1987), and that has been used to create the sectoral classification of those who are employed in the age group of 15–65 years (the economically active age group). The next sub-section presents the broad patterns of sectoral employment by classifying it across sex, regions – rural/urban and geographical zones and few other characteristics like economic status and caste.

8.4.2 *Gender and urban/rural comparison*

We consider the distribution of females and males aged 15 to 65 years across the sectors of the economy and those not in the workforce, excluding those who are attending an educational institution (Table 8.1). A large proportion of women are not in the workforce in urban areas and more so in the metros. Males in urban areas who are not in the labour force are unemployed. The services sector, which includes financial, public and other services, dominates as a source of employment in the metros for both women and men. Apart from agriculture, construction sector employment is dominant in rural areas as was observed from NSSO data as well in the previous section. The analysis in the remaining sections is on the basis of only those in the workforce: 40 per cent of women and 90 per cent of men.

8.4.3 *Regional distribution*

The contiguous states in India are grouped into six geographical zones. Interestingly, the states belonging to a zone are quite often similar in their human capital, infrastructure and economic development. The states corresponding to the zones are (i) North: Jammu and Kashmir, Himachal Pradesh, Punjab, Chandigarh, Uttarakhand, Haryana and Delhi; (ii) Central: Uttar Pradesh, Jharkhand, Chhattisgarh and Madhya Pradesh; (iii) West: Gujarat, Maharashtra, Goa, Rajasthan, Daman and Diu and Dadra and Nagar Haveli; (iv) South: Andhra Pradesh, Karnataka, Kerala, Tamil Nadu and Pondicherry; (v) East: Bihar, Sikkim, West Bengal and Orissa; and (vi) North-East: Arunachal Pradesh, Nagaland, Manipur, Mizoram, Tripura, Meghalaya and Assam.

Table 8.1 Distribution of the employed across industry groups for females and males (15–65 years): 2011–12

Sector	Females					Males				
	Urban		Rural by Level of Development)		All	Urban		Rural (by Level of Development)		All
	Metros	Other	High	Low		Metros	Other	High	Low	
Agriculture	0.6	4.5	32.8	33.1	23.5	1.7	6.3	40.7	38.1	27.8
Manufacturing-1	2.2	4.6	3.3	2.0	3.0	11.5	10.6	4.9	4.4	6.7
Manufacturing-2	0.6	0.7	0.6	0.7	0.7	10.1	9.8	4.4	5.8	6.8
Electricity and Constructions	0.6	2.3	8.0	7.0	5.6	8.9	12.5	19.0	25.6	19.1
Trade and Hotels	3.4	3.2	1.8	1.4	2.1	15.4	17.7	6.8	4.3	9.3
Transport and Communication	1.3	0.7	0.3	0.1	0.4	14.5	11.9	5.8	4.5	7.5
Financial Services	1.1	0.5	0.1	0.0	0.3	5.7	3.8	1.1	0.8	2.0
Public and Other Services	9.0	9.1	3.0	2.8	4.9	21.1	16.8	8.0	6.6	10.7
Not in Labour Force	81.2	74.4	50.2	52.8	59.5	11.1	10.5	9.4	10.1	10.1
Total	100.0	100.0	100.0	100.0	100.0	100.0	100.0	100.0	100.0	100.0

Source: Author's own estimates; manufacturing sub-sectors as defined in Appendix Table A1.

The distribution of the employed for each sector across these zones indicates that the tertiary sector predominates other sectors in the southern parts of the country, closely followed by the western region in some of the subdivisions of this sector (Table 8.2). These two regions also have a higher work participation rates for all as well as among the economically active age group of 15–65 years, and at the moment these two regions seem to be benefitting more from the demographic dividend than the other regions. Electricity

Table 8.2 Sector-level distribution of employed across geographical regions

Sectors↓ or Zones→	*North*	*Central*	*West*	*South*	*East*	*Northeast*	*Total*
Agriculture	6.3	25.3	25.6	24.4	16.3	2.0	100
	[28.7]	[39.5]	[47.0]	[40.7]	[40.6]	[23.9]	[40.1]
Manufacturing-1	8.4	24.0	17.8	28.7	18.2	3.0	100
	[7.2]	[7.0]	[6.1]	[9.0]	[8.5]	[6.7]	[7.5]
Manufacturing-2	9.8	35.6	21.3	21.2	10.3	1.8	100
	[6.3]	[7.7]	[5.5]	[4.9]	[3.6]	[3.0]	[5.6]
Electricity and Construction	8.3	30.5	16.8	21.0	18.6	4.9	100
	[17.2]	[21.6]	[14.0]	[15.9]	[21.0]	[26.5]	[18.2]
Trade and Hotels	10.4	26.1	20.1	23.6	16.7	3.1	100
	[10.3]	[8.9]	[8.1]	[8.6]	[9.1]	[8.3]	[8.8]
Transport and Communication	10.9	18.4	22.3	29.7	13.0	5.8	100
	[7.4]	[4.3]	[6.1]	[7.4]	[4.8]	[10.4]	[6.0]
Financial Services	14.1	18.2	21.7	31.0	12.4	2.6	100
	[2.8]	[1.2]	[1.7]	[2.2]	[1.3]	[1.4]	[1.7]
Public and Other Services	14.7	20.6	21.0	23.0	[15.2	5.5	100
	[20.1]	[9.6]	[11.6]	[11.5]	[11.3]	[19.8]	[12.0]
All Sectors	8.8	25.7	21.9	24.0	16.2	3.3	100
	[100]	[100]	[100]	[100]	[100]	[100]	[100]
Work Participation Rate (All)	36.2	35.4	41.0	42.4	33.1	34.0	37.7
Work Participation Rate (15–65 years)	50.5	54.4	57.9	57.2	49.9	46.9	54.3

Source: Author's calculations.

Note: The states included in the each of the geographical zones are as follows: North: Jammu and Kashmir, Himachal Pradesh, Punjab, Chandigarh, Uttarakhand, Haryana and Delhi; Central: Uttar Pradesh, Jharkhand, Chhattisgarh and Madhya Pradesh; West: Gujarat, Maharashtra, Goa, Rajasthan, Daman and Diu and Dadra and Nagar Haveli; South: Andhra Pradesh, Karnataka, Kerala, Tamil Nadu and Pondicherry; East: Bihar, Sikkim, West Bengal and Orissa; and North-East: Arunachal Pradesh, Nagaland, Manipur, Mizoram, Tripura, Meghalaya and Assam.

The values in brackets are shares of the sectoral distribution within a given geographical region.

and construction sectors and the manufacturing sector-2 are dominant in the central region. Across the central, eastern and north-eastern regions, the construction sector (including electricity) has the next higher share after agriculture. Financial services (the most remunerative, in terms of earnings per worker), of all sectors, has a very small share in each of the zones while employment in public services and trade and hotels is among the prominent service sub-sectors.

The western and southern regions are demographically well-balanced with close to 40 per cent among all and 60 per cent among those aged 15–65 years of the respective population in the workforce. These regions also dominate in terms of the sectors that provide more remunerative and well-secured job contracts, thereby adding to the regional imbalance in development. Given this variation in geographical spread of the different sub-groups of the services sector in particular and other sectors, it would create differences in economic benefits and hence the standard of living accruing to the workers across regions. This in turn would also influence the level of human capital formation, access to financial services and overall development.

8.4.4 Educational attainment and English language skills

Those without any schooling dominate the workforce. They are a little less than one-third of the employed and primarily in the agriculture or construction sector, as seen in Table 8.3. The next largest share is for those with middle school completion, and their share is higher in agriculture, manufacturing

Table 8.3 Sector-level distribution of employed across educational attainment

Educational Attainment→ Sectors↓	*Not Literate*	*Primary*	*Middle*	*Secondary*	*Higher Secondary*	*Post Higher Secondary*	*Total*
Agriculture	45.4	10.3	22.6	14.2	5.0	2.4	100
Manufacturing-1	23.2	10.5	32.3	20.4	7.4	6.4	100
Manufacturing-2	20.5	7.8	29.6	22.8	9.6	9.7	100
Electricity and Construction	36.9	10.6	30.1	14.9	4.6	2.8	100
Trade and Hotels	15.7	6.5	25.7	26.8	12.3	13.1	100
Transport and Communication	13.2	7.9	27.3	28.8	11.5	11.2	100
Financial Services	1.6	1.4	9.5	17.2	13.9	56.4	100
Public and Other Services	12.7	5.4	17.6	19.5	14.3	30.4	100
Total	31.5	9.0	24.8	17.9	7.7	8.9	100

Source: Author's calculations.

and construction as well. Those with middle school completion find employment in both manufacturing and services sectors like trade, hotel, transport and communication. Those with secondary schooling dominate in the trade and hotel and transport and communication. The financial services followed by the public and other services employ mainly those with post higher secondary level of education.

Public and other services include government programmes like MGNREGA, so there are a substantial proportion who are not literate, and this sector in that sense employs people from a wider range of educational qualification. This sector is dominated by the presence of the state, which provides a range of services and hence is able to employ people from varied skill segments.

Another aspect of employability is English language skills in the Indian context. Table 8.4 presents the pattern for those who have (self reported) none, little and fluent knowledge of English. About 75 per cent of those employed have no knowledge of English, about 20 per cent have little knowledge and 5 per cent have fluent knowledge. For financial services and so on, this skill is most in demand, but here also the share is not very high, perhaps due to a limited supply of labour. Therefore, if 'a little' and 'fluent' knowledge of English is an important aspect for generating high-quality employment, then a shortage of such skills would adversely affect their employability on the one hand and in turn also affect the capacity for innovation and hence productivity of several other sectors, particularly due to the interlinkage among financial, communications and related sectors with other sectors.

The sectors employing workers with higher educational levels would also have jobs that have better contracts and security. However, there could be some variation in the nature of security depending on the low- and

Table 8.4 Sector-level distribution of employed across English language skills

Sector	*None*	*A Little*	*Fluent*	*Total*
Agriculture	87.4	11.3	1.1	100
Manufacturing-1	76.4	19.7	3.9	100
Manufacturing-2	70.0	24.0	6.0	100
Electricity and Construction	84.1	14.0	1.8	100
Trade and Hotels	64.1	29.6	6.4	100
Transport and Communication	63.3	29.5	7.1	100
Financial Services	24.9	40.1	34.9	100
Public and Other Services	48.4	32.8	18.6	100
Total	75.7	18.9	5.2	100

Source: Author's calculations.

Note: English language skills are assessed only on the basis of spoken English, in terms of fluent, little and none.

middle-skilled segments and also whether they are self-employed, wage or salaried income earners. The next sub-section explores this feature of the labour market in India based on the India Human Development Survey data set.

8.4.5 *Work arrangement/job contract*

Apart from a large proportion of self-employed in agriculture, manufacturing-1 within the industrial sector and trade and hotels sector within the services sector have a substantial presence of self-employed. The majority of those in the financial and public services earn regular salaries, but in the construction sector men and women are largely paid daily or weekly wages and have weaker job contracts. Wage earners are there with a sizeable share in all the sectors except for financial services, trade and hotel and to a small extent in the public services. Some of the jobs like security services and housekeeping in the public sector are now being contracted out, and even though they get paid monthly salaries the contract is usually for less than a year. Further, the public and community services also include people who work in public works programme including MGNREGA and earn daily wages without any job contracts. Thus, the group of public and community services would account for both weakly and highly secure jobs.

Among the self-employed in the non-agricultural sector, there are three enterprise types: home-based, location not fixed (mobile enterprise) and those with a fixed location. Agriculture has both self-employed and wage earners, with a slightly higher share of wage earners than self-employed. Among the self-employed in agriculture, the individual is either a decision maker for farming and other activities or not. Those not self-employed are categorised in the database as (i) daily wage earners, (ii) having a contract for less than a year, (iii) piecework and (iv) regular salary earners.

In this analysis, we group these different types of job as discussed earlier into three categories: weak contracts, medium (semi-formal) contracts and strong (formal) contracts. Those not involved in decision making among the self-employed in agriculture, home-based enterprises and daily wage earners are considered as weak contracts, while those involved in decision making among the self-employed in agriculture, fixed location for enterprise and the regular salaried are considered as more secure employment types/contracts. The remaining two, that is, the mobile (not fixed) enterprises and piece-rate/short contract wage earners, are those with limited security in employment. This categorisation loosely fits our understanding of the Indian labour market, which could be categorised into informal, semi-formal and formal and enables one to combine all the sectoral divisions and the two broad employment types of self-employment and wage/salary earners as is available from the database.

Compared to the primary and secondary sectors, the tertiary sector comprising the services has better job contracts (Table 8.5). Expectedly in the

Table 8.5 Sector-level distribution (%) of employed across types of employment contracts

Sectoral Division of the Economy	*Type of Employment Contract*			*Total*
	Weak	*Medium*	*Strong*	
Agriculture	51.4	30.5	18.0	100
Manufacturing-1	56.2	19.9	23.9	100
Manufacturing-2	61.4	14.5	24.1	100
Electricity and Construction	87.7	7.5	4.8	100
Trade and Hotels	36.9	17.3	45.5	100
Transport and Communication	42.7	22.4	35.0	100
Financial Services	15.1	15.8	69.0	100
Public and Other Services	25.3	13.0	61.9	100
All Sectors	53.5	20.7	26.0	100

Source: Author's calculations.

Note: Weak contract: those not involved in decision making among the self-employed in agriculture, home-based enterprises in non-agricultural self-employment and daily wage earners; medium contract: the mobile (not fixed) non-farm enterprises and piece-rate/short contract wage earners; strong contract: those involved in decision making among self-employed in agriculture, fixed location for enterprise for non-agricultural self-employment and the regular salaried.

financial sector about 70 per cent of jobs provide strong (secure) contracts, with an equal distribution among the remaining two types of contracts. In comparison to this, public and other services have about 62 per cent with strong contracts, and about 25 per cent are with weak contracts with the least share for the medium type. Overall, strong contracts constitute only about 26 per cent of the three types of contracts, and the other two divisions are trade and hotel as well as transport and communication that have a higher share than this average. Weak contract jobs constitute a little above 50 per cent, with the largest share for the construction sector at 82 per cent, way above the average; the other sector having above-average rates is manufacturing. Since those in agriculture who are able to make decisions for cultivation and related activities have been classified as medium contract, this sector has the highest share in that category. Manufacturing-2 and transport and communications are the other two sectors with slightly higher than average rates for the medium type of contract. For this segment, it may perhaps be relatively easy to make some provisions and regulations to seek better social and economic security by accessing agricultural insurance, health insurance and employee provident funds, thereby improving their quality of employment and hence standard of life.

Given the education skills and type of job contract, one could expect that there would be an association between a household's economic status and the industrial sector and is analysed next.

8.4.6 Household economic status

Since wages are not reported for the self-employed, the returns to skills cannot be reported for all those who are employed. Hence, we connect them to their household's economic status. Economic status is measured on the basis of quintiles of asset index score estimated using principal component analysis based on possession of durable goods (excluding land) by the households. The individuals could belong to any one of the household asset quintiles, the topmost being the richest and the bottommost being the poorest in economic status. This measure of economic status is based on the stock of durable goods possessed by the households rather than on the basis of flow variable like income or total consumer expenditure.[7] Table 8.6 shows that those with better economic status are in the sub-group of financial services and public services. By linking education and quality of job contract, it could be expected that those in agriculture are among the poorest and poor segments of the population. Manufacturing, trade

Table 8.6 Sector-level distribution (%) of employed across economic status (%)

Sector	*Poorest*	*Poor*	*Middle*	*Rich*	*Richest*	*Total*
Agriculture	25.0 [54.7]	25.6 [49.3]	24.9 [45.5]	16.4 [32.2]	8.1 [17.8]	100 [40.1]
Manufacturing-1	11.4 [4.7]	19.0 [6.9]	24.0 [8.2]	26.0 [9.6]	19.6 [8.0]	100 [7.6]
Manufacturing-2	16.5 [5.1]	17.6 [4.7]	18.6 [4.7]	23.2 [6.4]	24.1 [7.3]	100 [5.6]
Electricity and Construction	26.2 [26.0]	27.9 [24.3]	22.6 [18.7]	16.2 [14.5]	7.2 [7.1]	100 [18.2]
Trade and Hotels	6.0 [2.9]	11.3 [4.7]	19.4 [7.7]	27.4 [11.8]	36.2 [17.2]	100 [8.8]
Transport and Communication	8.4 [2.7]	13.0 [3.7]	19.2 [5.2]	28.2 [8.2]	31.2 [10.1]	100 [6.0]
Financial Services	1.4 [0.1]	4.2 [0.4]	7.9 [0.6]	20.0 [1.7]	66.5 [6.2]	100 [1.7]
Public and Other Services	5.6 [3.6]	10.5 [6.1]	17.2 [9.4]	26.4 [15.5]	40.2 [26.2]	100 [12.0]
All Sectors	18.3 [100]	20.8 [100]	22.0 [100]	20.4 [100]	18.4 [100]	100

Source: Author's calculations.

Note: The economic status is classified in the basis of asset quintiles, with the poorest belonging to the lowest quintile and the richest belonging to the topmost asset quintile.

The bottom row shows that the distribution is not equal (20 per cent each) among the quintiles, as quintiles are based on household assets while the distribution is on the basis of only those in the labour market.

Values in brackets report the distribution within a wealth quintile.

and hotel and transport and communication are part of the middle and rich segments.

This classification overall fits our general understanding of those employed in different sectors and their living standards, except perhaps those in agriculture where by excluding landholding we may have overestimated their presence in the lower economic status.

8.4.7 Caste

Another important feature of the Indian sociodemographic structure is the caste system. Since the caste system was based on the occupations, there is a strong geographic and historic link to the type of occupation and employment pattern. The caste hierarchy also affects educational attainment and access to several public goods, which strongly impinges upon the intergenerational transmission of employment structure and well-being. Those lower in the social hierarchy are predominantly in agriculture and construction sectors and those in the middle like the OBCs and other castes have a substantial presence across all the sectors (Table 8.7). The upper-caste Hindus have a large presence in the financial services, well above their average share in the total employed, and also in public services and trade and hotel services. Due to the presence of the reservation policy, the SC and ST have a share in the public services similar to their average overall share among the employed. Thus, there is a clear segregation of castes across the sectors of the economy.

Table 8.7 Sector-level distribution of employed across caste groups

Industrial Sector	*Other Backward Castes (OBC)*	*Scheduled Castes (SC)*	*Scheduled Tribes (ST)*	*Upper-Caste Hindus (UCH)*	*Forward Caste and Others*	*Total*
Agriculture	43.0	24.3	12.3	2.6	17.7	100
Manufacturing-1	51.0	17.9	3.7	2.9	24.7	100
Manufacturing-2	43.1	25.2	7.4	3.8	20.5	100
Electricity and Constructions	38.6	30.7	14.0	2.4	14.3	100
Trade and Hotels	46.8	13.3	3.7	6.1	30.2	100
Transport and Communication	41.3	20.7	6.5	4.9	26.6	100
Financial Services	36.9	14.7	2.0	11.4	34.9	100
Public and Other Services	35.9	23.5	6.4	8.0	26.2	100
All Sectors	42.2	23.6	9.7	3.9	20.7	100

Source: Author's calculations.

8.5 Determinants of sector-level employment choice

In this section, we look at the factors that determine the probability of employment across different sectors of the economy. The descriptive statistics in Table 8.8 show that 40 per cent are in agriculture, 18 per cent are in construction and 12 per cent are in public and community services.

Table 8.8 Descriptive statistics of the variables in the regression model

Variable Name	*Mean*	*Standard Deviation*	*Variable Name*	*Mean*	*Standard Deviation*
Proportion Employed in:			Employment by residence (proportion employed)		
Agriculture and Allied	0.401	0.490	Metros	0.065	0.247
Manufacturing-1	0.075	0.264	Other Urban	0.223	0.416
Manufacturing-2	0.056	0.230	More developed village	0.306	0.461
Electricity & Construction	0.182	0.386	Less Developed Village (R)	0.407	0.491
Trade etc. & Hotels etc.	0.088	0.283	Northern (R)	0.088	0.283
Transport & Communications	0.060	0.237	Central	0.257	0.437
Financial Services	0.017	0.130	Western	0.219	0.413
Public and Other Services etc.	0.120	0.325	Southern	0.241	0.428
Age Years	38.44	12.50	Eastern	0.162	0.368
Women (Proportion of Employed)	0.326	0.469	North-Eastern	0.033	0.180
Education Level of Employed (Proportion of Employed)			Employed by Father's Education (Proportion of Employed)		
Not Literate	0.316	0.465			
Primary (R)	0.090	0.286	Not Literate (R)	0.654	0.476
Middle	0.248	0.432	Primary	0.114	0.317
Secondary	0.179	0.384	Middle	0.149	0.356
Higher Secondary	0.077	0.266	Secondary	0.052	0.222
Post Higher Secondary	0.090	0.286	Higher Secondary	0.015	0.124
English-None (R)	0.759	0.428	Post Higher Secondary	0.016	0.125
English-Little	0.189	0.392			
English-Fluent	0.052	0.223			

(*Continued*)

Table 8.8 (Continued)

Variable Name	*Mean*	*Standard Deviation*	*Variable Name*	*Mean*	*Standard Deviation*
Employment by Nature of Work Contract (Proportion of Employed)			Employed Religion (Proportion of Employed)		
Work Contract-Weak (R)	0.534	0.499	Hindus	0.837	0.369
Work Contract-Medium	0.206	0.405	Muslims	0.109	0.312
Work Contract-Strong	0.259	0.438	Christians	0.021	0.144
Employment by Social Groups (Proportion of Employed)			Other Religions (R)	0.033	0.212
Upper-Caste Hindus	0.039	0.193			
Other Backward Caste	0.420	0.494			
Scheduled Caste	0.235	0.424			
Scheduled Tribe (R)	0.097	0.296			
Other Hindu Castes	0.207	0.405			

Source: Author's estimates.

Note: The description of several variables like education groups and caste/religion are self-explanatory; for job contract types, refer to the text.

Sample size is 71645.

Except age, all other variables are categorical variables so that the numbers reported here are shares in that category.

(R) represents the category which is considered as the reference or omitted category for those categorical variables for the regression results reported in Table 8.9.

This composition excludes those not in the workforce and hence is slightly different from the distribution reported in Table 8.1. The mean age of those in the labour market is about 38 years and women constitute 33 per cent of the 15–65 years old among the employed. Illiterates constitute the largest share of 31.6 per cent, about one-fourth have a middle school education followed by secondary school education of about 17 per cent, and the share of tertiary education is close to 10 per cent. Comparing this with the educational attainment of the previous generation (father's) we see the share of illiterates has come down. Five per cent can speak English fluently, while 75 per cent cannot speak English and 20 per cent can speak little English. A little more than 50 per cent have weak employment contracts and those with strong contracts are higher than the medium contracts.

The results of analysis presented in Table 8.9 provide the relative risk ratio or odds ratio for the regressors compared to the reference sector of those employed in agriculture obtained from the multinomial logit regression as in equation 3. When a statistically significant coefficient is less than one, then

Table 8.9 Sectoral employment: multinomial logit model (RRR$)

Explanatory Variable	*Manufacturing-1*		*Manufacturing-2*		*Electricity & Construction*		*Trade etc. & Hotels etc.*	
	Coeff.	*Std. Err.*	*Coeff.*	*Std. Err.*	*Coeff.*	*Std. Err.*	*Coeff.*	*Std. Err.*
Age (Years)	0.99***	0.001	0.97***	0.001	0.99***	0.001	0.98***	0.001
Sex of the Individual (Male)								
Female	0.89**	0.05	0.16***	0.01	0.35***	0.01	0.09***	0.01
Education Level (Not Literate), English Knowledge (None), Type of Work Contract (Weak)								
Primary	1.54***	0.13	0.97	0.10	0.95	0.05	1.38***	0.14
Middle	2.06***	0.14	1.34***	0.10	1.21***	0.06	1.78***	0.13
Secondary	1.88***	0.14	1.32***	0.12	0.92	0.05	1.97***	0.16
Higher Secondary	1.74***	0.18	1.27**	0.14	0.79***	0.07	1.82***	0.19
Post Higher Secondary	2.23***	0.27	1.89***	0.24	1.10	0.13	2.37***	0.28
English-Little	1.25***	0.08	1.46***	0.11	1.37***	0.08	1.45***	0.10
English-Fluent	1.82***	0.28	2.62***	0.35	2.16***	0.28	2.06***	0.26
Contract Type-Medium	0.49***	0.03	0.35***	0.03	0.14***	0.01	0.77***	0.05
Contract Type-Strong	0.72	0.05	0.53***	0.03	0.10***	0.01	1.00	0.06
Caste (Scheduled Tribe), Religion (Others)								
Caste-UCH	2.01***	0.302	1.25	0.19	1.03	0.11	2.65***	0.37
Caste-OBC	2.33***	0.234	1.22*	0.13	0.92	0.05	2.09***	0.22
Caste-SC	1.70***	0.177	1.37***	0.15	1.03	0.06	1.31***	0.17
Caste-Others	1.90***	0.200	1.08	0.13	0.77***	0.05	2.01***	0.23
Religion-Hindus	0.97	0.12	1.14	0.16	1.08	0.11	0.73**	0.10
Religion-Muslim	2.81***	0.39	1.64***	0.25	1.29**	0.15	1.34**	0.19
Religion-Christian	0.64**	0.13	2.14***	0.42	1.90***	0.28	0.79	0.15

(*Continued*)

Table 8.9 (Continued)

Explanatory Variable	*Manufacturing-1*		*Manufacturing-2*		*Electricity & Construction*		*Trade etc. & Hotels etc.*	
	Coeff.	*Std. Err.*	*Coeff.*	*Std. Err.*	*Coeff.*	*Std. Err.*	*Coeff.*	*Std. Err.*
Father's Educational Qualification (Not Literate)								
Primary	1.11	0.08	1.14	0.11	1.01	0.05	1.07	0.08
Middle	1.38***	0.09	1.26***	0.09	1.19***	0.07	1.38***	0.09
Secondary	1.24*	0.14	1.38***	0.17	1.09	0.12	1.44***	0.15
Higher Secondary	1.30	0.23	1.34*	0.24	1.26	0.23	1.29	0.22
Post Higher Secondary	1.34	0.34	1.75***	0.36	1.32	0.31	1.88***	0.38
Location (Less Developed Village), Geographical Zones (North)								
Metros	71.88***	9.89	61.05***	8.63	15.71***	2.09	88.74***	12.10
Other Urban	16.84***	1.14	11.93***	0.82	4.35***	0.22	16.67***	1.08
More Developed Village	1.49***	0.10	0.93	0.07	0.98	0.04	1.38***	0.10
Zone-Central	1.03	0.09	1.31***	0.13	0.77***	0.04	0.82**	0.07
Zone-Western	0.47***	0.04	0.52***	0.05	0.43***	0.02	0.52***	0.04
Zone-Southern	0.67***	0.06	0.46***	0.05	0.39***	0.02	0.77***	0.06
Zone-Eastern	1.19*	0.11	0.51***	0.06	0.69***	0.04	0.75***	0.07
Zone-North-Eastern	1.97***	0.27	0.81	0.15	1.65***	0.15	3.09***	0.38
Intercept	0.11***	0.02	0.45***	0.08	2.26***	0.27	0.21***	0.03

Source: Author's estimates.

Note: $: RRR-relative risk ratio as in equation (3).

*, ** and *** are the statistically significant coefficients at 1 per cent, 5 per cent and 10 per cent levels of significance.

For the categorical variables, the group mentioned in the brackets is the omitted categories.

Table 8.9 Sectoral employment: multinomial logit model (RRR[$]) (Continued)

Explanatory Variable	*Transport & Communications*		*Financial Services*		*Public and Other Services etc.*	
	Coeff.	*Std. Err.*	*Coeff.*	*Std. Err.*	*Coeff.*	*Std. Err.*
Age (Years)	0.98***	0.002	0.99***	0.004	0.99***	0.002
Sex of the Individual (Male)						
Female	0.09***	0.01	0.44***	0.05	1.40***	0.06
Education Level (Not Literate), English Knowledge (None), Type of Work Contract (Weak)						
Primary	1.38***	0.14	2.58***	0.88	1.64***	0.13
Middle	1.78***	0.13	5.62***	1.52	2.08***	0.13
Secondary	1.97***	0.16	9.21***	2.44	2.72***	0.19
Higher Secondary	1.82***	0.19	14.78***	4.10	4.22***	0.37
Post Higher Secondary	2.37***	0.28	56.90***	16.09	9.47***	0.95
Little	1.45***	0.10	1.81***	0.21	1.52***	0.09
Fluent	2.06***	0.26	4.26***	0.67	2.99***	0.33
Contract Type-Medium	0.77***	0.05	1.02	0.13	0.61***	0.03
Contract Type-Strong	1.00	0.06	2.67***	0.35	2.78***	0.14
Caste (Scheduled Tribe), Religion (Others)						
Caste-UCH	1.50***	0.22	3.36***	0.88	1.48***	0.17
Caste-OBC	1.11	0.11	2.20***	0.55	1.09	0.08
Caste-SC	1.16	0.12	2.52***	0.62	1.68***	0.13
Caste-Others	1.07	0.11	2.21***	0.53	0.93	0.08
Religion-Hindus	0.73**	0.10	0.98	0.20	1.03	0.11
Religion-Muslim	1.34**	0.19	1.45	0.36	2.03***	0.24
Religion-Christian	0.79	0.15	1.05	0.29	1.27	0.19

(*Continued*)

Table 8.9 (Continued)

Explanatory Variable	*Transport & Communications*		*Financial Services*		*Public and Other Services etc.*	
	Coeff.	*Std. Err.*	*Coeff.*	*Std. Err.*	*Coeff.*	*Std. Err.*
Father's Educational Qualification (Not Literate)						
Primary	1.07	0.08	1.08	0.15	1.04	0.06
Middle	1.38***	0.09	1.47***	0.17	1.35***	0.07
Secondary	1.44***	0.15	1.84***	0.29	1.44***	0.13
Higher Secondary	1.29	0.22	1.21	0.27	1.49***	0.22
Post Higher Secondary	1.88***	0.38	1.30	0.29	1.47**	0.26
Location (Less Developed Village), Geographical Zones (North)						
Metros	88.74***	12.10	99.80***	22.99	59.50***	7.79
Other Urban	16.67***	1.08	20.07***	3.99	14.77***	0.80
More Developed Village	1.38***	0.10	1.35	0.29	1.31***	0.07
Zone-Central	0.82**	0.07	0.92	0.14	0.76***	0.05
Zone-Western	0.52***	0.04	0.39***	0.05	0.41***	0.03
Zone-Southern	0.77***	0.06	0.76**	0.10	0.43***	0.03
Zone-Eastern	0.75***	0.07	0.77	0.10	0.80***	0.06
Zone-North-Eastern	3.09***	0.38	1.38	0.29	1.98***	0.20
Intercept	0.21***	0.03	0.002***	0.00	0.08***	0.01

Source: Author's estimates.

Note: $: RRR-relative risk ratio as in equation (3).

*, ** and *** are the statistically significant coefficients at 1 per cent, 5 per cent and 10 per cent levels of significance.

For the categorical variables the group mentioned in the brackets is the omitted categories.

it means that the regressor is less in favour of that sector when compared to the agricultural (reference) sector. If the statistically significant coefficient has magnitude greater than one, then it implies that the odds are in favour of that regressor for a particular sector compared to the agricultural sector.

Compared to the agriculture sector, all other sectors have lower average age of the employed but the coefficient magnitude is close to one, indicating that the gap is not very large. The odds ratio for women is more than one for public and community services when compared to the agricultural sector, and the next largest employer for women seems to be the financial services sector. Compared to agriculture, the odds of finding a better-educated person is larger for all other sectors. Education is a strong predictor of employment choice in the financial services sector. The odds of being employed in the financial services sector compared to agriculture are almost 60 times keeping everything else the same for those with post higher secondary education. As can be expected, the construction and agriculture sectors are closer to each other in terms of education qualifications.

After controlling for education, the odds of fluent English knowledge are about two to one for all the sectors except in financial sector, where it is four times that for agriculture. Since in the agricultural sector, those who make their own decisions about cultivation and allied activities are considered as having a 'strong' contract, for all the other sectors excluding financial services the odds ratio is less than one compared to agriculture. Incidence of casual labour is high in the construction sector and hence has the least magnitude for medium and strong contracts compared to agriculture.

For caste, scheduled tribe is taken as the omitted category, and hence in many sectors all other castes have a higher likelihood of employment compared to agriculture. Construction as well as transport and communications are the two sectors to show no caste preferences in relation to the agricultural sector. Keeping other religions as the reference category, it is noted that Muslims and Christians are less likely to be in agriculture and have higher odds of participation in the manufacturing and public services compared to other sectors. Father's education is taken as a proxy for ability and has a positive role to play in the choice of employment in most sectors except in construction and financial services. As seen in Figure 8.2, the employment in the construction sector in rural areas is replacing agricultural employment. Given this, one could expect that father's education has a similar impact on the two sectors. However, for the financial sector the reasons may be completely different for lack of significance of the coefficients relating to father's education. This sector being a more recent one, after controlling for one's own education, father's education does not seem relevant in the sectoral employment choice.

By definition, the metros would offer a very high chance of non-agricultural employment, but in the construction sector we see that coefficients are of lower magnitude and corroborate the fact that they have a substantial presence in villages as well. Odds ratios for employment in both the modern and traditional services sectors are greater in urban areas than rural areas. Most regional zones show a lesser likelihood of non-agricultural employment compared to the Northern zone. But for financial services, once the metro and urban factors (dummy variables) are controlled for, the inter-zonal differences are not statistically significant, indicating that larger cities and towns across the different states are no different and provide similar employment in the financial services sector. For the remaining sectors, there are inter-zonal differences even after controlling for rural and urban residence.

Thus, overall, results of the sectoral choice model substantiate the findings that there is a gender, education, caste and regional segregation of employment in sectors which are known to be more remunerative and have better job contracts than the less remunerative ones. On the other hand, it is also important to note that the diversity within the services sectors also absorbs labour of varied skills.

8.6 Challenges and opportunities to improve diversity in service sector employment

Two aspects of employment that pose both opportunities and challenges are rural–urban differences and male–female gaps in sectoral choice of employment. For rural areas, the opportunities come from the fact that the growth in overall services sector employment was higher, albeit marginally, in rural areas at 2.6 per cent between 1993–94 and 2007–08 compared to that of 2.5 per cent for urban areas (Unni and Naik, 2011). Given the larger rural population, the marginal difference would still account for a large number of rural employed. However, the rural share in employment for communications within the modern services sector fell from 42 per cent to 34 per cent and from 30 per cent to 18 per cent in finance and insurance, while it increased in the traditional sectors from 39 per cent to 64 per cent (Unni and Naik, 2011). The causes that led to these changes in the rural sector need to be examined and appropriate policy intervention should be put in place. On the one hand, the limited and poor access to communications network and banking facilities shows a huge unmet demand for these two services in rural areas. Improving accessibility to these would increase the employment, and on the other hand innovative use of communication technology and extension services should also impact agricultural productivity. The fact that the more remunerative and productive sectors within the services have not sustained their momentum of the decade of the 1990s is clearly the challenge for rural areas. Incentives and state-level planning for inter-sectoral linkages should be promoted. It needs to be analysed whether the first phase of growth of services in the rural areas as reported in Unni and Naik (2011) happened in the more developed states and whether other states are yet to catch up.

Construction was the other sector that raised its employment share from 58 per cent to 65 per cent, but once again this is a less remunerative sector with weak employment contracts. However, migrants from the less developed states into the better off states may have benefitted in this process, and an analysis of this aspect is also needed. Inter-sectoral linkages through trade are another source of growth and employment potential for the rural areas. Trade either through e-commerce and or improved connectivity from better quality roads and transport facilities should enhance both agricultural and non-farm activities and hence employment.

Basic amenities like electricity, water, renewable energy, education and health services are yet to reach many households in rural areas. Here, the state has to take the responsibility for their provision so that social diversity in employment could be better ensured, as was observed form the results in this study for the public and community services sector. It is quite likely that the higher-end service activities and hence employment would still be expanding in the cities given the availability of better quality human and physical capital. So if the rural areas are not provided with access to better quality of basic amenities, then rural–urban inequality is bound to rise, posing a major challenge to equitable development.

The gender gap in employment has strong implications for overall GDP growth. It has been estimated that if women's participation rate increases to the current level of men, then it would add 16 per cent to India's GDP in the next ten years starting from 2015 (MGI, 2015). In another recent study, it was shown that though India has made progress in reducing the gender gap in education, constraints to participation in the labour market have not diminished, leading to a large potentially employable pool which is untapped and thereby affecting overall growth and equality (WEF, 2016). The study also reports that India has a long way to go in removing barriers to property ownership, most importantly land, access to financial services and legal systems so that more opportunities arise for women. On the one hand, fewer women are better educated and have a fluent knowledge of English, so that would work against their employability. On the other hand, a substantial proportion of well-educated women with fluent English knowledge are not economically active. The inability to employ the better skilled women or retain them to reach higher levels of decision making particularly in the private sector is clearly a loss in productivity arising from the loss of efficient employee due to difficult working conditions. As has been shown in this study, the community and public services sector is the only sector apart from agriculture that has 'preference' for employing women. Here too it was observed that this sector was not homogenous in its skills, as it also included employment in public work programmes including MGNREGA which has shown large participation by women.

The Wadhwani/Nathan Breakthrough Index shows that states which have no restrictions on women's working hours, have high conviction rates for workforce crimes, offers incentives for women entrepreneurs, and have higher female workforce participation rates (CSIS, 2016). Sikkim tops the list, while Delhi has very low FWPR and is at the bottom of the states partly due to weaker laws and legislations that would seem to hinder employment options for women. The findings by Bezbaruah (2012) for the Indian banking sector in the New Delhi region based largely on qualitative assessment shows that deeply entrenched cultural practices find their way into the organisational structures of the banking industry. This is irrespective of ownership (government, foreign or private) giving scope for ample discrimination in a covert and subtle manner. These factors, even at a highly skilled formal sector employment, would deter women to either not participate or withdraw or underperform. All of this would in turn have an impact on not being able to provide adequate quantity and quality of services that now seem to be very crucial in the face of increasing digitisation of financial transactions and financial inclusion, as is being taken up on priority by the union government. Clearly, a better ecosystem needs to be provided to include better skilled women in the workforce.

Mehrotra and Parida (2019) show that the growth of employment in recent years and more among youth has happened in the modern services sector compared to the traditional services sector. That there is more scope to do so in the health, education and financial intermediation sectors, which is largely part of formal sector and both government and private sector, could contribute to the same. Various recent studies including this one has been able to indicate the opportunities and challenges that remain in the service sector for employment generation, and the state needs to evolve a more integrated approach to create incentives for intra-sectoral linkage within the services sector as well as inter-sectoral linkages with industry and agriculture which could lead to inclusive growth.

Notes

1 The activity status on which a person spent relatively long time during the 365 days preceding the date of survey is referred to as the usual principal activity status. This activity status is broadly classified into three categories as, employed (in the workforce), unemployed and not in labour force.

2 A person in subsidiary status of employment could have pursued some economic activity for a shorter time throughout the reference year of 365 days preceding the date of survey or for a minor period, which is not less than 30 days, during the reference year. The principal activity status as per the major time criterion for this person could either be employed (in another 2-digit industrial classification) or unemployed or not in the labour force.

3 Usual status combines principal and subsidiary status information so that a person could be unemployed (available for or seeking work) as per major time or minor time criterion with a reference period of 365 days mentioned earlier. The current daily activity status assesses the major time (at least 4 hours in a day) accorded to an economic or non-economic activity in a given day for the week preceding the survey.

4 United Nations Central Product Classification (UNCPC) includes construction in services while National Industrial Classification (2008) does not. The UNCPC is internationally accepted.

5 Groups starting with 2 are referred as manufacturing-1 (includes mainly consumer products), and groups starting with 3 are referred as manufacturing-2 (includes intermediates and capital goods).

6 Multinomial logit model is the commonly used method to estimate when the dependent variable is discrete and with several mutually exclusive categories (Long, 1997). One of the earliest applications was for modeling occupational choice. The other methods of estimation could be multinomial probit model, conditional logit model or nested logit model.
7 The data set has information on household incomes and total consumer expenditure. The former could have measurement errors, and this data has missing observations as well. Total monthly consumer expenditure would be more smoothed across households and hence is not preferred in comparison to possession of durable goods.

References

Azam, M., A. Chin and N. Prakash (2013). 'The returns to English-language skills in India', *Economic Development and Cultural Change*, 61(2), 335–367.

Banga, R. and R. Bansal (2009). 'Impact of trade in services on gender employment in India', MPRA, UNCTAD-India Project, Munich Personal RePEc Archive Paper No. 35071. https://mpra.ub.uni-muenchen.de/35071/ (Accessed on 08/01/2017). MPRA Paper No. 35071, posted 28, November, 2011.

Basu, D. and D. Das (2016). 'Employment elasticity in India and the US, 1977–2011: A sectoral decomposition analysis', *Economic and Political Weekly*, 51(10), 51–59.

Bezbaruah, S. (2012). 'Gender inequalities in India's new service economy: A case study of the banking sector', Doctoral Thesis submitted to Queen Mary University London. https://qmro.qmul.ac.uk/xmlui/bitstream/handle/123456789/2479/BEZBARUAHGenderInequalities2012.pdf?sequence=1 (Accessed on 25/01/2017).

Chaudhary, R. and S. Verick (2014). 'Female labour force participation in India and beyond', www.ilo.org/wcmsp5/groups/public/@asia/@ro-bangkok/@sro-new_delhi/documents/publication/wcms_324621.pdf (Accessed on 07/10/2016).

CSIS (2016). 'Wadhwani/Nathan Breakthrough Index: Women in the workplace', *Nathan Associates and Center for Strategic and International Studies*, 1(2). www.csis.org/analysis/breakthrough-index-women-workplace (Accessed on 30/10/2016).

Desai, S. and R. Vanneman (2015, July 31). 'India Human Development Survey-II (IHDS-II), 2011–12. ICPSR36151-v2', Inter-university Consortium for Political and Social Research [distributor], Ann Arbor, MI. http://doi.org/10.3886/ICPSR36151.v2.

Eichengreen, B. and P. Gupta (2010). 'The service sector as India's road to economic growth?', Indian Council for Research on International Economic Relations (ICRIER) Working Paper Series No. 249, ICRIER, New Delhi. http://icrier.org/pdf/Working%20Paper%20249.pdf (Accessed on 22/12/2016).

GoI (2014). *Employment and Unemployment Situation in India: NSS 68th Round, July 2011–June 2012*, Ministry of Statistics and Programme Implementation, Government of India (GoI), New Delhi.

GoI (2015). 'Services sector', in *Economic Survey: 2014–15*, Ministry of Finance, Government of India, New Delhi.

GoI (2019). *Periodic Labour Force Survey: July 2017–June 2018*, Ministry of Statistics and Programme Implementation, Government of India (GoI), New Delhi.

ILO (2016). *India Labour Market Update*, International Labour Organisation (ILO) Country Office, New Delhi, India.

Joshi, S. (2004, September 11). 'Tertiary sector driven growth in India: Impact on employment and poverty', *Economic and Political Weekly*, 39(37), 4175–4178.

Kapur, S. and T. Chakraborty (2008). 'English language premium: Evidence from a policy experiment in India', Paper presented at the ISID Development Conference. www.isid.ac.in/~pu/conference/dec_08_conf/Papers/ShilpiKapur.pdf (Accessed on 20/12/2016).

Long, S.J. (1997). *Regression Models for Categorical and Limited Dependent Variables*, Sage Publications, New York.

Mazumdar, D. and S. Sarkar (2007, March 17). 'Growth of employment and earnings in tertiary sector, 1983–2000', *Economic and Political Weekly*, 42(11), 973–981.

Mehrotra, S. and J.K. Parida (2019). 'India's employment crisis: Rising education levels and falling non-agricultural job growth', CSE Working Paper, 2019-04, Center for Sustainable Employment, Azim Premji University, Bengaluru.

MGI (2015). *The Power of Parity: Advancing Women's Equality in India*, Mckinsey Global Institute (MGI). www.mckinsey.com/global-themes/employment-and-growth/how-advancing-womens-equality-can-add-12-trillion-to-global-growth (Accessed on 13/05/2016).

Mukherjee, A. (2013). 'The service sector in India', Working Paper No. 352, Asian Development Bank, Manila. www.adb.org/sites/default/files/publication/30285/ewp-352.pdf (Accessed on 20/12/2016).

National Industrial Classification-NIC (1987). 'Ministry of Statistics and Program Implementation'. http://mospi.nic.in/sites/default/files/main_menu/national_industrial_classification/twodigit_NIC1987.pdf (Accessed on 12/09/2016).

Nayyar, G. (2012). 'The quality of employment in India's services sector: Exploring the heterogeneity', *Applied Economics*, 44(36), 4701–4719.

Thomas, J.J. (2013, September 30). 'Economic growth that is not really jobless', *Livemint*, Monday. www.livemint.com/Opinion/boaY8zh2eH0Z3JOqe9qRfM/Economic-growth-that-is-not-really-jobless.html (Accessed on 15/08/2016).

Unni, J. and R. Naik (2011). 'Rural structural transformation: The case of the services sector in India', *Economic and Political Weekly*, 46(26–27), 196–200.

WEF (2016). *The Global Gender Gap Report: 2016*, World Economic Forum (WEF), Geneva. www3.weforum.org/docs/GGGR16/WEF_Global_Gender_Gap_Report_2016.pdf (Accessed on 31/10/2016).

Appendix 8.1

Two-digit classification under National Industrial Classification (NIC, 1987)

1 **Agriculture, hunting, forestry and fishing**

00 Agricultural production
01 Plantations
02 Raising of livestock
03 Agricultural services
04 Hunting, trapping and game propagation
05 Forestry and logging
06 Fishing (including collection of sea products)

2 **Manufacturing-1**

Mining and quarrying

10 Mining of coal and lignite, extraction of peat
11 Extraction of crude petroleum, production of natural gas
12 Mining of iron ore
13 Mining of metal ores other than iron ore
14 Mining of uranium and thorium ores
15 Mining of non-metallic minerals not elsewhere classified
19 Mining services not elsewhere classified

Part of manufacturing

20–21 Manufacture of food products
22 Manufacture of beverages, tobacco and related products
23 Manufacture of cotton textiles
24 Manufacture of wool, silk and man-made fibre textiles
25 Manufacture of jute and other vegetable fibre textiles (except cotton)
26 Manufacture of textile products (including wearing apparel)
27 Manufacture of wood and wood products, furniture and fixtures
28 Manufacture of paper and paper products and printing, publishing and allied industries
29 Manufacture of leather and products of leather, fur substitutes of leather
30 Manufacture of basic chemical and chemical products (except products of petroleum and coal)

3 Manufacturing-2

31 Manufacture of rubber, plastic, petroleum and coal products, processing of nuclear fuels
32 Manufacture of non-metallic mineral products
33 Basic metal and alloys industries
34 Manufacture of metal products and parts except machinery and equipment
35–36 Manufacture of machinery and equipment other than transport equipment (manufacture of scientific equipment, photographic/cinematographic equipment and watches and clocks is classified in Division 38)
37 Manufacture of transport equipment and parts
38 Other manufacturing industries
39 Repair of capital goods

4 Electricity, gas and water and construction

40 Electricity generation, transmission and distribution
41 Gas and steam generation and distribution through pipes
42 Water works and supply
43 Non-conventional energy generation and distribution
50 Construction
51 Activities allied to construction

5 Wholesale, retail trade and restaurants, hotels

60 Wholesale trade in agricultural raw materials, live animals food, beverages, intoxicants and textiles
61 Wholesale trade in wood, paper, skin, leather and fur, fuel, petroleum, chemicals, perfumery, ceramics, glass and ores and metals
62 Wholesale trade in all types of machinery equipment including transport equipment
63 Wholesale trade not elsewhere classified
64 Commission agents
65 Retail trade in food and food articles, beverages, tobacco and intoxicants (note: non-specialised retail trade establishments such as departmental stores super bazars and central stores are classified in group 688 along with non-store retail sale establishments engaged in house-to-house other ambulant sales)
66 Retail trade in textiles
67 Retail trade in fuels and other household utilities and durables
68 Retail trade n.e.c.
69 Restaurants and hotels

6 Transport, storage and communication

70 Land transport
71 Water transport

72 Air transport
73 Services incidental to transport n.e.c.
74 Storage and warehousing services
75 Communication services

7 Financing, insurance, real estate & business services

80 Banking activities including financial services
81 Provident and insurance services
82 Real estate activities
83 Legal services
84 Operation of lotteries
85 Renting and leasing (financial leasing is classified in financial activities) not elsewhere classified
89 Business services not elsewhere classified

8 Community, social and personal services and other services

90 Public administration and defence services
91 Sanitary services
92 Education, scientific and research services
93 Health and medical services
94 Community services
95 Recreational and cultural services
96 Personal services
97 Repair services
98 International and other extra territorial bodies
99 Services not elsewhere classified

Source: http://mospi.nic.in/sites/default/files/main_menu/national_industrial_classification/twodigit_NIC1987.pdf

Part III

Insights from sectoral experiences

Education, financial services and the IT industry

9 Production loan access and urban self-employed households

Shika Saravanabhavan and Meenakshi Rajeev

9.1 Introduction

The provision of financial services has long been recognised as a tool to effect development. These services include banking the unbanked by opening formal financial accounts, encouraging savings, and most importantly, the provision of credit to allow the poor to come out of the poverty trap. In India, in recent years the government has instituted a widespread financial inclusion drive focused on opening bank accounts for those previously excluded from the financial system. As a result, there has been a marked improvement in bank account ownership among Indians between 2011 and 2017 (Table 9.1).

However, account ownership is only the first step towards leveraging financial inclusion for development. When we look at the propensity to save, we do not see the same level of improvements in this 6-year period, where the percentage of Indians who reported saving at a formal financial institution rose only by 8 per cent. More worrisome is the fact that the global Findex survey reported a drop in the percentage of adults who borrowed from a financial institution over the same period. A lag in the use of formal institutions for saving or borrowing by the households, relative to having accounts in such institutions, is indicative of lack of access to such services.

Comparing India to other similar economies, we find that credit prevalence is lower than in most South Asian countries and other BRICS nations (Table 9.2). This indicates that there are credit access-related issues in India that need to be remedied.

The issue of credit access is particularly important in India given that self-employment contributes substantially to our economy, as it employs a vast majority of the population. Though this sector has large potential for income and wealth creation, most of the households get into self-employment more as a coping mechanism in the face of high unemployment and lack of opportunities in the formal sector than anything else (Banerjee and Duflo, 2011). In many cases, these enterprises are small in scale and scope, which makes it difficult for them to grow or even to sustain themselves over a long period. For instance, in our sample, we find that 26 per cent of the urban self-employed households in the non-farm sector has less than 3 lakhs as asset value. Several

Table 9.1 Financial inclusion in India

Year	*Account in a Financial Institution (% aged 15+)*	*Saved in a Financial Institution (% aged 15+)*	*Borrowed from a Financial Institution (% aged 15+)*
2011	35	12	8
2014	50	14	6
2017	80	20	7

Source: World Bank Global Findex Database (2018).

Table 9.2 Comparing credit access among developing countries in 2017

	Borrowed from a Financial Institution (% aged 15+) in 2017
India	7
Bangladesh	9
Sri Lanka	15
Pakistan	2
China	9
Russia	14
Brazil	9
South Africa	9

Source: World Bank Global Findex Database (2018).

studies have shown that one of the major constraints faced by these enterprises is lack of timely finance (Ayyagari, Demirgüç-Kunt and Maksimovic, 2008; Beck and Demirgüç-Kunt, 2006). Since these enterprises lack sufficient funds of their own, credit becomes essential to support even their working capital requirements; however, we observe that a large percentage of these enterprises are still unable to access formal credit.

An often-cited reason in such cases for the lack of access to formal credit is the absence of financial infrastructure (Demirgüç-Kunt, Beck and Honohan, 2008; Rajeev and Vani, 2017). However, the urban areas are much better endowed than the rural areas in terms of financial infrastructure. For instance, in March 2018, 34 per cent of the total bank branches were in the rural areas and the rest in urban, semi-urban and metropolitan regions (27 per cent in semi-urban, 19 per cent in urban areas and 20 per cent in metropolitan areas).[1] Better infrastructure should in principle ensure a higher level of credit inclusion, but our analysis shows that urban credit access for self-employed is still very low.

In the extant literature on credit access, the focus of most of the studies is rural agricultural credit access (Bell, 1991; Binswanger and Khandker, 1995; Gadgil, 1986; Kochar, 1997; Rajeev and Vani, 2012; Mohan, 2006), while studies on urban credit access are few and far between. In India, historically, a large majority of the households were engaged primarily in agriculture. Accordingly, the government also focused more on improving rural credit for farmers, and the policy recommendations, especially during the seventies and the eighties, were directed towards improving rural agricultural credit. During this period, compared to the substantial focus on rural credit, the non-agricultural self-employed households received only limited attention.[2] Things, however, are changing fast, as India is increasingly becoming urban and there is rising rural to urban migration because of the low income and agricultural problems in rural areas. Though the urban sector is growing fast in India, a large percentage of the urban population does not have the skills or education to get into jobs in the formal sector (Bhowmik, 2005). Hence, for many in the urban sector, self-employment has become an important means of employment. Furthermore, an important characteristic of urban self-employment is the dominance of service sector employment, especially in wholesale and retail trading. The National Sample Survey Organisation (NSSO) data shows that the self-employed account for around 34 per cent of the urban households,[3] and more than 70 per cent of these households are involved in the services sector (NSSO, 2013).

Given this background, this chapter is an attempt to understand access to credit to the urban self-employed. Initially, using descriptive analysis we examine the level of access to financial services (both formal and informal) and the terms and conditions of credit. We also examine whether credit access varies across regions and across different economic and social classes. Further, using econometric methods, we identify the factors that hinder or aid accessibility to financial services. Particularly, we seek to understand whether factors such as financial infrastructure play a major role in improving access to credit to the urban self-employed. The chapter uses 70th round NSSO All India debt and investment survey (AIDIS) data (with a reference period of January–December 2013), which is one of the few data sources that provides information on both formal and informal credit at the household level. Findings of such an analysis have valuable policy implications, as they would indicate the challenges faced by the formal financial institutions in providing access as well as indicate the specific groups of population lacking access to formal credit.

Though NSSO data provides important information on accessibility to credit at the household level, details of problems faced by the households in accessing financial services are not available from NSSO data. Therefore, to understand these issues in-depth we have conducted a field survey in the state of Karnataka. For this survey, we have selected a few major markets from Bangalore Urban district and Tumakuru district. Here, our focus is on the self-employed in the services sector, especially those engaged in retail trade, which is one of the major occupations for the households belonging to the services sector.

Following this introduction, the rest of the chapter is organised as follows. Section 9.2 provides a brief background for the study. Section 9.3 describes the theories underlying the analysis. Section 9.4 describes the data and methodology used. Section 9.5 examines the differential access to credit across the various states. Section 9.6 discusses the empirical analysis and section 9.7 presents the field survey and results. Section 9.8 concludes.

9.2 Self-employment and access to credit: a background

In most of developing countries including India, self-employment generally means 'survival self-employment' (Fields 2013). It is less of a choice and more of a compulsion. Also, most of the household enterprises in India are informal in nature. Informal units are characterised by low levels of investment, and the employment relations in these enterprises are mostly based on personal and social relationships or are casual in nature (European Commission et al., 2009). Although these enterprises have a level of 'autonomy' and 'economic independence'(NSSO, 2013), it is considered to be a 'survivalist response' that people are pushed into due to low education, skills and socioeconomic position (Temkin, 2009). Another type of informal self-employment is when people get into business in the informal sector on their own accord, to take advantage of the weaker regulations and legal constraints (De Soto, 1989). Though the latter type of informality might exist in India, it is the former type that forms a majority in India (Gurtoo and Williams, 2009).

Even though self-employment is a strategy for survival in most cases, it has large potential for improving income and employment generation (Banerjee and Duflo, 2011). Furthermore, these enterprises are also sometimes considered as a 'first unit of micro entrepreneurship' which could be developed into more efficient entities when the environment becomes conducive (Das, 2003). Another important aspect is the increasing number of women becoming self-employed (Daymard, 2015). Women are less educated and are limited in geographic mobility, and therefore self-employment is convenient for them. It is seen that access to formal finance actually increases the probability of women engaging in self-employment as compared to men (Menon and Rodgers, 2011). However, women-headed households are more likely to be credit-constrained than male-headed households (Ghosh and Vinod, 2017; Rajeev, Vani and Bhattacharjee, 2011; Williams and Gurtoo, 2011). If a woman has access to credit for entrepreneurial activity, she would have better control over household income and will improve her status at home, which in turn has a positive impact on the household welfare (Fletschner, 2009; Pitt and Khandkar, 1998; Swaminathan, Du Bois and Findeis, 2009). Many of these studies on women are for rural areas; urban microenterprises owned by women have not received much attention.

9.3 Theoretical perspectives underlying the analysis

Several scholars over time have highlighted the relevance of financial institutions in improving innovation and production processes in the economy (Evans and Jovanovic, 1989; King and Levine, 1993; Mckinnon, 1973; Schumpeter, 1934). Usually, starting a new enterprise requires funds and, in the absence of external resources, individuals or households have to depend on personal savings (Evans and Jovanovic, 1989). However, this is a major disadvantage for poor households who lack own resources for initial investment. Scaling up of existing enterprises also requires access to finance (Paulson and Townsend, 2004), and lack of insufficient finance leads to stagnation in growth. Though access to formal finance is crucial to small enterprises, we observe a general reluctance on the part of formal institutions to lend to small entrepreneurs or self-employed households (Beck and Demirguc-Kunt, 2006).

An important body of theoretical literature explains this based on the theory of asymmetric information. The well-known model by Stiglitz and Weiss (1981) talks about how information asymmetry between the lender and borrower results in credit rationing by financial intermediaries, which leads to less than optimal loan disbursement and inadequate investment. Also, in the absence of local knowledge about the borrowers, the banks generally insist on collateral or land-based security as a condition for lending, which the poor usually lack, and therefore it is the relatively richer households who get easy access to formal services. Furthermore, frequent visits to banks and cumbersome procedures impose large transaction costs on the borrowers (Rajeev and Vani, 2012).

9.4 Data and definitions

The 70th round NSSO-All India Debt and Investment Survey used in this study is the latest data we have at the household level on financial services. The survey was carried out during January through December 2013. This is the seventh survey conducted by NSSO on assets, investment and debt. The total sample of households was 62,135 in rural India and 48,665 in urban India for visit 1 and 61,650 in rural India and 46,771 in urban India for visit 2. Visit1 provides a comprehensive picture of a household's access to credit and socioeconomic characteristics of the household. Visit 2 covers only information regarding loans and transactions. The NSSO reports compute indicators such as incidence of indebtedness[4] and average amount of debt based on the data from visit 1, and we have also used the data from visit 1 itself as it gives comprehensive information on loans taken by the households. We restrict our analysis to urban self-employed households. If the household has at least one member who is self-employed, as an own account worker or an employer, we define it as a self-employed household.

For the primary survey, we have selected three prominent markets from Bengaluru Urban district – namely, 'City Market', 'K. R Puram Market' and 'Jayanagar Market', which are located in three non-contiguous localities in the city of Bengaluru. We have also selected two markets from the middle-income district of Tumakuru, namely, the 'Tumakuru' market and the 'Gubbi' market. The list of traders in each market was obtained from the local municipal office, and from these, 100 traders were randomly selected for a structured interview. Unavailable sample units were replaced by picking from the list once more. The sample units were selected from the respective lists at random without replacement. The first round of the survey was conducted in 2012, and subsequently recent visits were made in 2016 to assess any changes, although no significant changes were observed. A total of 500 traders have been surveyed as part of this study.[5]

9.4.1 Methodology for analysis

We first use descriptive analysis to explore patterns in data. In the later sections, we use a probit model with correction for sample selection bias to determine the factors that impact access to credit for the self-employed household enterprises. We have done our analysis at the household level, and Appendix 9.1 provides the descriptive statistics of the variables and their proportion in the sample.

We have further used ordered logistic regression model to analyse data from the primary survey. Here the dependent variable is ordinal in nature with categories being 'included', 'marginally excluded', 'severely excluded' and 'fully excluded' based on the score for each respondent.

9.4.2 Definitions and concepts used

NSSO defines a self-employed person as one who 'is engaged independently in a profession or trade on own account or with one or a few partners working in household enterprises'. It defines a household in an urban area to be self-employed if the major source of income during the 365 days preceding the date of survey was through self-employment of its members (NSSO, 2014). The self-employed persons are categorised as being own account workers, employers, and helpers in household enterprises. Own account workers operate the enterprises with or without partners and by not hiring outside labour. Employers, on the other hand, work as own account workers with or without partners and run the enterprise using hired labour, and finally the unpaid helpers assist the household enterprise without receiving any financial compensation (NSSO, 2014). If the household has at least one member who is self-employed as an own account worker or an employer we define it as a self-employed household.

Household enterprises can be broadly classified as being involved in manufacturing or the services sector. In this chapter we examine the non-agricultural household sector which includes the various enterprises which are run as individual enterprises, proprietorships and partnerships. We also give special emphasis to the household services sector which comprises a diverse group of activities such as retail and wholesale trade, hotels and restaurants, entertainment, transport, education, health, financial services and insurance. All the enterprises covered under NIC-2008, 2-digit codes 05 to 99 are considered as non-agricultural enterprises.

Finally, when we talk about access to credit services in India, it is important to discuss both formal/institutional and informal/non-institutional sources of credit. A household is said to have access to credit if it has outstanding credit on the date of survey (the date of disbursement of credit can be any date prior to the date of survey). In this chapter formal sources of credit include commercial banks and co-operative credit institutions, government loans, loans from Self Help Groups, NBFCs and other sources such as insurance and provident funds. Informal credit, on the other hand, are loans from sources such as professional private money lenders, relatives and friends.

9.5 Patterns of differential access to financial services for the self-employed household sector

Before we conduct our analysis using NSSO household-level data, we examine where India stands in terms of self-employment in comparison to a few other selected countries. Figure 9.1 provides the most recent estimates of

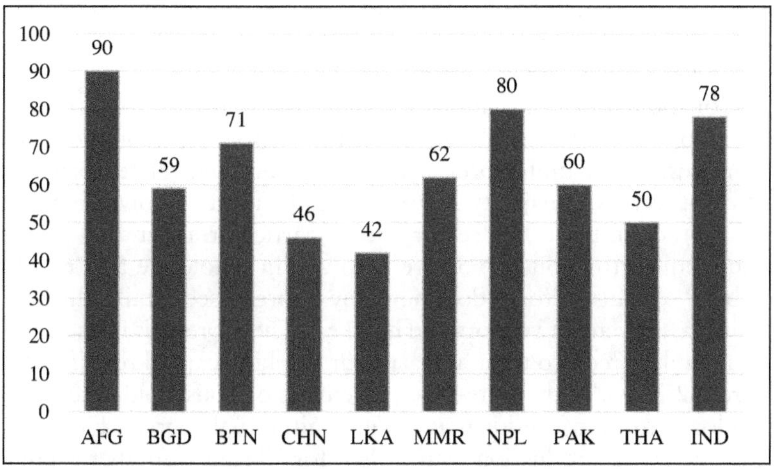

Figure 9.1 Self employed as a percentage of total employed across major developing countries of Asia: 2019

Source: Based on International Labour Organisation database. https://data.worldbank.org/indicator/SL.EMP.SELF.ZS

Note: AFG-Afghanistan, BGD-Bangladesh, BTN-Bhutan, CHN-China, IND-India, LKA-Sri Lanka, MMR-Myanmar, NPL-Nepal, PAK-Pakistan, THA-Thailand

Table 9.3 Major occupations of urban self-employed households in the non-farm-sector tertiary and secondary sectors

Occupation	*Percentage of households*
Wholesale and retail trade	40
Transport and storage	12
Accommodation and food	4
Financial and insurance activities	2
Real estate	2
Education related	2
Administration and support service activities	1
Professional, scientific and technical activities	3
Manufacture of food products	2
Textile, spinning and weaving	5
Manufacture of wearing apparel	8
Manufacture of furniture, other wood and straw material	2

Source: Authors' calculations using NSSO-AIDIS 70th Round data (2013).

Note: The categories are not mutually exclusive. The households may have their members working in different sectors.

self-employment in different countries of Asia. We observe that India is one of the top three countries with the highest rates of self-employment. Next, using the NSSO data, we look at the different sectors in which the self-employed households are involved.

Some of the major occupations in which the self-employed are involved include wholesale and retail trade, transport and storage, accommodation and food services, and manufacture of textiles, leather and related products. Of the different sectors, a majority of the self-employed are involved in wholesale and retail trade in the urban sector and in particular around 40 per cent of the non-farm-sector households are involved in wholesale and retail trade (see Table 9.3). This sector is dominated by unorganised retail, which include small kiranas, pavement vendors and hawkers. Therefore, this is a sector which requires regular credit to meet at least their working capital requirements.

Figure 9.2 provides the state-wise percentage of households accessing production loans from institutional and non-institutional sources. First and foremost, the access to production loans is low for all states. Southern states such as Andhra Pradesh (24 per cent), Kerala (21 per cent) and Tamil Nadu (18 per cent) have relatively higher access to production loans from the formal sector. Surprisingly, it is the southern states that have comparatively higher access to the informal sources of credit also. For instance, Andhra Pradesh (14 per cent), Tamil Nadu (10 per cent) and Telangana (11 per cent) show higher access to informal credit.

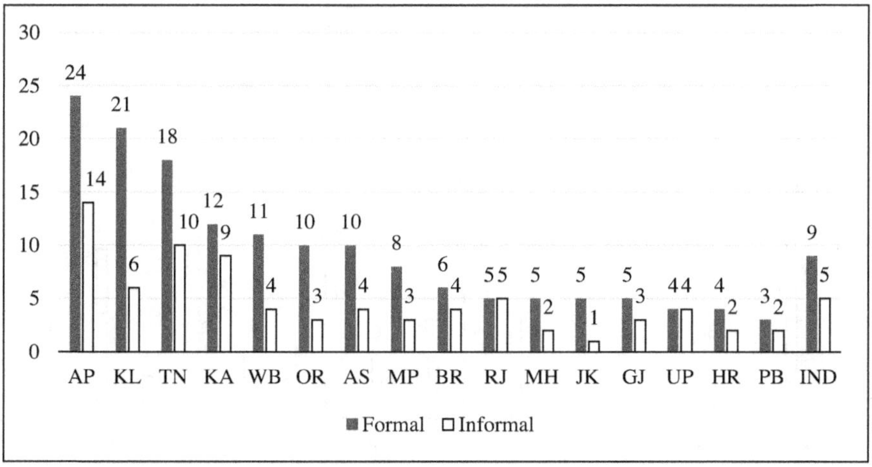

Figure 9.2 Percentage of Non-farm self-employed urban households with access to production loans (%)

Source: Authors' calculations using NSSO-AIDIS 70th Round data (2013).

Note: AP-Andhra Pradesh, KL-Kerala, TN-Tamil Nadu, KA-Karnataka, WB-West Bengal, OR-Orissa, AS-Assam, MP-Madhya Pradesh, BR-Bihar, RJ-Rajasthan, MH-Maharashtra, JK-Jammu and Kashmir, GJ-Gujarat, UP-Uttar Pradesh, HR-Haryana, PB-Punjab, IND-India.

Figure 9.3 presents access to production loans for services and manufacturing sectors in urban areas. We find that in both cases there are large variations across states. Here again the southern states fare better in access, both in the services sector as well as the manufacturing sector.

We now examine access to production loans by gender of the head of households. Our computations from NSSO data show that, out of the urban self-employed households, women-headed enterprises accessing formal credit are relatively lower, with only 3 per cent accessing credit from commercial banks and cooperatives as compared to 5 per cent of the male-headed enterprises. The majority of the women-headed enterprises that avail loans from formal sources are through self-help groups. Thus, availing individual-based loans from banks is an issue for women-headed enterprises. This could mainly be because of the lower educational level of women or lower level of exposure to finance-related matters. We also find that the women-owned enterprises have a lower percentage of households from the disadvantaged castes such as SC and ST who are taking loans from banks (Table 9.4).

Table 9.4 reveals the percentage of urban self-employed households accessing production loans, at different rates of interest, across different credit agencies. Focusing on the price of loan, we see that majority of the bank credit (commercial banks and cooperative banks) is taken at a rate of interest between 6 and 20 per cent (Table 9.5). Very high interest rates in formal sector

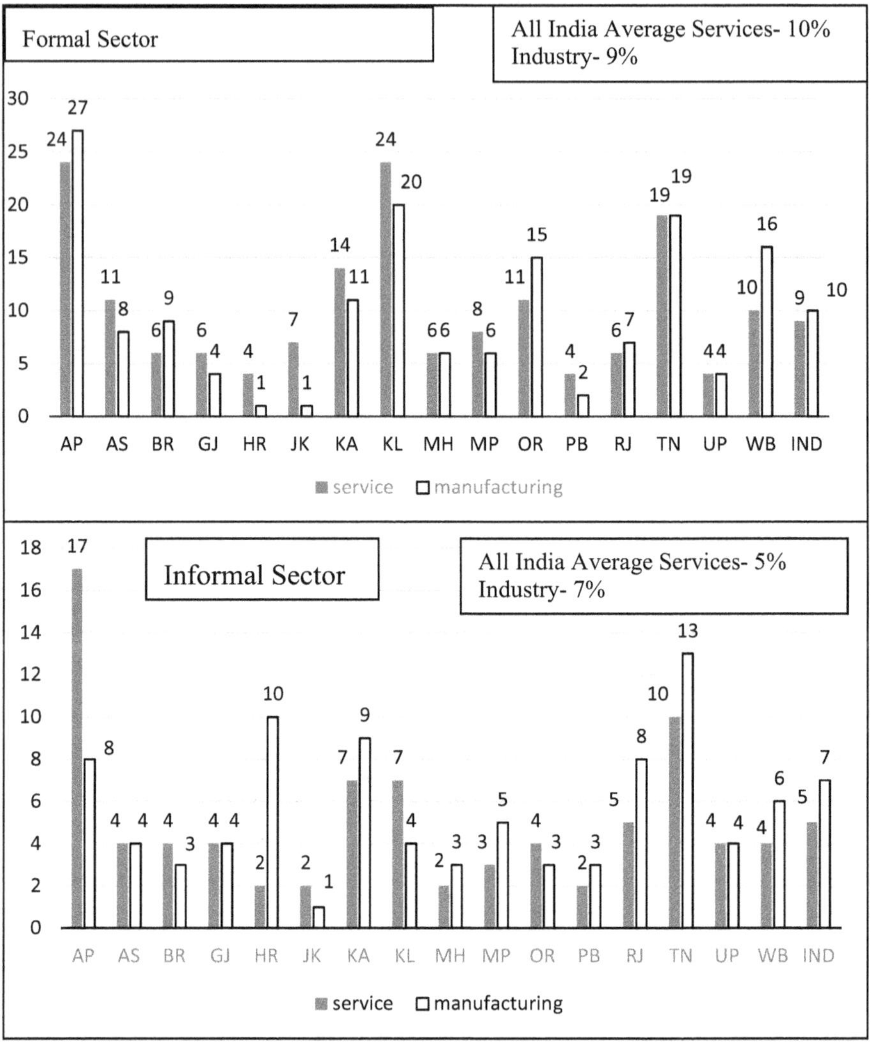

Figure 9.3 Percentage of non-farm self-employed urban households with access to production loans from formal and informal sources (%)

Source: Authors' calculations using NSSO-AIDIS 70th Round data (2013).

Note: Formal includes sources such as government, self-help groups, provident funds, insurance and other financial companies. Other informal includes relatives, friends, landowners and professionals.

AP-Andhra Pradesh, KL-Kerala, TN-Tamil Nadu, KA-Karnataka, WB-West Bengal, OR-Orissa, AS-Assam, MP-Madhya Pradesh, BR-Bihar, RJ-Rajasthan, MH-Maharashtra, JK-Jammu and Kashmir, GJ-Gujarat, UP-Uttar Pradesh, HR-Haryana, PB-Punjab, IND-India.

Table 9.4 Percentage of urban self-employed households accessing production loans by gender of head of the households

Caste groups	*Female-owned enterprises*				*Male-owned enterprises*			
	Bank	*Cooperatives*	*SHGBL/ SHG-NBFC*	*ML*	*Bank*	*Cooperatives*	*SHGBL/ SHG-NBFC*	*ML*
SC and ST	7	10	60	16	23	11	15	27
OBC	16	16	37	21	25	17	12	31
Others (general)	11	8	39	26	34	18	12	16
Total	13	12	40	22	28	17	12	25

Source: Authors' calculations using NSSO-AIDIS 70th Round data (2013).

Note: SHGBL-self-help groups bank linked, SHGNBFC-self-help groups non-banking finance corporation linked, ML-professional money lenders.

Table 9.5 Urban self-employed households accessing production loans by average annual rate of interest faced by households (%)

Source	*< 6%*	*6%–12%*	*12%–20%*	*20%–30%*	*≥30%*	*Total*
Banks	3	53	41	2	1	100
Cooperatives	2	43	53	2		100
SHGBL	5	59	14	17	5	100
SHGNBFC	1	21	26	47	5	100
Other formal sources	3	26	35	30	6	100
Money lenders	1	9	13	34	43	100
All*	2	33	33	20	12	100

Source: Authors' calculations using NSSO-AIDIS 70th Round data (2013).

Note: *Also includes sources of loans such as relatives and friends, landlord and all others.

SHGBL-self-help groups bank linked, SHGNBFC-self-help groups non-banking finance corporation linked, Money Lenders-professional money lenders.

loans may be outliers, arising due to loans remaining outstanding for a very long time and the resulting accumulated interest burden. We also observe that around 47 per cent of people who avail loans through self-help groups linked to NBFCs borrow at a high annual interest rate between 20 to 30 per cent.

In the case of production loans, informal loans are fewer and most of the households availing informal production credit from money lenders do so at annual interest rates of more than 30 per cent (see Table 9.5). The interest rates on loans from informal sources are much higher. However, people still access these loans possibly because of the difficulty in accessing banks (see Beck, 2013; Rajeev and Vani, 2017).

The earlier analysis reveals regional variations and lower access to credit by certain groups. To arrive at appropriate measures to enhance access to credit services to the self-employed households, who are supposedly in regular need of credit, it is necessary to identify the factors that influence access to credit. We use later a probit model corrected for sample selection to identify the determining factors of access to credit services by the self-employed households.

9.6 An econometric analysis

In this section, we present the econometric methods applied, variables and results of the analysis. The objective here is to study access to production loans to non-farm urban self-employed households. In doing so, we have to take care of two issues: how to model the household's decision to become self-employed and also their decision to take production loans.

Here we assume that these two processes are not independent of each other. The decision to become self-employed in the non-farm sector itself is a non-random decision, and also the household would need a production loan only if they decide to be self-employed. In such a scenario when we are modelling two dependent variables whose errors are likely to be correlated and when sample selection bias is suspected, a probit model with sample selection correction is generally used. According to Van de Ven and Van Praag (1981), there is an underlying relationship such that the outcome of interest y_i^p is observed only if

$$y_i^* = x_i\beta + u_{1i} \qquad (Latent\ Equation) \tag{1}$$

Or,

$$y_i^p = 1 \text{ if } y_i^* > 0 \text{ (Probit equation/Outcome Equation)} \tag{2}$$

The observations for the outcome variable, y_i^p, is not always observed; we observe y_i^p only if the selection variable is greater than zero.

$$y_i^s = Z_i\alpha + u_{2i} > 0 \qquad (Selection\ Equation) \tag{3}$$

Where i refers to household i, u_{1i}, $u_{2i} \sim N(0,1)$ *and* $Cov(u_{1i}, u_{2i}) = \rho$; when $\rho = 0$ a univariate probit model is sufficient.
Therefore, we have: $y_i^p = 1$ if a household decides to take a production loan, 0 otherwise;

$y_i^s = 1$ if a household decides to get into self-employment, 0 otherwise. Data for y_i^p is observed only if y_i^s is equal to one. So we have three types of observations in the sample:

y_i^p is equal to zero when y_i^s is equal to zero;
y_i^p is equal to 1 when y_i^s is equal to 1;
y_i^p is equal to zero when y_i^s is equal to 1.

The likelihood function is built upon these three observations and the model is estimated using maximum likelihood estimation technique (Greene, 2003). One important criterion for this model is that there should be at least one variable in the selection equation that is not included in the main outcome equation. In the absence of such a variable, the model is identified only by its functional form.

We estimate the following equations for this study:

9.6.1 Outcome equation

$$\begin{aligned} &\textit{Access to Production Loans} = \beta_0 + \beta_1 \textit{Bank branches} \\ &+\beta_2 \textit{ Service sector} + \sum \beta_{3j} \textit{ social group dummies} \\ &+\beta_4 \textit{ woman headed household} + \beta_5 \textit{ woman headed enterprise} \\ &+\beta_6 \textit{ Wealth} + \beta_7 \textit{Collateral} + \beta_8 \textit{Maximum educationin household} \\ &+\beta_9 \textit{Ratio f children to total household size} + \beta_{10} \textit{Age of household head} \\ &+\sum \beta_{11j} \textit{Regional dummies} \end{aligned} \tag{4}$$

9.6.2 Selection equation

$$\begin{aligned} &\textit{Self employed} = \gamma_0 + \sum \gamma_{1j} \textit{Bank branches} + \gamma_2 \textit{Service sector} + \\ &\sum \gamma_{3j} \textit{Social group dummies} + \gamma_4 \textit{woman headed household} \\ &+ \gamma_5 \textit{Wealth} + \gamma_6 \textit{collateral} + \gamma_7 \textit{Maximum education of household} \\ &+ \gamma_8 \textit{Ratio of children to total household size} + \gamma_9 \textit{Age of household} \\ &\textit{head} + \sum \gamma_{10j} \textit{Regional dummies} + \gamma_{11} \textit{Availability of unpaid helpers} \end{aligned} \tag{5}$$

(where subscript j refers to further components of the variable. These variables are further discussed below.)

9.6.3 Variables used

The dependent variable for the main 'outcome equation' is access to formal loans for non-farm production purposes, which is a binary variable. This variable takes the value of one for households which have production loans and zero otherwise. The dependent variable for the 'selection equation' is also binary, taking the value one if the household decides to be self-employed and is otherwise zero. In this type of regression, an exclusive variable is required which is included only in the selection equation and not in the outcome equation. In our analysis, this variable is the number of unpaid helpers.[6] Literature shows that unpaid workers play an important role in self-employed households and are also a common characteristic of small enterprises in developing countries (Margolis, 2014; Tambunan, 2009). The other explanatory variables used in this exercise are as follows.

First, we are interested in understanding the impact of financial infrastructure on access to credit. We have used the demographic reach of the bank branches as one of the explanatory variables. This variable is created by dividing the total number of urban bank branches in a state by the total adult urban population. We expect a positive relation between this variable and access to credit. Next, we have included a dummy variable which represents whether or not the household belongs to the service sector. It takes the value of one if it belongs to the service sector and zero otherwise. The service sector is the most dominant category and comprises a diverse group of activities such as retail and wholesale trade, hotels and restaurants, entertainment, transport, education, health, financial services and insurance. Another important explanatory variable that we used in the analysis is the urban land area owned by the household. Small enterprises generally do not have enough assets that they could use as security, and they often lack proper financial statements and performance reports through which the banks can assess whether they are credit worthy borrowers or not (Nikaido, Pais and Sarma, 2015). It is in this backdrop that we used the variable urban land area owned by the household, and we expect this variable to have a positive association with access to formal credit. Further, we have used the logarithm of total value of assets as a measure for the wealth of the household.

We have also identified various other household characteristics that are likely to be associated with the households' ability to access credit. First, maximum level of education attained by any of the members in the household can also determine whether the household is able to access formal loans or not. A certain level of education is required to be able to access formal loans (as these loans involve paper work). Education improves financial literacy, and therefore potential borrowers are aware of financial choices and are able to make more informed decisions. Studies show that lack of financial education can perpetuate financial exclusion in the case of low-income entrepreneurs (Birochi and Pozzebon, 2016). Other variables such as caste of the household and gender of the owner/employer have also been included. The caste variable comprises three categories: namely scheduled castes and tribes, other backward castes, and the general castes. The gender of the enterprise owner is represented by a dummy variable which is equal to one if the owner is female and zero otherwise. Other variables such as ratio of children, household size and regional dummies have also been included in the analysis.

9.6.4 *Findings*

We have used a probit model with correction for sample selection. Accordingly, we estimate the model in two stages. The first stage is based on choice of occupation (self-employment or other), and the second stage is based on access to loans. Thus, we have two dependent variables in our model: access to loans and choice of self-employment as an occupation. Appendix 9.2 reports the results of the probit regression. The Wald test for independent equations is significant, implying the existence of sample selection bias, and it supports the use of a probit model with sample selection as opposed to a univariate probit.

Outcome equation: access to credit services

Here the dependent variable is whether the household accesses production loans or not (conditional on whether the household is self-employed). The results (Appendix 9.2) show a non-linear relationship between the number of bank branches and the outcome variable. The coefficient of outreach of bank branches is negative and the coefficient of its squared term is positive, indicating the non-linear relationship. This implies that in regions where the number of bank branches is low, we see that it has a negative impact on access to production loans; however, in regions where the number is higher the access improves. Thus, this result indicates that one needs a threshold level of bank branches to observe improvement in access to credit. In regions where bank branches are low in number, it could be that the banks cater to the large borrowers and the smaller borrowers get crowded out. When there are large numbers of banks in an area, the large borrowers get spread out among the many branches and the banks may find it profitable to provide services to smaller borrowers too. Therefore, there is a need for supply-side efforts to increase the number of bank branches to cater to the rising urban population, especially in regions where the numbers are low.

We find that the coefficient of the dummy variable which proxies the households belonging to the services sector is positive and significant. This implies that the households which are self-employed in the service sector have a higher likelihood of access to formal credit as compared to manufacturing. The total urban land area owned by a household is relevant in predicting access to formal credit, and it has a positive and significant association with the likelihood of access to formal credit. This brings to the fore the importance of immovable property as security in obtaining formal credit. This also reaffirms the lure of informal credit institutions to the poor, as such institutions may not mandate physical security to provide loans, and instead it makes use of the local knowledge and influence in place of the security. However, as we have seen earlier in our descriptive analysis, the costs of these loans are much higher.

Households that have primary education do not show any significant difference in accessibility to credit vis-à-vis illiterate households. But households with secondary or higher education show a positive impact. While women-owned enterprises and socially deprived castes do not show a significant effect on access to credit, we observe that these categories have a significant negative impact on becoming self-employed.

Selection equation: decision to be self-employed

We now present the results of the selection equation which is a required step for obtaining unbiased results for the loan equation. Here the dependent variable is whether the household became self-employed or not. Though the focus of the present chapter is to understand the determinants of access to urban production loans, these results are also of interest to us (column 2 in Appendix 9.2). Here too, we see a non-linear relationship with the number of bank branches. In regions where there are higher number of branches (after a threshold point), the negative effect reduces and the possibility of becoming self-employed increases. The larger the number of banks, the more intense the competition among them, leading to more favourable environment to obtain start-up funds and establishment of enterprises.

The households belonging to other backward castes or the general caste have a higher probability of becoming self-employed as compared to the scheduled tribes. As the wealth of the household increases, the likelihood of becoming self-employed also increases. This could suggest the importance of an initial endowment in starting an enterprise, as discussed by Banerjee and Newman (1993). Also, here we find that households with higher educational levels, such as primary and secondary, are more likely to become self-employed as compared to households with below a primary level of education.

The earlier analysis provides a broad picture of accessibility to credit services by self-employed households, and we observe that access to credit is low for the self-employed. Also, we have identified the various factors that impact access to credit for these households. Further, to understand the ground realities with regard to access, we have conducted a field survey in major markets of two districts of Karnataka. As mentioned earlier, around 74 per cent of the urban self-employed are in the services sector according to NSSO data, and hence it is of interest to us to take this sector for our field study. The largest component of the services sector is trading and therefore we consider traders in these markets as our respondents.

9.7 Experiences from the field

The 70th Round NSSO-All India Debt and Investment Survey, conducted between July 2012 and June 2013, shows that Karnataka's position is low in terms of proportion of self-employed urban households accessing credit, and it has a relatively higher reliance on informal loans as well (Figure 9.1). This happens despite having good urban financial infrastructure. However, Karnataka is also a state with relatively larger share of urban poor. To understand the underlying reasons, we have selected two markets from the Bengaluru Urban district as well as from Tumakuru district for a primary field survey.

9.7.1 *Urban financial exclusion: lessons from Bengaluru and Tumakuru*[7]

This section focuses on the urban self-employed in the services sector, especially those who are engaged in retail trade. Bengaluru Urban district has a vibrant and dynamic information and technology sector, which has arguably brought several improvements to the city that should also have a positive impact on the level of financial inclusion among its population, including our respondent population. Tumakuru, on the other hand, is a smaller town and provides us perspectives of a relatively less urbanised region.

Most of the respondents of our sample are male (90 per cent of them are male and 10 per cent female). About 70 per cent of the respondents established their business in the decade of 2000, and their initial levels of investment varied from below Rs 1,000 to Rs 50,000. About 33 per cent of the respondents have invested between Rs 1,000 to Rs 5,000 and another 25 per cent between Rs 5,000 to Rs 10,000. About 70 per cent of the respondents lived in rented houses. There is a fair prevalence of illiteracy among them (35 per cent of the respondents are illiterate). Only 40 per cent attended school up to the primary level. This low level of education of the self-employed is a matter of concern as it may hamper their ability to attain familiarity with financial services.

The present survey provides data on several indicators that are otherwise not available from secondary sources. It has helped in arriving at a more comprehensive measure of financial inclusion (or exclusion) among this trader community. We do not just rely on a binary classification that indicates whether someone is accessing a service or not; rather, a graded measure is utilised here which has helped us to show the extent of accessibility to financial services among different groups. To this end, we have constructed and utilised an ordinal measure of financial inclusion that captures some of the different possible levels of inclusion that we are likely to encounter. This measure aggregates a score which is a function of the access to different services that an individual trader is reported to have availed. The absolute number of the score in this regard is of little importance except to order the level of access to financial services.

The scoring pattern adopted is as follows. If a respondent has a current account in a bank or has taken a loan for the purpose of business/trade from the formal sector s/he gets a score of 10. If the loan is obtained for the purpose of consumption from a formal agency (such as vehicle, housing, education), 8 points are assigned. Possessing a savings account that is operated regularly (at least once in 3 months) gives a score of 6. In the case that at least one family member has a bank account, the score assigned is 4. Occasional usage of banking services (once a year to less than once in 3 months) for term deposits, remittances, and so on gives a score of 2. Traders who have not accessed any of these services were assigned a score of 0. Following the assignment of scores, we further classified respondents into different grades of financial inclusion/exclusion, with higher scores indicating better inclusion. The threshold scores for the different grades were as follows. Traders were considered to be financially 'included' if they obtained an aggregate score of 10 points or greater. Traders scoring between 6 and 10 points were considered to be 'marginally excluded'. A score between 2 and 6 warranted their classification as 'severely excluded'. Those with a score of 0 were considered to be 'fully excluded'.

Following this methodology, we obtained a distribution of exclusion levels among surveyed traders in Bengaluru (also in Tumakuru), the details of which are presented in Appendix 9.3. It is striking that a large minority (44 per cent) of those surveyed are completely excluded, and this level of exclusion is comparable to the rural scenario before the financial inclusion drive in Karnataka. Our survey reveals that, in case of Bengaluru (Appendix 9.3), only 8.3 per cent are completely included, 13.5 per cent are marginally excluded, 33.8 per cent are severely excluded and as high as 44 per cent are fully excluded (see also Rajeev and Vani, 2017). Overall, this data reveals that the trader community leans more towards the side of financial exclusion than towards that of inclusion. This is a serious problem, as these traders have a reasonably good amount of income (on an average around Rs 20,000 per month) and have regular need of credit for their working capital needs, but surprisingly they never approached the formal banking system. On the other hand, they took credit from the informal sector (such as their wholesalers) and used informal savings facility such as chit funds. Another noteworthy feature is that unlike the case of their rural counterparts, physical accessibility to formal banks is not an issue for these respondents, as there are several bank branches in the areas of survey.

Selected markets in Tumakuru also show a similar picture. We see that a marginally higher percentage are fully included (12 per cent) than in Bengaluru, and fewer are fully excluded (36.3 per cent) compared to Bengaluru traders (see Appendix 9.3). This trend is mainly due to a proactive bank official who took interest in providing credit to the trader community: a pattern which is not so common in large metropolitan regions.

Testing the association of the levels of inclusion with different characteristics of traders in Bengaluru provides some interesting results. Firstly, there is a significant increase in the level of financial inclusion with increase in the education level of respondents. The type of business, too, shows a significant correlation with inclusion insofar as those who dealt in consumer durables and electronics are more included than others. A positive relationship exists with the level of initial investment, mirroring the previous result, since these businesses require higher initial investments than the others. Similarly, those who reported having relatively better economic status are more financially included than others. Lastly, we found that the flower traders were all women and they are the most financially excluded group in the sample. From this, we may infer the existence of some gender bias in the level of financial inclusion towards males (Rajeev and Vani, 2017 provide further details).

Similar to the pattern seen in Bengaluru, we find that education, type of business, and economic status is significantly and positively correlated with the level of financial inclusion among those surveyed in Tumakuru. In addition, it is also observed that the location of business had an important effect, whereby those operating from regular shops were more financially included than the rest (those doing business from pavements or unsheltered structures), which is not seen in Bengaluru, where traders having regular shops are as excluded as the pavement traders. However, bribes are not as prominent an aspect of achieving shop location in Tumakuru as they are in Bengaluru.

A multivariate analysis, following this bivariate analysis, provides some interesting observations. For the multivariate analysis, we have selected an ordered logistic regression and utilised the ordinal levels of the measure of financial inclusion detailed earlier, among traders in Bengaluru, as the dependent variable. The results of this regression are provided in Appendix 9.4 (see also Rajeev and Vani, 2017). Consistent with our earlier findings, income and education are significant factors in improving financial inclusion among traders. Furthermore, an insignificant difference between those with primary education and illiterates points towards the existence of a threshold level of education for accessing financial services, that is, traders must have studied at least until the secondary level to fully avail the benefits of financial services. While age of the self-employed or shop location (pavement, unstructured shelter or regular shop) did not influence the dependent variable significantly, the type of business did. We find that consumer durables and electronics traders who have a higher level of investment are more likely to display a higher level of financial inclusion than the other categories.

Performing a similar regression analysis of the survey responses in Tumakuru, we once again find that education plays a significant role in determining the level of financial inclusion. This, however, becomes apparent only among those who are graduates, unlike in Bengaluru, which had a lower threshold. While those retailing consumer durables and electronics are more included than the rest, as seen before, we also observed that age and shop location (regular shop, pavement or unstructured shelter) played a significant role, unlike in the prior regression. This is possibly due to certain bank officials concentrating efforts on those who are relatively younger (younger than 40 years) and who operated from regular shops in Tumakuru.

9.7.2 *Problems faced by traders*

Recognising the widespread problem of lack of utilisation or access to financial services among traders, we queried further some of the constraints they may have faced in this regard. A negative perception was common among respondents about the complexity of banking procedures and the need for collateral or security. Furthermore, this shared antipathy appeared to stem more from a herd mentality within the community rather than from individual experiences with banks. Financing for enterprises are primarily derived from own savings and, in a few cases, from informal sector loans. Approximately 88 per cent of the respondents reported having a negative attitude towards banks, and 52 per cent reported perceiving banking procedures as complicated. Thus, we observe that even though geographical distance to the bank is not much, there is substantial psychological distance.

A widespread apathy towards banks among traders prompted us to delve deeper into the issue, and we attempted to understand the problem from the perspective of bank officials in this regard.

9.7.3 *Crowding-out effect*

Banks in urban areas are usually geared towards servicing the needs of middle-income and high-income customers with a good educational background and high financial literacy. Owing to this, they are unable to effectively meet the financial needs of small traders, who are, thus, 'crowded-out' of the system.

9.7.4 *Transaction costs*

Self-employed traders are often own account workers and thereby need to attend to their businesses throughout the day, leaving little time for visits to banks. Added to this, banks work on a rigid schedule and are open for only a relatively short time during the day, during which traders are unable to make trips on account of high opportunity cost from lost business. On the other hand, informal lenders are often willing to visit them at their workplace and thereby make suitable arrangements to provide financial services.

In fact, as mentioned earlier, in Tumakuru district, it was found that some traders were able to access credit owing to innovative arrangements by one bank. The branch manager of a bank in Tumakuru assigned one of the staff members to act as a field officer, who forwarded loans and thereby collected Rs 1000 a week as a part of repayment from flower vendors who availed this facility. It was found that more than 70 per cent of the borrowers fully repaid the loan.

Indeed, our discussions with some of the traders revealed that the doorstep collection practiced by money lenders was far more beneficial to their repayment performance. Banks are unlikely to pursue repayment, and this left little motivation among borrowers to make timely repayments, and mounting dues would put borrowers into a default status with large dues. The respondents, therefore, consider doorstep collection of the dues a useful practice followed by the informal lenders.

Added to these two issues, procedural features also act as a deterrent to availing financial services. Documentation requirements and procedures, such as 'know your customer' norms, tend to alienate small traders from the financial system due to lack of adequate education and knowledge. Therefore, the introduction of innovative and user-friendly banking practices for this section of society appears to be very beneficial in improving their access to formal credit and banking services.

To understand the more recent scenario, especially after the introduction of 'Jan Dhan Yojana', we visited the same survey areas again. These subsequent visits to the field showed us that the Jan Dhan Yojana has resulted in a few of the larger traders opening accounts and availing small loans, which is a positive outcome of the drive. However, there are several small traders who have not benefitted. Thus, there is scope for improving financial access of relatively poorer sections of the urban self-employed.

Improving the business correspondents (BC) banking model with local kiosks may be useful in this respect. While the RBI introduced new guidelines for this type of banking in 2006, to improve banks' ability to provide financial services, financial viability of such a model has limited their growth. However, when there are large number of traders in one location, a BC may get good business and financial viability may not be an issue. Similarly, when main bank branches are also in the vicinity, monitoring BCs will not be a major issue. Mobile technology can further help in this regard to reach out to customers.

9.8 Concluding observations

Among the various financial products, access to credit is critical in an economy where self-employment is the norm. Unlike most other studies, which look at access to credit for the rural population, we have focussed here on the self-employed population in the urban sector. The self-employed urban poor often face a different business environment as compared to the self-employed poor in rural areas, and therefore banking norms developed for the benefit of the latter are not always helpful to the former. For instance, the self-employed in rural areas are primarily farmers and they benefit by priority sector lending norms for agriculture. There is no such dedicated initiative for urban poor who are self-employed in small businesses, especially in the services sector. Given the importance of the issue and existing research gaps, initially, through the analysis of NSSO data, we look at the regional imbalances in access to production loans across India. We find that access to production loans by the urban self-employed is quite low in India. However, comparatively the southern states are slightly better off for both the service sector as well as the manufacturing sector households.

From our regression analysis using NSSO data, we affirm the importance of financial infrastructure in improving access to credit. We find a non-linear relationship between financial infrastructure and access to production credit. When the number of bank branches is low, we see that it has a negative impact on access to production loans; however, in regions where the number is higher, access to production loans for urban self-employed households improves. In the states belonging to the lower range of demographic coverage of bank branches, households have a lower likelihood of accessing production loans. The government focus has largely been on improving infrastructure in the rural areas (as emphasised earlier in the chapter); however, our findings highlight the rather low accessibility of financial services for the urban self-employed, and, therefore, urban infrastructure improvement and access should be given importance in the current context of increasing urbanisation.

The analysis also shows that self-employed households in the services sector have a higher possibility of accessing formal loans than in the manufacturing sector. However, from our descriptive analysis we find that the percentage of overall access for both services and manufacturing sectors is very low. Most of these enterprises are forced to depend on their own resources for investment, which is negligible in the case of poor households. Many of these households turn to informal sources of finance, and we see a higher use of informal finance by the self-employed in manufacturing.

Over the years, several government initiatives have been brought out to improve access to loans for the small and microenterprises such as the Credit Guarantee Fund Trust for Micro and Small Enterprises (CGTMSE) started in 2000, the establishment of the Small Industries Development Bank of India (SIDBI) in 1999 and most recently the Micro Unit Development and Refinance Agency (MUDRA) launched in 2014 with the intention of encouraging the development of the micro enterprise sector in the country. However, in view of the potential for the funds to be appropriated by the well-off, implementation of these programmes needs to be well supervised.

The analysis also brings to the fore the impact of collateral requirements in obtaining formal loans. We find that 26 per cent of the urban self-employed households in the non-farm sector have less than 3 lakhs as asset value and are therefore poor, and formal banks could tap this clientele by providing easier and less costly access to timely finance. In view of this, credit bureaus can play a useful role in providing information about the creditworthiness of the individual, thus reducing the information asymmetry that exists between the banks and the customers. A good credit history can reduce the need for collateral and can decrease the cost of obtaining a loan. Thus, developing a reliable credit information system is in the interests of the financial institutions, as it reduces the risk involved as well as enables customers to obtain reasonably priced loans. A good public credit registry system under the Reserve Bank of India needs to be created to remove the information asymmetry. There is a Central Repository of Information on Large Credits (CRILC) that has been set up by the RBI in 2014; however, this is for large credit amounts. A more comprehensive system that stores and disseminates information on the borrowers of smaller loan amounts, especially in the case of small and medium enterprises, could help in developing a credit history for the borrowers that can be used in future to assess their creditworthiness. Furthermore, it could help the banks in making more informed decisions about lending and thereby reduce the accumulation of non-performing assets.

Yet another aspect that needs discussion in the light of our analysis is the role of education. The importance of education comes out strongly in the field survey analysis. The analysis shows the existence of a threshold level of education for accessing financial services, which means that traders should have at least secondary education for proper access to financial services. This result is similar in both the primary and secondary data analysis. From our primary data analysis, the wedge between the urban (self-employed) poor and banks is clear even in their level of basic financial inclusion. Even in Bengaluru, which is a developed region, 45 per cent of traders reported that they have never approached a bank despite operating in close proximity. From the primary data analysis, we see that economic status and education positively impact respondents' levels of financial inclusion, indicating that there is little inclusion among the poorer sections of society who are economically and socially deprived. Our field study also reveals that the financial inclusion drive under the Jan Dhan Yojana succeeded in bringing some of the relatively larger traders into the formal financial and credit coverage, but the smaller traders are crowded out.

Discussions held with bank officials highlighted three important issues, viz., a crowding out of traders in favour of more educated and higher-net-worth borrowers, high opportunity costs for the self-employed as a result of frequent visits to bank to manage accounts and loan repayment, and difficulties in documentation and procedural norms which created significant barriers in availing credit. Localised kiosk-based services brought through business correspondents (BCs) can be one solution, especially for the trader class. Since they operate in the marketplace, there can be enough business for the banks. Besides, in the urban regions, monitoring BCs may not be an issue. Joint liability group formation can also be another option. Furthermore, improvements in banking facilities such as streamlined documentation procedures and reduced wait times are important as well.

Notes

1 RBI bank branch statistics. RBI has classified the centres according to the size of the population: rural with fewer than 10,000, semi-urban with above 10,000 and fewer than 1 lakh, urban with above 1 lakh and fewer than 10 lakh and metropolitan with 10 lakh and above.
2 UNDP (2009): India Urban Poverty Report 2009.
3 This also includes a small percentage of households who are involved in self-employment, but their main sources of income is some other means.
4 The NSSO considers a household to be indebted if it has any cash loan outstanding as on June 30, 2012 (date of reference). Percentage of indebted households in total household gives us incidence of indebtedness. As richer states and richer households are more indebted, we consider incidence of indebtedness as a pointer towards accessibility to credit rather than a debt-ridden situation, even though this latter possibility cannot be ruled out.
5 We thank B.P. Vani and Jaisimha K. Rao for their help in this work.
6 Here we are discussing access to production loans from banks. The banks are not concerned about the number of unpaid helpers in the enterprise and, therefore, it will not impact the decision on whether the banks lend money to the specific

microenterprise or not. However, having unpaid workers can increase chances of households becoming self-employed as they provide free labour and help which are crucial for micro enterprises which lack capital or funds to hire external help. Literature shows that unpaid workers play an important role in self-employed households and also it is a common characteristic of small enterprises in developing countries (Margolis, 2014; Tambunan, 2009).

7 A part of this work was carried out during an earlier project on the same theme. I thank Ms. B.P. Vani for her support. For more details of this work, see Rajeev and Vani (2017).

References

Ayyagari, M., Demirgüç-Kunt, A. and V. Maksimovic (2008). 'How important are financing constraints? The role of finance in the business environment', *World Bank Economic Review*, 22(3), 483–516. https://doi.org/10.1093/wber/lhn018.

Banerjee, A.V. and E. Duflo (2011). *Poor Economics: A Radical Rethinking of the Way to Fight Global Poverty*, 2011th ed., Random House Publishers Private Limited, New Delhi.

Banerjee, A.V. and A.F. Newman (1993). 'Occupational choice and the process of development', *Journal of Political Economy*, 101(2), 274–298.

Beck, T. (2013). 'Banking finance for SMEs-lessons from the literature', *National Institute Economic Review*, 225(1), R23–R38.

Beck, T. and A. Demirguc-Kunt (2006). 'Small and medium-size enterprises: Access to finance as a growth constraint', *Journal of Banking and Finance*, 30(11), 2931–2943. https://doi.org/10.1016/j.jbankfin.2006.05.009.

Bell, C. (1991). 'Interactions between institutional and informal credit agencies in rural India', *The World Bank Economic Review*, 4(3), 297–327.

Bhowmik, S.K. (2005). 'Street vendors in Asia: A review', *Economic and Political Weekly*, 40(22/23), 2256–2264.

Birochi, R. and M. Pozzebon (2016). 'Improving financial inclusion: Towards a critical financial education framework', RAE Revista de Administracao de Empresas. https://doi.org/10.1590/S0034-759020160302.

Binswanger, H.P. and S.R. Khandker (1995). 'The impact of formal finance on the rural economy of India', *The Journal of Development Studies*, 32(2), 234–262. https://doi.org/10.1080/00220389508422413.

Das, M.B. (2003). 'The other side of Self-employment: Household enterprise in India', Social Protection Discussion Paper Series, No. 0318, Social Protection Unit Human Development Network, The World Bank, Washington, DC.

Daymard, A. (2015). 'Determinants of female entrepreneurship in India', OECD Economics Department Working Papers, No. 1191, OECD Publishing, Paris. https://doi.org/10.1787/5js4rfh5gtbq-en.

Demirgüç-Kunt, A., Beck, T. and P. Honohan (2008). 'Access to finance and development: Theory and measurement', in *Finance for All? Policies and Pitfalls in Expanding Access*, World Bank Policy Research Report, The World Bank, Washington, DC.

De Soto, H. (1989). *The Other Path: The Invisible Revolution in the Third World*, Harper and Row, New York.

European Commission, International Monetary Fund, Organisation for Economic Co-operation and Development, United Nations and World Bank (2009). *System of National Accounts 2008*, European Commission, International Monetary Fund,

Organisation for Economic Co-operation and Development, United Nations and World Bank, New York.

Evans, D.S. and B. Jovanovic (1989). 'An estimated model of entrepreneurial choice under liquidity constraints', *Journal of Political Economy*, 97(4), 808–827. https://doi.org/10.1086/261629.

Fletschner, D. (2009). 'Rural women's access to credit: Market imperfections and intrahousehold dynamics', *World Development*, 37(3), 618–631.

Gadgil, M.V. (1986). 'Agricultural credit in India: A review of performance and policies', *Indian Journal of Agricultural Economics*, 41(3), 282–309.

Ghosh, S. and D. Vinod (2017). 'What constrains financial inclusion for women? Evidence from Indian micro data', *World Development*, 92, 60–81. https://doi.org/10.1016/j.worlddev.2016.11.011.

Greene, W.H. (2003). *Econometric Analysis*, 5th ed., Pearson Education, London.

Gurtoo, A. and C.C. Williams (2009). 'Entrepreneurship and the informal sector', *The International Journal of Entrepreneurship and Innovation*, 10(1), 55–62. https://doi.org/10.5367/000000009787414280.

King, R.G. and R. Levine (1993). 'Finance and growth: Schumpeter might be right', *The Quarterly Journal of Economics*, 108(3), 717–737.

Kochar, A. (1997). An empirical investigation of rationing constraints in rural credit markets in India', *Journal of Development Economics*, 53(2), 339–371.

Margolis, D.N. (2014). 'By choice and by necessity: Entrepreneurship and self-employment in the developing world', *European Journal of Development Research*, 26(4), 419–436. https://doi.org/10.1057/ejdr.2014.25.

Mckinnon, R. (1973). *Money and Capital in Economic Development*. Brookings Institution, Washington, DC.

Menon, N. and Y. Van der Meulen Rodgers (2011). 'How access to credit affects self-employment: Differences by gender during India's rural banking reform', *Journal of Development Studies*, 47(1), 48–69. https://doi.org/10.1080/00220381003706486.

Mohan, R. (2006). 'Agricultural credit in India: Status, issues and future agenda', *Economic and Political Weekly*, 41(11), 1013–1023.

Nikaido, Y., Pais, J. and M. Sarma (2015). 'What hinders and what enhances small enterprises' access to formal credit in India?', *Review of Development Finance*, 5(1), 43–52. https://doi.org/10.1016/j.rdf.2015.05.002.

NSSO (2013). *All India Debt and Investment Survey*, NSSO, Ministry of Statistics and Programme Implementation, Government of India (GoI), New Delhi.

NSSO (2014). *Key Indicators of Debt and Investment in India (2013)*, Ministry of Statistics and Programme Implementation, Govt of India. New Delhi.

Paulson, A.L. and R. Townsend (2004). 'Entrepreneurship and financial constraints in Thailand', *Journal of Corporate Finance*, 10(2), 229–262. https://doi.org/10.1016/S0929-1199(03)00056-7.

Pitt, M.M. and S.R. Khandkar (1998). 'The impact of group-based credit programs on poor households in Bangladesh: Does the gender of participants matter', *The Journal of Political Economy*, 106(5), 958–996.

Rajeev, M. and B.P. Vani (2012). 'Farm sector in Karnataka: Farmers indebtedness and risk management', Project Report No. CESP/93, Institute for Social and Economic Change, Bangalore.

Rajeev, M. and B.P. Vani (2017). *Financial Access of the Urban Poor in India: A Story of Exclusion*, Springer Briefs in Economics, New Delhi.

Rajeev, M., Vani, B.P. and M. Bhattacharjee (2011). 'Credibility of equal access to credit: Does gender matter?', *Economic and Political Weekly*, 46(33), 76–79.

Schumpeter, J.A. (1934). *The Theory of Economic Development: An Inquiry into Profits, Capital, Credit, Interest, and the Business Cycle*, Harvard University Press, Cambridge.

Stiglitz, J.E. and A. Weiss (1981). 'Credit rationing in markets with imperfect information', *The American Economic Review*, 71(3), 393–410.

Swaminathan, H., Du Bois, R.S. and J.I. Findeis (2009). 'Impact of access to credit on labour allocation patterns in Malawi', *World Development*, 38(4), 555–566.

Tambunan, T. (2009). 'Women entrepreneurship in Asian developing countries: Their development and main constraints', *Journal of Development and Agricultural Economics*, 1(2), 27–40.

Temkin, B. (2009). 'Informal self-employment in developing countries: Entrepreneurship or survivalist strategy? Some implications for public policy', *Analyses of Social Issues and Public Policy*, 9(1), 135–156. https://doi.org/10.1111/j.1530-2415.2009.01174.x.

UNDP (2009). 'India: Urban poverty report 2009', www.in.undp.org.

Van de Ven, W.P.M.M. and B. Van Praag (1981). 'The demand for deductibles in private health insurance: A probit model with sample selection', *Journal of Econometrics*, 17(2), 229–252. https://doi.org/10.1016/0304-4076(81)90028-2.

Williams, C.C. and A. Gurtoo (2011). 'Evaluating women entrepreneurs in the informal sector: Some evidence from India', *Journal of Developmental Entrepreneurship*, 16(3), 351–369. https://doi.org/10.1142/S1084946711001914.

Appendix 9.1

Description summary statistics of variables used in the study – NSSO data

Variable	*Description* *Dependent variables*	*Mean*	*Std. Dev.*
Access to production loan	= 1 if household accesses production loan	0.123	
Self-employed	= 1 if household is self-employed	0.418	
	Explanatory variables		
Demographic penetration of bank branches	Number of bank branches divided by urban population	2.516	0.759
Services sector	= 1 if household is self-employed in services sector	0.316	
Log of total asset value	Log value of total assets owned	13.137	2.557
Urban land area owned	Area of urban land owned	0.108	0.509
SC and ST	=1 if household belong to scheduled castes/tribes	0.219	
OBC	=1 if household belongs to other backward castes	0.384	
General	= 1 if household belongs to general	0.396	
Female-headed household	= 1 if household is female-headed	0.124	
Female-headed enterprises	= 1 if enterprise owned by female	0.087	
Below primary	= 1 if highest education in household is below primary	0.090	
Primary	= 1 if highest education in household is primary	0.198	
Secondary	= 1 if highest education in household is secondary	0.379	
Tertiary	= 1 if highest education in household is tertiary	0.333	
Age of household head	Age of household head	47	13.516

(*Continued*)

(Continued)

Variable	*Description* *Dependent variables*	*Mean*	*Std. Dev.*
Household size	Household size	4.525	4.525
Ratio of children	Ratio of children to total household size	0.222	0.219
Number of helpers available	Total number of helpers available for enterprise	0.164	0.546
North	=1 if Northern administrative zone	0.159	
South	=1 if Southern administrative zone	0.243	
Central	=1 if Central administrative zone	0.182	
North-East	=1 if North-eastern zone	0.105	
East	=1 if Eastern zone	0.165	
West	=1 if Western zone	0.147	

Source: Calculated by the authors, based on NSSO (2014).

Appendix 9.2
Probit regression with sample selection

Variables	*Outcome*	*Selection*
	Access to production loans	*Self-employed*
No. of bank branches	-0.3403*	-0.2435**
	(0.182)	(0.106)
No. of bank branches	0.0492*	0.0340**
	(0.028)	(0.016)
Service sector	0.1950***	
	(0.070)	
Log of total asset value	0.0070	0.0573***
	(0.028)	(0.016)
Total land area owned-urban	0.1224**	-0.2786***
	(0.054)	(0.067)
(Base-SC and ST)		
OBC	0.0392	0.2568***
	(0.077)	(0.043)
General	0.0382	0.2842***
	(0.084)	(0.046)
Women-headed enterprises	0.0429	
	(0.063)	
Women-headed household	-0.0119	-0.1347***
	(0.089)	(0.052)
(Below primary)		
Primary	0.1254	0.2188***
	(0.106)	(0.055)
Secondary	0.2387**	0.2100***
	(0.106)	(0.055)
Tertiary	0.3242***	-0.0206
	(0.111)	(0.060)

(*Continued*)

(Continued)

Variables	*Outcome*	*Selection*
	Access to production loans	*Self-employed*
Ratio of children	0.2684*	0.0995
	(0.151)	(0.092)
Age of household head	0.0141	0.0186**
	(0.014)	(0.008)
Age of household head square	-0.0001	-0.0002**
	(0.000)	(0.000)
Household size	-0.0249	0.0778***
	(0.015)	(0.009)
(Base-South)		
North	-0.2743***	-0.3619***
	(0.099)	(0.051)
North-East	0.0092	-0.3236***
	(0.210)	(0.086)
East	0.2745***	-0.2739***
	(0.086)	(0.052)
Central	-0.0328	-0.5416***
	(0.095)	(0.047)
West	-0.0799	-0.5515***
	(0.109)	(0.054)
Helpers		0.4302***
		(0.051)
Constant	-0.5406	-2.0156***
	(0.717)	(0.344)
Observations	27,308	27,308
Rho	11.7***	

Source: Authors' estimates.

Note: Robust standard errors in parentheses.
*** $p < 0.01$, ** $p < 0.05$, * $p < 0.1$.

Appendix 9.3

Level of financial exclusion among respondents

Level of Exclusion	*Bengaluru*	*Tumakuru*
High Level of Inclusion	8.3	12.1
Marginally Excluded	13.5	14.3
Severely Excluded	33.8	37.4
Fully Excluded	44.4	36.3
Total	100.0	100.0

Source: Authors' Field Survey and Rajeev and Vani (2017).

Appendix 9.4

Regression results (ordered logistic regression, using field survey data)

Variable	*Bengaluru*	*Tumakuru*
	Coefficient	*Coefficient*
age_yng	0.2098 (0.5095)	−0.844*** (0.464)
old_est	−0.1384 (0.5109)	−1.717* (0.451)
Income	−0.0001* (0.0000)	0.000* (0.000)
edu_pri (primary education)	−0.4268 (0.4982)	0.447 (0.784)
edu_sec (secondary education)	−1.5319* (0.5175)	−0.447 (0.777)
edu_coll	–	−2.179** (1.023)
veg_fru (vegetable and fruit traders)	1.5489*** (0.8966)	−1.537*** (0.829)
con_good (light consumer goods)	1.4435*** (0.8753)	−0.648 (0.527)
Flower	2.1986** (0.9537)	1.542** (0.754)
reg_shop	−0.1902 (0.4380)	−1.087 (0.656)
/cut1	−4.1857 (1.2201)	−7.174 (1.329)
/cut2	−2.9143 (1.2001)	−6.124 (1.295)
/cut3	−0.9174 (1.1220)	−3.654 (1.198)

Source: Authors' estimates and Rajeev and Vani (2017).

Note: Robust standard errors in parentheses.
*** $p < 0.01$, ** $p < 0.05$, * $p < 0.1$

Dependent variable: level of financial exclusion defined as

Highly Included = 1, Marginally Excluded = 2, Severely Excluded = 3, Fully Excluded = 4

Explanatory variables

Education: Illiterates constitute the base category;
Type of business: Consumer durables, electronic goods is base category;
age_yng are those traders who are younger than 35 years of age and old_est are the establishments that came up prior to 2000;
reg_shop: those who own regular shop

The cutoff points are the threshold points that distinguish between the levels of the outcome variable. Hence, in our variable we have three cutoff points as we have four different levels: included, marginally excluded, severely excluded and fully excluded. cut1, cut2 and cut3 are the estimates of these cutoff points. For example, cut1 is the estimated cutoff point used to differentiate fully excluded from severely excluded, marginally excluded and included. cut2 is used to differentiate fully excluded and severely excluded from marginally excluded and included.

10 Contribution of education to GDP growth

Measurement and policy issues

P. Duraisamy

10.1 Introduction

The Indian economy has witnessed a higher growth trajectory since the thrust given to economic reforms in the 1990s. Like many South East Asian countries during the 1980s and the BRICS group of countries (Brazil, Russia, India, China and South Africa) in recent times, India moved from its modest rate of growth of around 3–4 per cent per annum until the 1980s to an average growth rate of 6–7 per cent since the 1990s. Notably, India's high growth in recent decades is not due to strong growth in the manufacturing sector, as observed in many developed countries, or export-led growth of the South East Asian countries. Rather, it is a *service sector led economic growth* (Papola, 2009). The prominent changes in the structure of the Indian economy – in terms of composition of output and employment – and growth patterns since 1950 can be summarised as follows:

1 The primary sector's (agriculture and its allied activities) share has declined from 55 per cent in 1950–51 to 14.4 per cent in 2018–19. The growth rate of this sector was 2.9 per cent, and the share of employment has fallen sharply from 64.8 per cent in 1993–94 to 43.2 per cent in 2019 (World Bank, 2019). There has been a remarkable shift of workers from agriculture to the other two sectors of the economy.
2 The share of the secondary sector, mainly consisting of the manufacturing industry, has risen slightly from 20 per cent in 1950–51 to 23.1 per cent in 2018–19. Evidence suggests that the 1950s and 1960s saw a fast rate of growth of 7 per cent per annum, partly due to the thrust given to heavy industries in the first and second five-year plans, followed by a growth rate of around 4 per cent in the next decade. With the introduction of economic reforms at a modest level in the 1980s and the liberalisation, privatisation and globalisation policies post-1991 crisis, the growth rate picked up to 6 per cent per annum. A somewhat moderate progress is witnessed in the share of employment from 15.6 per cent in 1993–94 to 24.9 per cent in 2019.

3 Importantly, the service sector GDP witnessed an average growth rate of 4 per cent before 1980, which increased to 6–8 per cent until 2011–12 and 8–10 per cent thereafter. Its share, including construction, in overall GDP has increased from 30 per cent in 1950 to 62.5 per cent in 2018–19. The service sector's share of employment has gone up from 19.7 per cent in 1993–94 to 31.9 per cent in 2019.

It is amply evident that not only is the service sector a major contributor to GDP but it is also the one which has grown at a much faster rate than the other two sectors. Thus, the high growth trajectory of the Indian economy since the implementation of economic reforms is mainly led by the consistently high growth observed in the service sector. The fast growth of the service sector is, however, not unique to India but a worldwide phenomenon observed in several countries. The service sector growth is important for a capital-scarce country like India as the sector's value added per unit of capital is high relative to the other sectors.

The growth pattern of the service sector has been extensively studied, focusing on the drivers of growth at the overall economy level as well as at the broad sectoral level, namely agriculture, manufacturing and services (Bosworth, Collins and Virmani, 2007; Das et al., 2013). Using disaggregated industrial classification, the India KLEMS project analysed the contribution of a number of sectors to GDP and the growth pattern from 1980–81 to 2008–09 (India KLEMS, 2014).

Questions have been raised in the earlier studies on whether the high growth of the service sector is sustainable in the long run. These studies reveal that the future growth of the Indian economy depends on sustaining and improving the contribution of service sector to GDP. Among the two conventional inputs – labour and capital – in the production of goods and services, the productivity of labour depends on education, skill, and training. Development of education and skills is, therefore, critical for sustaining the high growth rate of the service sector also, and analysing the contribution of education to economic growth assumes relevance. In the knowledge-based modern economies, the role of higher education is even more important. Despite its important contribution, the role of human capital to economic growth, particularly education, has not been given due attention, perhaps owing to problems surrounding measurement of output of the education sector.

The focus of this chapter is on the contribution of education to GDP in the Indian context, on which there is a significant gap in research today. The direct contribution of the education sector to GDP and its indirect contribution in the production process through improvements in labour quality, skill and so on are examined. The changes in the productivity of education in the labour market is analysed based on the estimates of the returns to education since 1980 using earnings function methodology. The study also focuses on the issues pertaining to growth of education sector, measurement of education sector's output and policies to revitalise this sector.

The chapter is structured as follows: section 10.2 discusses the methodological issues pertaining to measurement of the service sector's output in general and education sector in particular and also an alternative methodology developed and being implemented in many Organisation for Economic Cooperation and Development (OECD) countries and a few other countries. Section 10.3 presents the trends in direct contribution of the service sector and the educational sector to GDP. The major contribution of education stems from the improvements it makes to labour quality and through the role of labour as an input in the production process. For individuals, investment in education is rewarded by way of higher earnings in the labour market. These effects are denoted as 'indirect contribution' of education, and sections 10.4 and 10.5 are devoted to account for these effects. Section 10.6 presents the challenges facing the education sector, policies needed for revitalising the sector and concluding remarks.

10.2 Measuring the output of the educational sector: methodological issues

Measuring the output of the service sector, particularly the education sector, is much more difficult compared to that of industry and agriculture. The output of the education sector is not directly measurable and hence the expenditure method is used to compute the contribution of education sector to GDP. Hence, value added by the education sector (E) to GDP is measured as product of value added per worker (V_i) multiplied by number of workers (L_i) in kth educational level and summed over all educational levels. The value added per worker is computed by subtracting all input cost from total expenditure of the education sector excluding labour cost (wages) used in the production of services. That is,

$$E = \Sigma_i L_i{*}V_i, i = 1, 2, \ldots k \text{ education levels} \qquad (1)$$

There are several problems associated with this approach: (i) Since the value of output is measured by the value of inputs, the ratio of output to inputs does not measure productivity performance for that sector and it is also hard to study the changes in productivity over a period of time (Gu and Wong, 2012); (ii) the data on both the number of workers and value added are normally based on sample surveys such as NSS, Annual Survey of Industries (ASI), enterprises surveys and the Population Census. As these surveys/census are conducted with a gap of 5 to 10 years, data for inter-survey years are computed using some interpolation method. Hence, this method of estimating output is prone to be inaccurate, and there is no way of assessing whether the contribution of the service sector is under- or overestimated.

Two approaches are employed to estimate the output of education sector: (i) cost of investment in human capital, developed by Kendric (1976), and (ii) the income approach in which the investment is measured using information on the stream of future earnings by Jorgenson and Fraumeni (1989, 1992). The National Accounts System in India uses the cost of human capital investment approach. That is, the output of the education sector is measured using the amount of current budgetary expenditure incurred on public institutions and an estimate of the total cost of inputs used in the case of private educational institutions (CSO, 2007). As shown in the following section, the estimates of the education sector's contribution to GDP seems to be grossly underestimated, as evident from the fact that the share of education to GDP is stagnant while the sector witnessed a huge expansion of educational institutions and enrolment in the past two decades.

10.2.1 *Measuring education's contribution: alternative methodology*

An alternative to the cost of inputs approach is the income approach proposed and applied by Jorgenson and Fraumeni (1989, 1992) and Jorgenson, Landefeld and Nordhaus (2006). It involves estimating the present discount value of lifetime labour income weighted by educational levels and adjusting for the cost of investment in education and training. The lifetime income approach provides a broader accounting framework in the sense that it has the potential to include the contribution of non-market activities such as home production, especially of women, in the estimates of national income. The volume of education output is measured as the weighted sum of product of student enrolment and value of education, where the latter is calculated using the difference in the present discounted value of lifetime earnings between two successive levels of education. Theoretically both the cost and income methods should yield the same estimate; in practice it differs to the tune of 17–19 times in the case of the US, as shown by Jorgenson and Fraumeni (1989). The main reasons are subsidiaries to education expenditure, liquidity constraints on borrowings and risk-taking behaviour of the individuals in investing in human capital.

In the last decade, the Organisation of Economic Cooperation and Development (OECD) has developed methods to estimate output-based measures of education services (OECD, 2010). Nine OECD countries have implemented output-based measures of education services, and a number of other OECD countries are expected to implement this approach in due course. More recently, the US Bureau of Economic Analysis has developed experimental output-based measures for the US primary- and secondary-education sectors. Gu and Wong (2012) show that in the case of Canada the income-based estimate is about 6.8 times as large as the cost-based estimates in 2015.

An output-based measure of education has been applied to estimate education's contribution for several countries such as the United States. Australia, Canada, France, New Zealand, Norway, Poland, and Spain and the OECD launched a project to apply this approach to more than 20 countries. Such estimates have also been developed for China. Estimates based on such an approach are yet to be made available, and it is necessary to move towards this approach in order to capture the real contribution of education to national income.

10.3 Education services contribution to service sector and overall GDP

It is now amply evident that the service sector is the largest contributor to our economy. The share of service sector to GDP over the period 1980–81 to 2018–19 based on National Accounts Statistics is shown in Figure 10.1. It may be noted that the share of service sector to GDP has recorded a sharp rise from 38 per cent in 1980–81 to 62 per cent in 2018–19. The service sector consists of four sub-groups. Data for the year 2018–19 reveal that (i) finance, real estate, dwelling and business services are the major contributors to GDP, that is, 22 per cent, followed by (ii) trade, hotels and restaurants with a share of 19 per cent. The other important contributors are (iii) public administration, defence and other services which include education (13 per cent) and (iv) construction (8 per cent).

Education emerges as a powerful tool in fuelling the growth of the service sector. All the groups rely on skilled and semi-skilled human resources generated by our primary, secondary and tertiary education systems; the third group in particular is substantially more human capital–intensive in the production process compared to the others and it employs the scientific, engineering and technical human resources created by the education sector. It would be useful to trace the contribution of education to GDP and also the expansion of the education sector.

The share of education to GDP is available only for the period 1980–81 to 2008–09 (India KLEMS Data), which is shown in Figure 10.1. The curve depicting the share of the education sector to GDP is rather flat, implying a slow increase, and it has remained close to 4 per cent since 2000. This seems quite surprising given the huge size of the education sector and the striking growth in enrolment since 1950–51, which is discussed below:

The growth in enrolment by educational levels from 1950–51 to 2015–16 is shown in Figure 10.2. There is a huge increase in enrolment in schools, that is, from 24 million in 1950–51 to 106 million in 1980–81 and to 261 million in 2015–16. This has resulted in a steady increase in gross enrolment ratio (GER) at all levels of education (Figure 10.3). During the period 1980–81 to 2015–16, the GER at the primary level of education increased from 81 per cent to 99 per cent. Data also indicate a massive increase in enrolment at the middle and secondary levels, leading to increase the GER from 42 per cent to 93 per cent at the middle school level and from 29 per cent to 80 per cent at the secondary school level during the same period.

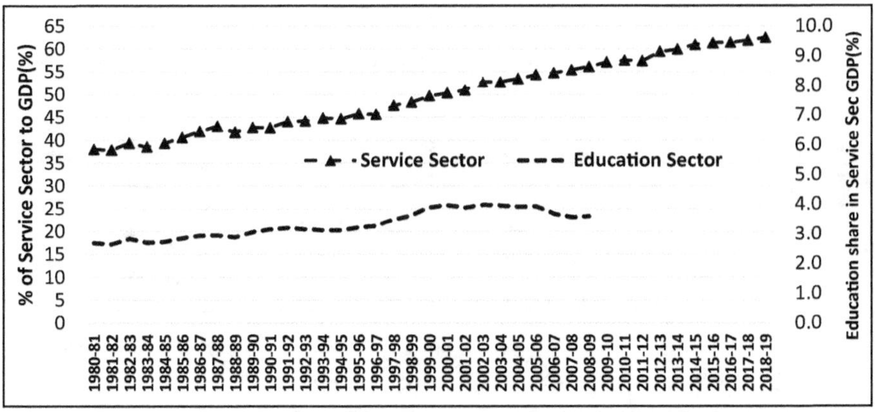

Figure 10.1 Share of service sector and education sector to GDP, 1980–2018

Source: CSO (Various Years), RBI (2020) and KLEMS Data Base from RBI Website (www.rbi.org.in/Scripts/KLEMS.aspx).

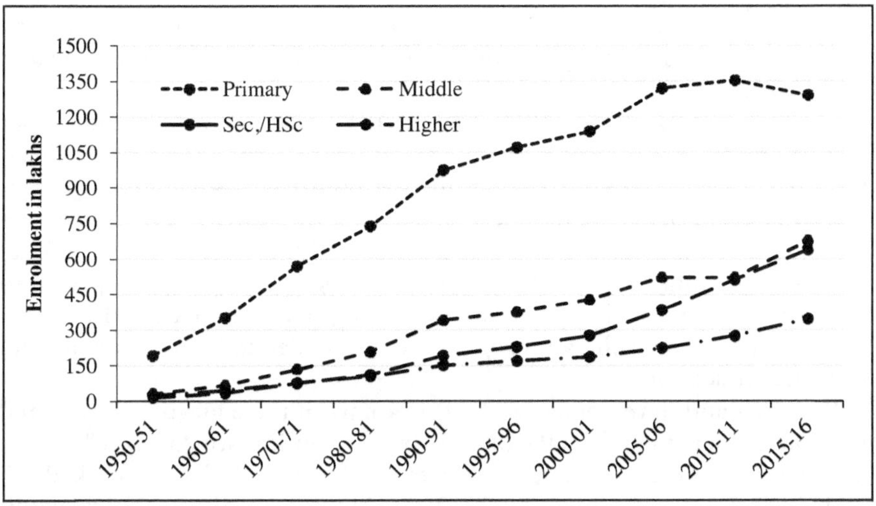

Figure 10.2 Trends in school enrolment by levels, 1950–2016

Source: SES (Various Years) and AISHE (Various Years).

Enrolment in higher education too witnessed a phenomenal expansion since 1980–81. The student enrolment in higher education institutions (HEIs), shown in Figure 10.2, indicate that the enrolment increased from 11 million in 1980–81 to 34.6 million in 2015–16 and 37.4 million in

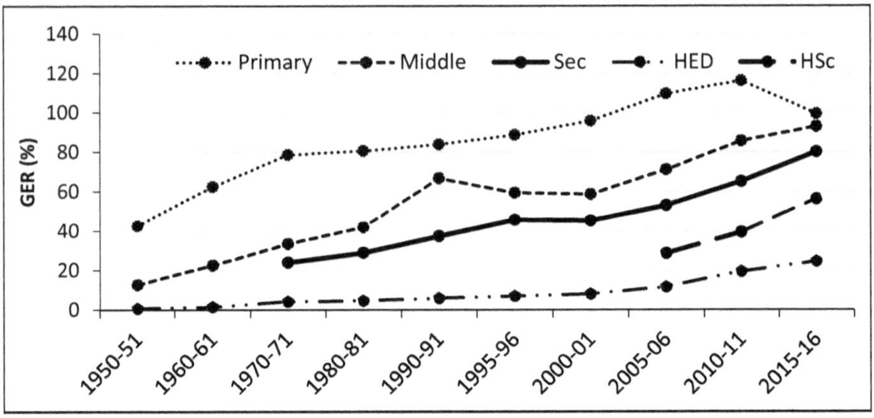

Figure 10.3 Gross enrolment rates by educational levels, 1950–2016
Source: SES (Various Years) and AISHE (Various Years).

2018–19. The GER also surged from a meagre 4.7 per cent in 1980–81 to 24.5 in 2015–16 and to 26.3 per cent in 2018–19. Thus, India has transitioned from 'elitism' in higher education to 'massification' (Duraisamy and Duraisamy, 2016).

The massive expansion of the education sector, especially the higher education sector, is due to growing private participation in higher education (66 per cent of enrolment), while the progress of school education is due to two national programmes, namely District Primary Education Programme (DPEP) and Sarva Shiksha Abhiyan (SSA). The recent constitutional guarantee – Right to Education (RTE) – in school education is expected to help achieve universal elementary education, while the RUSA (Rashtriya Uchchatar Shiksha Abhiyan) programme is intended to improve the quality of higher education.

Research and development (R&D) is a part of the education sector, and the country has made significant achievement in investment in R&D and also in terms of the contribution of scientific research. India was ranked 7th globally in R&D investments in 2012, 9th in the number of scientific publications and 12th in the number of patents filed (Prasad, Sathish and Singh, 2014). The changing technology and delivery mechanism will drive investments in educational software development, skill enhancement, IT training and e-learning (Prasad et al., 2014).

The spectacular expansion of the education sector is, however, not reflected in its contribution to GDP, clearly indicating a gross underestimation of education services' share due to problems in appropriately measuring educational services, data limitations and also the methodology adopted in estimation.

10.4 Indirect contribution of education to GDP through improvements in labour quality in the production of goods and services

The major contribution of education is through improvements in labour quality which is an input (human capital) in the production process, similar to physical capital. These effects are captured by estimating an aggregate production function. The aggregate growth accounting procedure takes this into account, and the educational attainment of the workers is used to estimate quality-adjusted labour input and its contribution to growth of the economy as a whole and that of the sub-sectors. Education is also included as an input in the aggregate production function. The growth accounting framework has been widely used to identify the sources of growth, the major contributors being land, labour (increased employment), physical capital and human capital (educational attainment/health) and TFP or improvements in the basic efficiency of resource use. This method is used to account for the contribution of education as described here.

10.4.1 Growth accounting method

The growth accounting method is based on an aggregate production function which is specified as,

$$Q_t = A_t f(K_t, L_t), t = 1, 2, \ldots T \text{ years/Quarters} \tag{2}$$

where K and L refer to physical capital and labour inputs, respectively, and A is the efficiency parameter. Assuming perfectly competitive markets and that factors are paid according to their marginal product, it can be shown that

$$\Delta \ln Q = \alpha \, \Delta \ln (K) + \beta \, \Delta \ln (L) + \Delta \ln TFP \tag{3}$$

For simplicity, studies use Cobb-Douglas production function with constant returns to scale (CRTS) to estimate the factor shares

$$Q_t = A_t \, (K^{\alpha}_t, L^{\beta}_t), \beta = (1 - \alpha) \text{ (CRTS)} \tag{4}$$

A question to address is how to identify the role of education or human capital in the growth accounting. Education influences the quality of labour and the quality weighted labour input weighted (L^*) is measured as

$$L^* = e^{\delta S} \, L_S, \tag{5}$$

s = years of schooling, L quantity of labour and δ is the labour productivity.

Using the earlier approach, Bosworth, Collins and Virmani (2007) estimated the contribution of each of the factors of production to output and

Table 10.1 Contribution of education in the production process: 1980–2005

Period	*Output*	*Employment*	*Output per worker*	*Contribution by*			
				Capital	*Land*	*Education*	*Factor productivity*
All	5.8	2.0	3.7	1.4	–	0.4	2.0
Agriculture	2.8	1.1	1.7	0.4	–0.1	0.3	1.1
Industry	6.4	3.4	3.0	1.6	–	0.3	1.1
Service	7.6	3.8	3.8	0.7	–	0.4	2.7

Source: Bosworth, Collins and Virmani (2007).

Note: Figures are annual percentage rate of change.

also total factor productivity (Table 10.1). They also included education as a factor of production. The results reveal that 0.3 to 0.4 per cent of the GDP increase of 5.8 per cent per year during the period 1980–2005 is due to education. The study also shows that the impact of education in the service sector is much higher than that in the other two sectors. The growth of output and TFP of the service sector are also found to be significantly higher than those in the other two sectors.

10.4.2 *Impact of education on growth differences across the Indian states*

In one of the earliest studies, Duraisamy and Mahal (2006) estimated the impact of human capital (education and health) on state-level output using a Cobb-Douglas aggregate production function given here:

$$\ln Y_{it} = \ln A + \alpha \ln K_{it} + \beta \ln L_{it} + \gamma \ln H_{it} + \delta S_{it} + \mu_{it} \text{ where } \mu_{it} = \lambda_{it} + w_{it} \quad (6)$$

i = 1.2 . . . N states and t = 1.2 . . . T years

where Y is aggregate output, A is a technology parameter, K is physical capital stock, L is labour force, H is health (life expectancy), all expressed in natural logarithmic form (ln), and S is mean years of schooling. The error term μ_{it} consists of two components – w_{it}, a random disturbance and λ_{it}, an unobserved time-and state-specific fixed effect. The study estimated the effect of the inputs K, L, S and H, taking into account the endogenous nature of inputs and using fixed effects model on a panel data of 14 major states for a period of three decades. The results showed that both education and health have positive and statistically significant effects on the changes in state income. An increase in the schooling of the population by one year was found to increase the net state domestic product (NSDP) by 0.1 per cent, while a 1 per cent increase in LEB increased NSDP by 1–2 per cent. These results clearly suggest that the states which had higher levels of educational attainment and health status witnessed higher NSDP.

10.5 Education's impact on productivity in the labour market

The human capital theory advocates that education enhances productivity of the people and leads to higher rewards in the labour market (Schultz, 1961). Evidence also points out that education increases the chances of being employed and reduces the waiting time for jobs. The effect of education on labour market earnings has been extensively studied using the earnings function approach specified as follows:

$$\ln W_i = \alpha + \Sigma_k \beta_k S_{ik} + \nu_1 E_i + \nu_2 E_i^2 + \delta L_i + u_i, \quad (7)$$

i = 1, 2, . . . n workers; k = 1, 2, . . . k educational levels
where *W* is the wage rate, *S* refers to schooling levels, *E* stands for experience and *L* denotes location (rural or urban); α, β, ν and δ are the parameters to be estimated; and *u* is the random disturbance term.

The methodology of estimating returns to education is elaborated in Duraisamy (2002), and the study also provided the first set of estimates on returns to education based on NSS unit level data for the years 1983 and 1993–94. Duraisamy and Duraisamy (2016) provide estimates of earnings functions for the years 1983, 1993–94, 2004–05 and 2011–12. The estimates of the returns to education for India from various rounds of NSS data for the period 1983 to 2012 are given in Table 10.2. The results show that the returns to education increase with increase in the level of education. Over the years, the returns to higher education, especially technical education, have increased.

The returns to education vary between 8 and 12 per cent per year of schooling, and the returns have been decreasing over the years (Table 10.2). The returns to primary education range from 6 to 12 per cent. Although the returns to secondary education were higher than primary education before

Table 10.2 Changes in the labour market returns to education in India

Education	*1983*	*1993–94*	*1999–00*	*2004–05*	*2007–08*	*2009–10*
Years of Schooling	12.1	12.7	7.0	8.7	12.4	8.3
Primary	8.2	7.9	11.4	11.7	11.5	5.8
Secondary	13.7	13.8	4.3	5.4	9.6	6.0
Tertiary	11.0	11.7	20.2	18.7	27.7	20.8

Source: Duraisamy (2002), Duraisamy and Duraisamy (2016), Montenegro and Patrinos (2014).

1990, they have declined since then and the returns to higher education have been increasing. This suggests that higher education is rewarded more perhaps due to service sector–led growth of the Indian economy. The estimates lead to interesting finding that the returns to education are more or less equal to or even more than the returns to investment in physical capital. Thus, investment in human capital is highly rewarding both for the individual as well as the nation.

10.6 Challenges, policy issues and concluding remarks

The contribution of education services to GDP as currently estimated in the National Accounts Statistics hovers around 4 per cent. The methodology presently adopted by the CSO leads to an underestimation of the education sector's contribution to GDP. Alternative methods have been developed and applied in several countries. Instead of an expenditure- or input-based approach, estimates based on the lifetime earnings approach, as followed in the OECD, China and other countries, may better capture the share of education sector in GDP and it is worthwhile experimenting with this approach in the Indian context. This approach will not only give more realistic estimate of the contribution of education but also increase GDP as evident from the estimates.

Human capital in general and education in particular affects the quality of labour, which in turn augments labour productivity and thus economic growth. Programmes and policies to improve the quality of education and skill development of the workforce are the need of the hour.

The education sector is currently facing several challenges: 26 per cent of the population is illiterate (2011 Census) and the average years of schooling of the population is just 4.9 years, which is far lower compared to about 7.5 years for China, Thailand and Indonesia and 9.5 years for Malaysia. Efforts to achieve universal primary education are still elusive. Poor quality of school education and high dropout rates are important issues in this context. India needs to strengthen vocational streams and skill development at the school level.

Higher education too is facing many challenges. Although there is evidence of massive expansion of the education sector in recent years, India still lags behind many developing countries in terms of educational attainment of the population. The NASSCOM-McKinsey report of 2009 shows that only 26 per cent of India's engineering graduates were employable. The Associated Chambers of Commerce and Industry of India (ASSOCHAM) survey of 2012 reported that only 10 per cent of master of business administration (MBA) graduates from Indian B-schools get a job right after completing their course. About 19 per cent of sanctioned seats in engineering lie vacant leading to closure of several engineering and management programmes/institutions. Regional and disciplinary imbalances in engineering education have been widening. There are wide disparities among gender and social groups in educational attainment as measured by GER in higher education. Data show that the GER of males is 24.5 per cent, while that of females is 22.7 per cent. Further, the GER in higher education for social groups, namely, SCs and STs are 18.5 per cent and 13.3 per cent, respectively, which are far below the national average of 23.6 per cent. To overcome the problem of non-employability, education must be linked to skill development. There is also an urgent need to address the issues of disciplinary, regional imbalances and disparities by gender and social groups in their access to quality education.

References

AISHE (Various Years). *All India Survey on Higher Education*, Ministry of Human Resources Development, Government of India, New Delhi.

Bosworth, B., Collins, S. and A. Virmani (2007). 'Sources of growth in Indian economy', National Bureau of Economic Research Working Paper No. 12901 https://ssrn.com/abstract=966115.

CSO (2007). *National Accounts Statistics: Sources and Methods*, Central Statistics Office, Government of India, New Delhi.

CSO (Various Years). *National Accounts Statistics*, Central Statistics Office, Government of India, New Delhi.

Das, D.K., Erumban, A.A., Aggarwal, S. and S. Sengupta (2013). 'Revisiting the service-led growth in India: Understanding India's service sector productivity growth', Paper presented at the IARIW-UNSW Conference on *Productivity: Measurement, Drivers and Trends*, held at Sydney, Australia during November 26–27. www.iariw.org/papers/2013/DasPaper.pdf.

Duraisamy, P. (2002). 'Changes in returns to education in India, 1983–94: By gender, age-cohort and location', *Economics of Education Review*, 21(6), 609–622.

Duraisamy, P. and M. Duraisamy (2016). 'Gender wage gap across the wage distribution in different segments of the Indian labour market, 1983–2012: Exploring the glass ceiling or sticky floor phenomenon', *Applied Economics*, 48(43), 4098–4111.

Duraisamy, P. and A. Mahal (2006). 'Health, poverty and economic growth in India', *Financing and Delivery of Health Care Services in India*, National Commission on Macroeconomics and Health (NCMH) (Section I, pp. 3–17), Ministry of Health & Family Welfare, Government of India, New Delhi.

Griliches, Z. (ed.) (1992). *Output Measurement in the Service Sectors*, Chicago University Press, Chicago.

Gu, W. and A. Wong (2012). *Measuring the Economic Output of the Education Sector in the National Accounts*, Economic Analysis (EA) Research Paper Series, Statistics Canada Analysis Branch, Economic Analysis Division Minister of Industry, Canada. www150.statcan.gc.ca/n1/en/pub/11f0027m/11f0027m2012080-eng.pdf?st=y5Tymsny.

India KLEMS (2014, July). *Estimates of Productivity Growth for Indian Economy*, ICRIER and RBI. www.rbi.org.in/Scripts/PublicationReportDetails.aspx?TYPE=QUICK&PARAM1=2014&PARAM2=0.

Jorgenson, D.W. and B.B.M. Fraumeni (1989). 'The accumulation of human and nonhuman capital', in R.E. Lipsey and H. Stone Tice (eds.) *The Measurement of*

Saving, Investment and Wealth, pp. 227–281, University of Chicago Press, Chicago, IL.

Jorgenson, D.W. and B.B.M. Fraumeni (1992). 'The output of the education sector', in Z. Griliches (ed.) *Output Measurement in the Service Sector*, pp. 303–338, University of Chicago Press, Chicago, IL.

Jorgenson, D.W., Landefeld, J.S. and W.D. Nordhaus (eds.) (2006). *A New Architecture for the U.S. National Accounts*, University of Chicago Press, Chicago.

Kendrick, J.W. (1976). *The Formation and Stocks of Total Capital*, Columbia University Press, New York.

KLEMS Data Base. www.rbi.org.in/Scripts/KLEMS.aspx), downloaded from RBI website.

Montenegro, C.E. and H.A. Patrinos (2014). 'Comparable estimates of returns to schooling around the world', WPS 7020, The World Bank, Washington, DC.

OECD (2010). *The OECD Human Capital Project: Progress Report*, Organisation for Economic Co-operation and Development, Paris.

Papola, T.S. (2009). 'India: Growing fast, but also needs to industrialise!', *The Indian Journal of Labour Economics*, 52(1), 57–69.

Prasad, H.A.C., Sathish, R. and S.S. Singh (2014). 'Emerging global economic situation: Opportunities and policy issues for service sector', Working Paper No. 1/2014-DEA, Ministry of Finance, Government of India, New Delhi.

RBI (2020). *Handbook of Statistics on Indian Economy 2018–19*, Reserve Bank of India, Mumbai. www.rbi.org.in/.

Schultz, T.W. (1961). 'Investment in human capital', *American Economic Review*, 51(1), 1–17.

SES (Various Years). *Selected Educational Statistics*, Ministry of Human Resource Development, Government of India, New Delhi.

World Bank (2019). *World Development Indicators*. https://databank.worldbank.org/source/world-development-indicators.

11 Learning to 'walk on two legs'?

Divergent trajectories and the future of India's ICT services

Balaji Parthasarathy

11.1 Introduction

The global revenues of the Indian information and communication technology (ICT) services industry grew from US$81 million in 1985–86 to US$151.4 billion in 2017–18 (Table 11.1). As the share of exports grew to 82.8 per cent of revenues, the Indian industry commanded an estimated 55 per cent of the world outsourcing market (MeitY, 2017–18: 91). To Schware (1992), a World Bank economist, the disproportionate reliance of the Indian software services industry on exports, or a tendency to not 'walk on two legs', was a sign of weakness. Schware argued that the experience gained in the domestic market, in software production and innovation, is crucial to broaden exports and to 'catch-up' in an industry where the technologies originate elsewhere. For instance, learning to organise and manage capital, skills, and new technologies, in domestic software production would allow firms to undertake larger and more complex software projects, and develop quality consciousness and the institutional support infrastructure, for business growth.

In the quarter century since Schware propounded his argument, the Indian experience has suggested that his emphasis on the importance of the domestic market for export growth was misplaced. Although the domestic market has been growing in recent years, it is happening much *after* exports came to characterise the industry, a phenomenon not explained by Schware. This chapter will explain not only why and how the Indian industry adopted a 'walking on one leg' strategy but also the significance of turning its gaze to the domestic market only later.

To understand why Schware's argument about the need for a domestic market for the software industry is misplaced, it is useful to appreciate how ICTs have shaped an increasingly 'informational, global and networked'[1] economy with 'the capacity to work as a unit in real time on a planetary scale' (Castells, 2000) in which anything that can be digitised and 'delivered electronically over long distances with little or no degradation in quality' (Blinder, 2006) will become tradable. This applies especially to impersonal services whose provision does not demand location-specific attributes, such

Table 11.1 India's information and communication technology services – global revenues and exports (in millions of US dollars, 1985–86 to 2017–18)

Year	*Revenues in millions of current US$ (a)*	*Exports*	
		as share of revenues	*as share of STPs (a)*
1985–86	81	29.6%	
1990–91	243	52.8%	
1995–96	1,253	60.2%	29.0%
2000–01	8,386	75.1%	70.7%
2005–06	30,300	77.9%	97.0%
2010–11	76,200	77.4%	80.1%
2014–15	118,800	82.4%	48.9%
2017–18	151,400	82.8%	44.0%

Source: Revenue and exports data until 2000–01 is from the National Association of Software and Services Companies (NASSCOM) (www.nasscom.in); for subsequent years the data is from the Ministry of Electronics and Information Technology (MeiTy) Annual Report, various years (http://meity.gov.in/content/annual-report).

Note: Global revenues and exports includes income from subsidiaries abroad; the share of STPs in exports has declined after the financial incentives for exports were removed in 2011.

as face-to-face contact, or a trust-based relationship. Thus, distant markets can be served whether or not there is a domestic market.

However, not all domestic markets can be served from a distance because developing software is about abstracting the practices in various sectors or domains of human activity, such as education, health and governance, before encoding those practices with digital technology. In other words, ICTs are general purpose technologies which have not only emerged as an important sector in their own right but also have the potential 'to transform an economy by finding new applications and fusing with existing technologies to rejuvenate other, pre-existing sectors of the economy' (David, 2000). While technological advancement has led to strides in the ability to code and deliver it over a distance, finding new applications by abstracting social practices in pre-existing sectors remains stubbornly difficult (Brooks, 1995). One reason is that many practices, even within the same sector, vary by location and possess a 'tacit dimension' (Polanyi, 2009). Physical proximity to practitioners in various sectors and potential users of ICTs, to facilitate 'learning-by-interacting', is one way of overcoming the challenge of tacitness that encoders face (Gertler, 2003). This is especially relevant in India where an increasingly important segment of the domestic market is the country's vast underprivileged population which has been served with little or no technology thus far.

With the brief explanation of the characteristics of ICTs to explain *why* the Indian services industry has acquired its characteristics, the rest of the chapter will explain *how* those characteristics were acquired. Section 11.2 will provide an analytical framework to understand how national contexts, including comparative advantage and state policy, shape the competitive advantage of firms in the ICT industry and influence the relative importance of global and domestic markets. Section 11.3 will use the framework to describe how the Indian ICT services industry gained international prominence despite a relatively small domestic market. It will point to the industry's role in the international division of labour as a producer of software by providing technical and managerial skills while relying on customers for domain knowledge. Section 11.4 will discuss the significant efforts, including the pursuit of new organisational alliances, to understand the needs of underprivileged users before the deployment of any technology. In essence, as the concluding discussion in section 11.5 will argue, the Indian software services industry is defined by at least two different trajectories, each with a distinct source of knowledge and organisation of production, rendering references to 'walking on two legs' irrelevant. But the section will also highlight a possibility of the phrase gaining relevance as these distinct trajectories, which will define the future of the Indian ICT services industry, show signs of overlapping, although not in ways that Schware could have predicted.

11.2 The role of markets, international and domestic

Neo-classical economics' trade theory explains international markets and globalisation by drawing on the idea of comparative advantage: differences in factor endowments and in productivity across countries and regions lead to differences in the relative cost of production, thereby providing an incentive to trade for mutual benefit in various sectors. But, as Porter (1998) argues, the comparative advantage provided by the availability of factor endowments such as natural resources, low-wage labour, and debt capital, is a necessary but insufficient basis for the *competitive* advantage for firms from a region, in any sector, in the global economy. Any factor pool is a depreciating basis for sustained advantage unless constantly upgraded, and a strong factor-creating institutional mechanism is more important than the absolute factor stock at a given time.

To Porter, a relatively poor country trying to develop an internationally competitive sector must reinforce any initial advantage conferred by factor endowments, or by chance (such as new inventions or technological discontinuities, major shifts in input costs or exchange rates, or other political factors such as war), for sustained economic performance. Further, it is the availability of various sector-specific factors that will determine the sectors in which firms from a country will be competitive. Since this is unlikely to happen autonomously where market information is at a premium, state action can provide signals to economic actors. These actions may include creating additional factors, such as communications infrastructure, or investing in R&D institutions, for select sectors in which the nation may have a comparative advantage. Thus, competitive advantage derives from the dynamic *construction* of comparative advantage, which depends on 'a complex evolution of competitive and cooperative ties among local firms, on government policies, and on a host of other political and social institutions' (Evans, 1995).

There are two aspects to Evans' point about the competitive and cooperative ties between states, markets and firms of significance to this chapter. First, while technological and institutional changes have facilitated increased flows and rising trade of expanded production between firms from various regions, such flows are unlikely to occur without mutual comprehension and compatibility. Thus, the need for international standards has grown to reduce information asymmetries between anonymous buyers and sellers separated by long chains of transactions (Varian, Farrell and Shapiro, 2004). Standards are particularly crucial in markets for products such as software, where supply-side economies of scale (declining marginal cost of production) are reinforced by demand-side economies of scale (or positive network externalities). Of interest to ICT firms is joining technology-driven commodity chains (TDCCs), which are global 'production networks where control over technological design, standards and trajectories is the central element of business power' (O'Riain, 2004). The role of government policy and standards in the export-led growth of the Indian ICT services industry are described in the next section.

Second, the outcomes of ties between firms and other institutions are brought out in Saxenian's (1994) seminal work on the ICT industry in Silicon Valley. Crucial to innovation in the region is the mobility of professionals between firms, whether established ones or start-ups. Supporting the firms is a network of institutions including service providers, such as intellectual property lawyers, market research firms, and venture capitalists, who specialise in issues of relevance to the industry. In addition, Stanford University and the University of California, Berkeley, have been the source of many new technologies. Professionals moving between these firms and institutions play different roles as buyers, producers or financiers, which leads to the sharing, validation and diffusion of ideas. Such sharing and validation simultaneously acknowledges and lowers the risk inherent in new ventures. To Saxenian, the blurred boundaries between firms and other institutions are critical to what she terms the regional industrial system of the Valley. This system helps firms in the Valley innovate and develop new products and services that are compatible with the technical and commercial needs of the market. Often, they are simultaneously shaping the market by establishing the standards to which firms elsewhere must conform.

If firms in the Valley sit atop their TDCCs, it is because the industrial system that Saxenian refers to does not belong to a hermetically sealed region. Saxenian (2006) documents the importance of 'ICs' – not integrated circuits, but Indians and Chinese (initially Taiwanese, but increasingly mainland Chinese) – in new-firm formation in Silicon Valley.[2] Critical to the entrepreneurial success of these skilled immigrants has been their membership in organisations, such as the Chinese Institute of Engineers or the Indus Entrepreneurs, which promote professional networking by harnessing and reinforcing ethnic identity and a shared educational background. Through seminars, conferences, and other formal and informal means, Chinese and Indian organisations serve as channels for investment, technical and labour market information. They also serve as forums where older entrepreneurs play role models and mentor younger counterparts.

These ethnic organisations are, however, not isolated enclaves that shun mainstream business and technology networks. Prominently, members of these organisations use their social and professional ties, especially with university classmates and alumni, to bridge firms in the Valley with firms in their countries of origin. Even if they do not return home for good, many operate simultaneously from the Valley and the countries they emigrated from, as the 'new argonauts', establishing access to technologies and markets that did not previously exist. 'Brain circulation', as an alternative to brain drain, has proven beneficial to the Valley and to regions that the argonauts connect, especially because it facilitates rapid flows of information in an industry with shrinking product cycles. For instance, Taiwanese firms partner with firms in the Valley to offer reliable and flexible manufacturing and integration, besides providing access to customers in Asia. Similarly, firms in India are an important source of software, as described later.

Saxenian's work on how Silicon Valley firms draw on local institutional strengths for global competitive advantage is illustrative of the importance of tacit knowledge and 'learning-by-interacting' in close proximity, which was mentioned in the Introduction. Egan (2000) reinforces this point by describing the evolving spatial organisation of the US software industry. Between 1970 and the 1990s, he points to a decentralisation of the industry without deconcentration, that is, a 'spatial drift' as older agglomerations lost their share of employment, not due to any general dispersal of the industry, but because employment grew in new agglomerations.

Egan explains the emergence of these new agglomerations in terms of a new spatial division of labour in the software industry based not on a distinction between low-skill/high-skill labour, but on a distinction within high-skilled labour, between those working on general-purpose technology and those developing applications for specific sectors. The standardisation and consolidation of general purpose software, which tends to emerge from regions like Silicon Valley, stimulates the demand for downstream applications based on the sector-specific information-processing practices. These demands are, increasingly, addressed in specialised agglomerations by independent software firms which form in proximity to lead users in those sectors, users who 'provide the stimuli for most global products and processes. . . . Local innovations in such markets become useful elsewhere as the environmental characteristics that stimulated such innovations diffuse to other locations' (Bartlett and Ghosal, 1990).

Egan refers to such specialised agglomerations as 'application districts' and points to Houston as an instance. Houston is not only the leading centre for employment and value-added in the oil and natural gas sector in the US, being home to most of the world's technological leaders in the sector, but also dominates the production of software for the sector.[3] To the extent that competitive advantage in oil and gas in the future continues to depend upon the effective use of ICTs, Egan argues that Houston is likely to capture even more of the value-added in the sector by developing the critical technology that all industry participants will need, and by setting the standards for global dominance in this specific application of software technology. The relevance of lead users for a growing domestic market in India is discussed in section 11.4.

11.3 The growth and transformation of Indian ICT services exports

The PC (personal computer), networking, and the internet revolutions of the 1970s, the 1980s and the 1990s, respectively, led to a proliferation of computer usage in various economic sectors and triggered a demand for software (Campbell-Kelly, 2003). However, while automated, capital-intensive operations permit the mass production of reliable hardware, software production, in comparison, has remained a craft-like, labour-intensive affair, plagued by uneven productivity and quality (Brooks, 1995). The result is that software development is notoriously prone to 'bugs', delays and cost overruns. Despite the development of a field of software engineering, along the lines of industrial engineering, to automate and rationalise software development, there is no 'silver bullet' to overcome this 'software bottleneck'. With Kraft's (1977) prediction that managing the software development process would lead to a division of labour between mental and manual labour proving wrong, overcoming the bottleneck has required the deployment of more skilled software professionals.

Although the question of whether or not there is a shortage of skilled labour is controversial, especially in the US, there has been agreement about the shortage of specific coding skills: whether for older mainframe systems until the 2000s (Koch, 1998) or for emerging technologies such as artificial intelligence (Stein, 2017). Faced with a shortage of people with specific skills, and the pressure to limit the costs of labour-intensive projects, firms were forced to look elsewhere for labour with a high skill–cost ratio. Among the countries with a favourable ratio, a 1992 World Bank sponsored survey found that US and European firms ranked India as the top choice for on-site and off-shore ICT services, ahead of Israel, Ireland, Mexico, Singapore, China, Hungary and the Philippines (InfoTech Consulting, 1992).

One indicator of skills availability in India is the annual output of graduates with a bachelor's degree in engineering. This output grew from 247 at the time of independence in 1947 to 237,000 in 2006 (Banerjee and Muley, 2009).[4] Although the colonial legacy meant that this labour is mostly educated in English, India's most pointed advantage came, however, from the skills embodied in the labour. In the 1980s, as the government undertook limited computerisation of its activities, it encouraged the use of Unix as the operating system of choice. This led local firms to modify the Unix source code to run on hardware they designed (Heeks, 1996). It is impossible to overemphasise the importance of familiarity with Unix. Developed initially at AT&T Bell Labs in 1969, its use spread rapidly as liberal licensing to universities led to the collaborative development of a truly open operating system, various versions of which were widely adopted by the world's leading computer vendors (Salus, 1994). As circumstances forced Indian programmers to adopt Unix,

> India entered the 1990s in a position of special advantage. Indian programmers are not only well educated and English-speaking, but out of necessity they're keenly focussed on client/server or multiuser solutions for PCs running DOS (with Netware) or Unix – just the kinds of solutions that US and European companies are rushing to embrace.
>
> (Udell, 1993)

Of course, the availability of a skill-cost advantage will not automatically guarantee the profitable exploitation of a global opportunity without a supportive socioeconomic environment for firms. Indeed, although India established the Department of Electronics (DoE) (renamed Ministry of Electronics and Information Technology since 2016) in 1971 to formulate electronics policy, the DoE's domination by a scientific community, committed to self-sufficiency and self-reliance, within a broader, state-dominated, autarkic, import-substitution led industrialisation strategy pursued since the 1950s, proved inimical to innovation and entrepreneurship (Sridharan, 1996). Under this policy regime, there was no Indian ICT industry in the private sector to speak of (Subramanian, 1992).

In the early 1980s, India's relatively poor economic record led to cautious efforts to liberalise policies to encourage private investment and trade (Sridharan, 1996). This opportunity was seized upon by a group of technologically and commercially pragmatic bureaucrats at the DoE, especially after Rajiv Gandhi became Prime Minister. They were keen that the globalisation of the software industry not bypass India. This resulted in the Computer Policy of November 1984 which, besides easing the local manufacture and availability of computers, recognised software as an 'industry', making it eligible for investment allowance and other incentives. The Computer Software Export, Development and Training Policy of December 1986 followed with a 'flood in, flood out' policy that gave easy access to imported software with the explicit goal of increasing India's share of world software production and exports. Industry was to be independent, with the government stepping in only to provide infrastructure and to play a promotional role. Overall, these policies were an explicit rejection of import-substitution led industrialisation policies in the software sector. Thus, it was software that led the growth of the Indian ICT services sector.

Despite these policy initiatives, exporting in the 1980s typically involved little more than bodyshopping, or the practice of providing inexpensive on-site (i.e., at customer locations overseas) labour on an hourly basis, for low value-added programming services.[5] The practice had its advantages and limitations. On one hand, it meant 'input-less exports', requiring only a contact overseas, a little finance, and the names of local programmers who could be hired and sent on-site (Heeks, 1996). On the other hand, it underutilised the skills of well-trained engineers, many of whom quit to seek more challenging and better-paying jobs once sent overseas. The high turnover only reinforced the tendency of firms from India to compete on low costs rather than being able to fall back on a repository of technical and managerial expertise acquired from previous projects.

Although bodyshopping seems like a quick-buck strategy, there were not too many alternatives for firms from a country that had previously merited little consideration as a source of ICT products. Banerjee and Duflo's (2000) study of 230 projects across 125 firms in India shows that reputation matters in software contracting, even after controlling for project, firm and client characteristics. While Indian engineers had the necessary technical skills, they were trained in a closed economy. Onsite services provided exposure to management processes and socially specific communication protocols, besides emerging technologies and various application domains.

The official encouragement given to bodyshopping reflected a limited understanding of the industry among policy makers: software was widely perceived as being 'hitech' without adequate distinction made between the different stages of production or the corresponding value added. According to Sen (1994), the euphoria following the growth in software exports in the 1980s encouraged the opinion that the software industry needed little policy support. Paving the way for a better understanding of the industry and policy support was a shift in the approach to policy making. Based on inputs from the industry which, in 1988, formed the National Association of Software and Services Companies (NASSCOM), subsequent policy measures promoted the industry more proactively. The clearest instance of this was the establishment, in 1990, of the software technology parks (STPs). As export zones dedicated to the software industry, the STPs were, in the language of Porter, a sector-specific factor that offered data communication facilities and financial incentives, such as tax-free export earnings. STPs allowed firms to offer offshore services, that is, services provision from India, instead of having to work at customer sites overseas.

In 1991, the year after the STPs were established, there came a balance-of-payments crisis induced shift in economic policies, including devaluation of the Rupee, trade liberalisation and duty rationalisation, openness to foreign investment, and a new industrial policy that removed entry barriers for new firms, a process that is still underway.[6] Even as these economy-wide changes benefited the software industry, many sector-specific policy changes also emerged from constant interaction with the industry, especially NASSCOM. Examples include income tax exemption on profits from services exports in 1992; elimination of import duties on software by 1997; and permission to grant ADR (American depository receipts)/GDR (global depository receipts) linked employee stock options in 1998.

The shift to offshore provision in a more liberal economic environment marked the beginning of a new relationship between the Indian ICT services industry and the global market. According to Sen's (1994) analysis of quarterly export growth, between 1987 and 1992–3, a linear equation provided the best fit for the growth. From 1992–93 (until 1994, the last year for which Sen had data), however, an exponential equation provided a better fit. Sen also projected that if exports maintained the exponential trajectory, they would reach US$630 million by 1997. Since actual exports in 1995–96 were US$750 million (Table 11.1), there was clearly a change in the growth characteristics of Indian software exports.

There were a couple of reasons for the change in growth characteristics. First, firms capitalised on the policy changes since the 1980s, especially the availability of data communication facilities, to establish offshore development centres (ODCs). The ODCs replicated the infrastructure, technology, training programmes, productivity tools and methodologies of the customer workplace. They brought professionals under one roof, instead of having them scattered at customer sites across the world, which helped firms build a repository of knowledge to compete for subsequent projects.

At the ODCs, firms also pioneered a global offshore delivery model, a highlight of which was the adoption of industry-wide certification norms, such as the ISO-9001/9000–3 standards prescribed by the International Standards Organisation, and the Software Engineering Institute's five-level Capability Maturity Model (SEI-CMM), to codify quality procedures in the development process. By June 2002, 85 firms were certified at Level 5, the highest level of the SEI-CMM, compared with 42 in the rest of the world. Following a certified process enables firms to acquire more profitable turnkey projects. Turnkey projects force firms to manage a wider range of tasks than just programming and take responsibility for the overall project schedule, quality and productivity, in contrast to bodyshopping, which is little more than resume selling (Arora and Asundi, 1999).

Second, the liberal economic climate of the 1990s also witnessed an influx of multinational corporations (MNCs) to establish ODCs to take advantage of the STPs and to capitalise on Indian skills.[7] As ODCs proved popular among Indian firms and MNCs, by 2017–18, the share of exports from India, that is, not including revenues from subsidiaries from abroad, increased to

Table 11.2 International trade in software services (2007–08 to 2017–18, by mode of supply)

Year	*Mode 1*	*Mode 2*	*Mode 3*	*Mode 4*
2007–08	60.4%	0.6%	13.9%	25.1%
2008–09	56.3%	0.1%	16.8%	26.8%
2009–10	64.6%	0.0%	17.6%	17.8%
2010–11	67.4%	0.1%	14.8%	17.7%
2011–12	69.0%	0.5%	15.4%	15.1%
2012–13	74.7%	1.6%	9.4%	14.3%
2013–14	69.0%	0.1%	13.7%	17.1%
2014–15	68.4%	0.1%	14.4%	17.1%
2015–16	64.8%	0.2%	18.9%	16.1%
2016–17	66.5%	0.2%	19.4%	13.9%
2017–18	69.5%	0.1%	17.4%	13.0%

Source: Reserve Bank of India Surveys on Computer Software and Information Technology Enabled Services Exports, various years (https://rbi.org.in/scripts/Pr_DataRelease.aspx?SectionID=364&DateFilter=Year).

Note: Mode 1 refers to cross border supply, Mode 2 to consumption abroad; Mode 3 to commercial presence, Mode 4 to presence of natural persons.

Mode 1 can be considered the equivalent of offshore services provision, Mode 3 as revenues from subsidiaries abroad, and Mode 4 as on-site services provision.

82.6 per cent (Table 11.2). The popularity of STPs within industry is also reflected in the growth of STP centres from 3 to 52 between 1990 and 2011 (DIT, 2011: 69), and the share of software exports passing through STPs rose to 97 per cent by 2005–06 (Table 11.1).

Notwithstanding the organisational innovations and the transformations in software services exports in the 1990s, the industry in India was characterised by the near absence of innovative offerings. Although the availability of skilled labour, at relatively low wages, confers an advantage in terms of development costs, the distance from final markets meant that firms were unable to react quickly to meet the emerging needs of users. Despite the instantaneous access which modern data communication infrastructure provides to distant markets, most firms in India were stuck at the lower end of the business to the extent that the tacit knowledge required to develop innovative services is difficult to convey over long distances. To invoke Egan (2000), firms from India could neither set the standards for general purpose software nor distinguish their offerings by being a part of sector-specific application districts with access to lead users.

The turn of the millennium, however, led to a qualitative transformation in services exports from India. Facilitating this shift, ironically, was the global slump in demand for ICT products following over-investment in the 1990s.[8] Despite this slump, the Indian ICT services industry and exports continued to grow after 2001 (Table 11.1). One reason for the growth was the efforts by firms worldwide to control costs by outsourcing not just software but also a range of ICT-enabled services, ranging from R&D and engineering services at one end of the skill spectrum,[9] to business processes, such as voice-based customer support centres (call centres) or medical transcription, at the other (Srinivas and Jayashankar, 2002). The growing importance of high-value-added services is evident in the 10.5 per cent contribution of product development and engineering services to exports from India by 2017–18 (Table 11.3). This table understates the importance of these activities to Indian firms since they typically require greater proximity to customers for reasons mentioned earlier and, as will be pointed out later, are increasingly being undertaken in subsidiaries abroad. At the other end of the skill spectrum, business process outsourcing (BPO) grew to account for 24.6 per cent of exports.

Table 11.3 Composition of India's information and communications technology service exports (as percentage share of total exports, 2007–08 to 2017–18)

Year	*Software Services*	*Product Development*	*Engineering Services (a)*	*BPO Services (b)*	*Total Exports (c)*
2007–08	67.2%	9.4%	3.2%	20.2%	34,841
2008–09	64.0%	8.9%	4.1%	22.9%	36,636
2009–10	60.7%	8.2%	7.6%	23.5%	38,753
2010–11	68.8%	4.9%	4.7%	21.6%	47,600
2011–12	66.8%	8.3%	3.9%	21.0%	51,800
2012–13	66.3%	5.6%	5.0%	23.2%	62,600
2013–14	68.0%	6.4%	5.4%	24.6%	71,300
2014–15	67.8%	4.3%	6.2%	21.7%	82,000
2015–16	67.0%	4.2%	5.6%	23.2%	88,000
2016–17	66.0%	3.2%	7.1%	23.7%	97,100
2017–18	64.9%	3.4%	7.1%	24.6%	108,400

Source: Reserve Bank of India Surveys on Computer Software and Information Technology Enabled Services Exports, various years (https://rbi.org.in/scripts/Pr_DataRelease.aspx?SectionID=364&DateFilter=Year).

Note: (a) refers to embedded solutions; product design engineering (mechanical and electrical but excluding software); architectural and other technical services; and any other services. (b) refers to customer interaction services; finance and accounting, auditing, book keeping and tax consulting services; human resource administration; legal services (including IP management); business and corporate research; medical transcription; content development, management and publishing; and any other service. (c) This figure is not the same as in Table 11.1 as the RBI does not count income from subsidiaries abroad as exports (unlike NASSCOM and MeitY), i.e., the component break-up is calculated on the basis of Modes 1, 2 and 4 (Table 11.2)

Another reason was access to more skilled labour for high-value-added services and the deepening of the local labour market which, in part, was an unforeseen consequence of US immigration policies. After the Immigration Act of 1965 gave priority to immigrants with scarce skills, the US drew huge numbers of educated professionals such as engineers, predominantly Asian (Saxenian, 2006). Indians were also significant beneficiaries. This trend was reinforced by the Immigration Act of 1990 which established the H-1B visa programme to enable the employment, up to six years, of workers in a specialty occupation which requires the theoretical and practical application of knowledge requiring completion of at least a bachelor's degree. As the programme was used extensively by firms of Indian origin and MNCs, Indians became the largest beneficiaries of H-1B petitions approved (Table 11.4).

Following the demand slump in the US in 2001, India's share of H-1B admissions declined (Table 11.4). Singh (2003) cites a NASSCOM estimate that 35,000 professionals returned to India. Of the returnees, an estimated 70 per cent were H-1B visa holders, while another 10–15 per cent had been

Table 11.4 India's share of approved H-1B petitions: 2000–18

Year	*Total petitions approved*	*Indian petitions*	
		Approved	*% Share*
2000	257,640	124,696	48.4%
2001	330,521	161,561	48.9%
2002	197,092	64,980	33.0%
2003	217,031	79,166	36.5%
2004	287,418	123,567	43.0%
2005	266,640	118,520	44.4%
2006	270,981	135,329	49.9%
2007	281,444	147,559	52.4%
2008	276,652	149,629	54.1%
2009	214,721	103,059	48.0%
2010	192,990	102,911	53.3%
2011	269,653	156,317	58.0%
2012	262,569	168,367	64.1%
2013	286,773	187,270	65.3%
2014	315,857	220,286	69.7%
2015	275,317	195,247	70.9%
2016	345,262	256,226	74.25%
2017	365,682	276,423	75.6%
2018	323,558	243,994	75.4%

Source: US Department of Homeland Security. *Characteristics of H1B Specialty Occupation Workers, Annual Report to Congress*, various years (www.uscis.gov/tools/reports-and-studies).

abroad for at least 10 years. These people returned not only because of shrinking international opportunities but also because they saw India as a place for innovation (Krishnadas, 2003). Even if they did not return permanently, many began to operate simultaneously from the US and India as argonauts (Saxenian, 2006).

As the Indian services industry widened its offerings, there was a parallel development as firms of Indian origin began to locate overseas, either in, or close to, their main markets: by 2017–18 these firms had established more than 1000 delivery/development centres in more than 200 cities across 80 countries (MeitY, 2017–18: 91). One reason, especially in the case of the US, was increasingly antagonistic political rhetoric. For instance, during the passage of a Customs and Border Protection Law in August 2010, which increased the 'filing fee and fraud prevention and detection fee' by US$2000 for H-1B visa applications made by firms with more than 50 employees, and with a US workforce in which more than 50 per cent were on those visa categories,[10] Senator Charles Schumer referred to

> chop shops that outsource good, high-paying American technology jobs to lower wage, temporary immigrant workers from other countries. These are companies such as Infosys. But it will not affect the high-tech companies such as Intel or Microsoft that play by the rules and recruit workers in America.
>
> (Sharma, 2010)[11]

While the law authorised collection of the higher fee until September 2014, the filing fee for H1-B visas was once again increased to US$4000 on December 18, 2015.[12]

On April 18, 2017, President Trump signed an executive order to 'Buy American and Hire American', which included to a call for 'reforms to help ensure that H-1B visas are awarded to the most-skilled or highest-paid petition beneficiaries' (Trump, 2017). In the spirit of that call, a policy memorandum dated March 31, 2017, tightened the definition of a 'specialty occupation' by saying that, although a bachelor's degree was a necessary condition for a H-1B specialty occupation visa, a generic degree could not justify the granting of a petition. It also noted that it would be hard to 'consider the position of programmer to qualify as a specialty occupation', that is, being employed as a computer programmer, and using information technology skills and knowledge to help on the job, is insufficient to establish the position as a specialty occupation. The memorandum called on petitioners to make the case for a specialty occupation by identifying the distinctiveness of wage levels, complexity of the job duties and the level of judgement and understanding required to perform them, and the amount and level of supervision required United States Citizenship and Immigration Services (USCIS) (2017).

Another policy memorandum issued on February 22, 2018, tightened the rules for deploying workers (H-1B beneficiaries) at client (third-party) sites

(UNCIS, 2018). Petitioning employers had to demonstrate that they would maintain an employer–employee relationship with the worker for the validity period of the visa. It also required them to provide contractual evidence of a 'specific and non-speculative qualifying assignment' in a 'specialty occupation based on requirements imposed by the end-client who uses the beneficiary's services'. Besides wages and benefits, contractual evidence could take the form of 'work assignments including technical documentation, milestone tables, marketing analysis, cost-benefit analysis, brochures, and funding documents'. When workers are to be placed at the premises of many clients, a full itinerary of dates, locations and a contractual agreement with each client is to be provided. These two memoranda issued by the Trump administration increased the bureaucratic procedures and associated costs for petitioners, with other changes being discussed also promising to be at least as burdensome (Bhattacharya, 2018).[13]

Aside from political uncertainty, the move by firms of Indian origin to work either in their main markets, or in 'near-shore' facilities in countries such as Mexico or Poland, must also be understood as an organisational response to the challenges they face. Thus, Tata Consultancy Services opened an innovation centre in Cincinnati, in proximity to its large clients in the midwestern US, because the centre represents 'the bridgehead of its ambitions to go beyond being merely an outsourced back-office and coding shop and take-on such consultancy giants as IBM, Hewlett-Packard (HP) and Accenture on their home turf' (Economist, 2011). Opening such centres enables firms to kill two birds with one stone. They not only hire locally to blunt political arguments about being low-cost firms who undermine the welfare of US workers but are also a means of addressing emerging opportunities as customers in various sectors transform their operations by adopting new technologies such as artificial intelligence and machine learning (MGI, 2017). Thus, despite India's high share of H-1B visas, Table 11.2 shows a steady decline on the reliance on Mode 4 (presence of natural persons) for exports and an increasing reliance on income from Mode 3 (subsidiaries abroad) for revenues.

11.4 Serving the BoP market with domain knowledge from India

After nearly two decades of export growth from India, many firms and entrepreneurs began turning their attention to the domestic market. For MNCs from the Global North,[14] facing declining populations and consequent saturation in many product segments, the growing populations in the emerging markets of the Global South are attractive, especially if their needs can be met by existing offerings.[15] However, according to a Pew Center study, a global middle class, with consumption patterns similar to those of the North, is more promise than reality (Kochhar, 2015). In India, for instance, while some estimate the middle class to be as high as 600 million (see Krishnan and Hatekar, 2016), and 49 per cent of respondents in a 2014 survey conducted by the University of Pennsylvania identified themselves as middle class (Kapur and Vaishnav, 2016), the Pew report says that barely 50 million in the country is middle *income*, that is, with a per capita income of more than US$10 a day.[16]

As this recognition of a limited 'middle class' market set in, the rhetoric shifted to the fortune to be made at the bottom of the pyramid (BoP), or the opportunity offered by an estimated 4 billion customers earning less than US$2 a day, mostly in the Global South (Prahalad, 2009). Tapping this 'fortune', however, poses challenges (Aoyama and Parthasarathy, 2016). First, limited affordability is a major reason that this segment of the population was not viewed as a viable market until recently. Second, the BoP is found in locations where infrastructure, such as power or communication networks, which are often taken for granted in affluent contexts, is typically weak to nonexistent. Third, the BoP is not socioculturally homogenous, and it is characterised by relatively limited skills and low levels of literacy.

While there are many possible locations that can provide firms the opportunity to acquaint themselves with the BoP market, India is sought after because it has a huge population that is socially and culturally diverse, a large proportion of which lives in poverty and illiteracy amidst inadequate infrastructure.[17] Although such circumstances, an unpredictable regulatory environment, and corruption in public life, can prove chaotic and challenge firms, it only leads Venkatesan (2013) to proclaim 'win in India, win everywhere'.

There are at least two other reasons why India is an ideal location from which to serve the BoP market. First, the availability of skills which made India the largest exporter of ICT services can also be used to design and deploy technology to address the challenges of the BoP. Second, India has more NGOs than any other country – an estimated 1.2 million, approximately one for every 600 people, compared to one police officer for every 963 people (Godfrey, 2015). NGOs have stepped in to make up, at least partially, for state failure to provide various forms of social and physical infrastructure (Jenkins, 2010). In their role as activists, or advocates for various ideals, NGOs not only hold the state to account for developmental failures but also target the practices of firms (Spar and La Mure, 2003). While the activist/advocate role often makes NGOs take on adversarial positions, they are increasingly sought after for their service provider role.

The growing attention to NGOs is the result of difficulties in designing services for the BoP, especially in the absence of lead users. Thus far, lead users have been usually sought in affluent economies, where high per capita incomes affords consumers the exposure to new technologies and innovations, and allows them to evaluate alternatives in an environment with robust and reliable infrastructure (Grabher, Ibert and Floher, 2008). Since the BoP has hitherto merited little consideration for deploying technologies to launch services, there are few, if any, benchmarks to understand how these markets may use new technologies (Aoyama and Parthasarathy, 2016). As

NGOs have long cultivated the grassroots linkages to design services and programmes using approaches centred round community participation, they are of particular interest as a source of domain knowledge from the BoP. In other words, as the reach of NGOs has grown, they provide crucial 'last mile connectivity' to the lead users in local markets and offer spatially 'sticky' tacit knowledge that firms, and MNCs in particular, find hard to obtain on their own. For NGOs, partnering with firms gives them access to resources and technologies they might otherwise lack to address various developmental challenges.

The state has also reached out to NGOs, especially since India's 11th Five Year Plan (2007–2012) emphasised inclusive development to empower the poor. The plan called for the involvement of different stakeholders, including the private sector, citizens' groups and the voluntary sector, to work with and improve the efficacy of government action for inclusiveness. The role of NGOs within the new framework of inclusive development began to change with various legislative initiatives,[18] of which the passage of the National Rural Employment Guarantee Act (NREGA) 2005 is prominent.[19] NGOs became active in the social audits that are mandated to check corruption in the implementation of NREGA, which guarantees 100 days of unskilled manual work in a financial year to adult members in every household. Similarly, the National Rural Health Mission (NRHM), which was launched on April 12, 2005, to make the public health delivery system functional and accountable and thereby provide accessible, affordable, and quality health care to the rural population, declared that 'involvement of non-governmental sector organisations is critical for the success of the NRHM'.[20] NGOs have also benefitted from the passage of the Companies Act 2013 which requires firms to achieve the goals of a publicly articulated corporate social responsibility (CSR) policy in partnership with local authorities, business associations and civil society/NGOs.[21]

An instance of the emerging partnership amongst the state, an MNC and the private sector is in the domain of education. In 2005, the US MNC Microsoft established a Microsoft Research (MSR) lab in Bangalore. The lab is home to a Technology for Emerging Markets group, which has no equivalent in any of the other 10 MSR labs across the world.[22] This group consists of technologists and social scientists who work closely with various external partners, including NGOs, universities, government, and private firms, to focus on communities that can consume computing technologies and services but for whom computing remains largely out of reach.

Against the backdrop of this agenda, researchers at MSR Bangalore set out to investigate how students used computers in rural government schools where computer-aided learning was supported to different degrees by an NGO, the Azim Premji Foundation (itself established by Azim Premji, the founder of Wipro).[23] At these schools, where there were far fewer PCs than students, the researchers observed many children usually crowded around a single machine. One student typically dominated interaction with the PC, which not only limited the learning opportunities for the others but, more fundamentally, challenged the notion of a *personal* computer in a resource-constrained context. To increase interaction with the PC for all the children huddled around it, MSR came up with the idea of a multipoint mouse, or multiple mice with multiple cursors, for a single machine. It thus became possible for at least half a dozen children to share a PC at a fraction of the cost of acquiring PCs for all. The multipoint mouse went well beyond cost saving, as studies provided statistically significant evidence to support the hypotheses that collaboration leads to better learning and tangible educational value (Pawar et al., 2007).

Microsoft's Education Products group eventually devised a software development kit which allows pedagogic material to be written on a single PC for up to 25 users. Together, the cost savings and collective learning benefits led the multipoint mouse to be deployed in many countries. The multipoint mouse is an example of what Microsoft's founder Bill Gates (2008) has referred to as 'creative capitalism – an approach where governments, businesses, and nonprofits work together to stretch the reach of market forces so that more people can make a profit, or gain recognition, doing work that eases the world's inequities'. This is also what Govindarajan and Trimble (2012) refer to as 'reverse innovation', that is, when the ability to design products and services for demanding conditions provides a basis 'glocalising' similar products in more affluent markets.[24]

11.5 A concluding discussion

This chapter explains how India's emergence as the world's largest exporter of ICT services, with considerably smaller production for the domestic market, challenges Schware's proposition about the importance of 'walking on two legs' for the software industry: that experience gained from the domestic market is critical to export success. But the domestic market, with a focus on BoP customers and an attendant organisation of production, gained significance much *after* exports came to characterise the Indian industry. The new opportunity shows that, instead of a unique trajectory, where a domestic market provides the basis for exports, there are at least two trajectories characterising the Indian industry. This chapter provides an explanation for these distinct trajectories which Schware did not.

Although independent India long had a large pool of relatively low-wage, English-speaking technical labour – thanks to investments made by the state – the broader policy regime made it difficult to valorise those skills whether in the domestic or the export market. But, then, what Porter terms chance played a role as technological changes in the Global North generated demand for software and led to the emergence of an ICT services industry. Labour-intensive ICT services production began to globalise in a quest for relatively low-cost skills. That this round of globalisation of this sector did not bypass India was due to sector-specific policies that were facilitated by political and bureaucratic changes in the mid-1980s, although the initial policies only resulted in bodyshopping. But, economy-wide policy changes and more sector-specific policies in the 1990s, especially establishing the STPs, led to rapid growth of the ICT services industry, as firms were able to build ODCs to develop and deliver services more profitably from India.

The growth of Indian services exports into the 1990s was not on the basis of technological leadership; instead, it was because of being technologically conversant with the widely accepted Unix operating system. The availability of skilled personnel familiar with a dominant technological standard and the availability of infrastructure to undertake offshore work allowed more firms from India to meet global quality norms better than from any other country. The decade also witnessed the deepening of the global connections as an increasing number of MNCs came to India to establish ODCs. Another indicator was the growing exchange with the US thanks to the H-1B visa programme of which Indians became the biggest beneficiaries. When the global industry faced a decline in demand at the turn of the millennium, many who were employed on these visas, amongst others, returned home to take advantage of their knowledge of industry practices in the US and the unfolding opportunities with the growing outsourcing of R&D and other tasks. To the extent that many retained a foot in both countries, they became the quintessential argonauts that Saxenian identifies.

Even as services exports grew in the new millennium to make India the largest exporter, the domestic market began to matter in unanticipated ways. In an effort to seek new markets in locations with growing and underserved populations, firms and MNCs from the Global North in particular began to turn their attention to the markets of the Global South. But the poverty, the illiteracy, the infrastructural deficiency and the sociocultural diversity in the Global South was not going to permit mere low-cost versions of products and services offered to more affluent populations. To meet the needs of the hitherto ignored BoP population, it was not enough for MNCs to be present with their technical skills in proximity to their potential users. They also had to work with partners, such as adversarial NGOs, who had gained a deep understanding of the BoP by serving them for years. India became a preferred location to identify the needs of the BoP as its ability to offer a combination of skills, a large BoP population, and active NGOs, within state policy that increasingly seeks 'inclusion', is matched by few countries. The opportunities for 'creative capitalism' in India are evident in the multipoint mouse example at MSR.

What do these different trajectories of the Indian ICT services industry mean for its future? Critical to understanding the future is to acknowledge that the social and economic value of ICTs lies not in technology *qua* technology, but in abstracting and encoding practices in various sectors. Consequently, the importance of lead users and the spatial drift toward application districts that, according to Egan, characterises the software industry in the US was in evidence among Indian firms, even *before* the shrill political rhetoric in the US against off-shoring to India (Bhattacharya and Punit, 2017). This acknowledges that the competitive advantage of the Indian industry is best gained from an ability to deploy new technologies with insights into the evolving needs of customers. Thus, firms of Indian origin will likely continue moving some of their operations close to their North American and European customers, or at least near-shoring to Latin America and Eastern Europe. This will happen as long as firms from India are unable to claim technological leadership, and those customers are more significant than domestic customers as sources of domain knowledge, irrespective of the vicissitudes of domestic politics in the main markets.

Similarly, the growing interest in the BoP, especially among MNCs from the Global North, who are often technology leaders, demands a presence in India to gain insights into how the lives and practices of the BoP users/customers will influence the design and appropriation of technology, a vantage that cannot be gained from, say, Silicon Valley. But, however technologically proficient, an isolated presence in India is hardly a sufficient condition. Insights into BoP service domains crucially demand partnerships with institutions including the state and civil society organisations, such as NGOs, who have long worked with the underserved. With the BoP population representing a significant market opportunity, especially as population growth stagnates in the more affluent parts of the world, the tendency to develop and offer more services from a country with India's socioeconomic diversity, and to indulge in reverse innovation, will likely continue even if sections of the BoP prosper.

In closure, the Indian software services industry grew primarily by relying on exports; that is, it initially adopted a 'walking on one leg' strategy. The subsequent attention to a domestic BoP market hardly validates Schware's proposition since the two markets have little or no connection, as they rely on very different sources of domain knowledge. But, to the extent that the domain knowledge of the two trajectories of the industry begin to overlap, that is, as the BoP provides a sustained basis for reverse innovation, the Indian ICT services industry could be justifiably described as 'walking on two legs' to finally validate Schware.

Notes

1 It is informational as the productivity and competitiveness of its units is dependent upon their capacity to 'generate, process and apply efficient knowledge based information'. It is global as 'its core activities of production, consumption and circulation are organised and generated on a global scale either directly or through a network of linkages between economic agents'. It is networked as 'its productivity is generated through and competition is played out in a global network of interaction between business networks' (Castells, 2000).

2 By 2000, Chinese- (from mainland China and Taiwan) and Indian-born engineers accounted for 14 per cent and 13 per cent, respectively, of Silicon Valley's engineers and scientists (Wadhwa et al, 2007:). Between 1995 and 2005, the Chinese were key cofounders in 12.8 per cent of start-up firms in the region, while the figure for the Indians was 15.5 per cent.

3 In 1997, the Houston metropolitan statistical area accounted for 68 per cent of oil and gas packaged software employment in the US (Egan, 2000).
4 The corresponding figure for the US in 2006 was 104,200 (*ibid*).
5 Unless otherwise mentioned, the narrative in the next seven paragraphs draws from Parthasarathy (2012).
6 For a description and assessment of various aspects of the reforms, see the collection of essays in Bhagwati and Panagriya (2013) and in Hope et al. (2013).
7 By 2015, 928 MNCs had established 1165 R&D centres in the country. www.slideshare.net/zinnov/executive-summary-talent-report-final.
8 For instance, in the US, spending on information technology, after growing by 16 per cent in 2000, fell by 6 per cent in 2001 (Economist, 2002). In aggregate terms, technology spending declined from nearly 5 per cent of GDP in 2000 to about 4 per cent by 2003 (Economist, 2003). The US mattered in particular since it remains India's biggest market for ICT services.
9 On the domestic front, firms were helped by legal changes, important amongst which was the passage of the Semiconductor Integrated Circuits Layout-Design Act 2000, which provided for the registration and protection of IC layouts and designs for a 10-year period (Krishnadas, 2000).
10 www.gpo.gov/fdsys/pkg/PLAW-111publ230/pdf/PLAW-111publ230.pdf
11 Fueling such political rhetoric, especially against firms of Indian origin using H-1B workers, were inputs from researchers to US lawmakers. For instance, testifying to the Senate Subcommittee on Immigration and the National Interest of the Judiciary Committee hearing on the Impact of High-Skilled Immigration on U.S. Workers on March 1, 2016, Ron Hira (an American of Indian origin) raised three objections to the H-1B programme. First, employers were bringing H-1B workers with an eye on profitability, rather than the 'best and brightest', whether measured by educational achievement or by wages. A consequence was that, although the H-1B annual cap of 85,000 visas since 2004 includes 20,000 for those with a master's degree or higher from a US institution, the education levels of most H-1B workers in the period 2005–12, for the 20 top H-1B employers in 2014, was 'no more than ordinary'; that is, they only possessed a bachelor's degree. Second, since it is employers who petition for and hold the H-1B visa, they wield disproportionate power over workers, including the threat of termination. A worker whose services are terminated becomes 'out-of-status' and must leave the US immediately. Similarly, data for the top 20 H-1B employers for 2013 showed that the wages of H-1B workers were typically far below accepted levels in the information technology industry. Hira provided anecdotal cases of such workers not only replacing better-paid and -skilled American workers but also being trained by the very workers they replaced. This, he claimed, was a step toward off-shoring and the loss of jobs in the US. Third, the H-1B programme is a guest worker programme. But rather than use the programme as a bridge to legal permanent residence (obtaining a green card), data from 2014 showed that few H-1B workers were sponsored for a green card. The continued reliance on temporary labour was also indicative to Hira of the desire to outsource jobs overseas, thereby distorting the local labour market (www.epi.org/publication/ congressional-testimony-the-impact-of-high-skilled-immigration-on-u-s-workers-4/).
12 www.uscis.gov/forms/h-and-l-filing-fees-form-i-129-petition-nonimmigrant-worker.
13 This memorandum was rescinded by another memorandum issued on 17 June 2020 (USCIS, 2020), after a court struck down 'the itinerary requirement for employers, removed the requirement that the petitioning employer provide contracts that span the entire requested period of stay, and held that the recent USCIS practice of limiting the H-1B validity periods was arbitrary and capricious' (DeBrine, Drozdowski and Parshad, 2020). For employers of H-1B visa holders, rescinding the 2018 memorandum was a welcome easing of onerous paperwork.

14 The Global North is used in this chapter as a shorthand reference to affluent countries in general and to North America, Western Europe and Japan in particular.

15 The attraction of the BoP market goes beyond the traditional bottom line, as firms began to increasingly view their operations in terms of the triple bottom line (economic, social and environmental returns) (Elkington, 1997), amidst broader shifts in the normative conception of development as something more than economic growth. The adoption of the Millennium and Sustainable Development Goals are emblematic of these shifts.

16 The variation in estimates is because Krishnan and Hatekar count anyone with an income over US$2 a day as middle-income. But, as the Pew Center report points out, US$2 to US$10 a day is better described as low-income. A US$10 a day is when people tend to have economic security and are 'insulated' from falling back into poverty. The survey reported by Kapur and Vasihnav was aspirational and participants self-identified.

17 According to UNDP (2016), India's Human Development Index ranked 131 among 188 countries. The number of people earning less than $3.10 a day (purchasing power parity) was 52.9 per cent, against the world figure of 32.5 per cent, and only 72.1 per cent of adults (15 years and older) were literate, against the world figure of 84.3 per cent.

18 Interview with the executive director of a Bangalore-based NGO, September 17, 2012, Bangalore.

19 The full text of the Act is available at: http://nrega.nic.in/rajaswa.pdf.

20 For details of the NRHM, see http://nrhm.gov.in/images/ pdf/about-nrhm/nrhm-framework-implementation/nrhm-framework-latest.pdf.

21 For details, see: www.mca.gov.in/Ministry/pdf/CompaniesAct2013.pdf. Section 135 of the Act requires firms with a net profit of INR50 million or more, during any financial year, spend, in every financial year, at least 2 per cent of the average net profits of the three immediately preceding financial years, on CSR activities specified by Schedule 7 (such as eradicating poverty, improving health and promoting education).

22 Details of MSR are from http://research.microsoft.com/en-us/labs/india/.

23 Unless otherwise mentioned, this paragraph and the next draw from https://blogs.msdn.microsoft.com/ multipoint/2008/11/06/the-birth-of-multipoint/.

24 For more cases of creative capitalism and reverse innovation, involving various kinds of players in different domains, and a more comprehensive theoretical framework, see Aoyama with Parthasarathy (2016).

References

Aoyama, Y. with B. Parthasarathy (2016). *The Rise of the Hybrid Domain: Collaborative Governance for Social Innovation*, Edward Elgar, Cheltenham, UK.

Arora, A. and J. Asundi (1999). 'Quality certification and the economics of contract software development: A study of the Indian software industry', Working Paper 7260, National Bureau of Economic Research, Cambridge, MA.

Banerjee, A.V. and E. Duflo (2000). 'Reputation effects and the limits of contracting: A study of the Indian software industry', *Quarterly Journal of Economics*, 115(3), 989–1017.

Banerjee, R. and V.P. Muley (2009). *Engineering Education in India*, Macmillan, Noida, India.

Bartlett, C.A. and S. Ghosal (1990). 'Managing innovation in the transnational corporation', in C.A. Bartlett, Y.L. Doz and G. Hedlund (eds.) *Managing the Global Firm*, Routledge, Abingdon, UK.

Bhagwati, J. and A. Panagariya (eds.) (2013). *Reforms and Economic Transformation in India*, Oxford University Press, New York, NY.

Bhattacharya, A. (2018, December 27). 'In 2018, the American dream began to fade for Indian techies', *Quartz India*. https://qz.com/india/1325074/h-1b-visa-woes-worsened-for-indian-techies-in-2018/.

Bhattacharya, A. and I.S. Punit (2017, February 3). 'Indian IT firms have been preparing for changes in H-1B visa laws for nearly a decade', *Quartz India* https://qz.com/901292/indian-it-firms-like-wipro-tcs-and-infosys-have-been-preparing-for-changes-in-h1b-visa-laws-and-donald-trumps-america-for-several-years/.

Blinder, A.S. (2006). 'Offshoring: The next industrial revolution?', *Foreign Affairs*, 85(2), 113–128.

Brooks, F.C. (1995). *The Mythical Man-Month: Essays on Software Engineering*, 2nd ed., Addison Wesley Longman, Singapore.

Campbell-Kelly, M. (2003). *From Airline Reservations to Sonic the Hedgehog: A History of the Software Industry*, MIT Press, Cambridge, MA.

Castells, M. (2000). *The Information Age: Economy, Society and Culture: Volume 1: The Rise of the Network Society*, 2nd ed., Blackwell, Oxford, UK.

David, P.A. (2000). 'Understanding digital technology's evolution and the path of measured productivity growth', in E. Brynjolfsson and B. Kahin (eds.) *Understanding the Digital Economy: Data, Tools and Research*, MIT Press, Cambridge, MA.

DeBrine, E., A.G. Drozdowski and S. Parshad (2020). Recent USCIS settlement offers substantial relief to H-1B employers, *National Law Review*, X(143), https://www.natlawreview.com/article/recent-uscis-settlement-offers-substantial-relief-to-h-1b-employers.

Department of Information Technology (DIT) (2011). *Annual Report*, https://meity.gov.in/ writereaddata/files/annualreport2010-11.pdf.

The Economist (2002, August 22). 'High-tech companies: IT grows up', www.economist.com/business/2002/08/22/it-grows-up.

The Economist (2003, October 2). 'Spending on information technology: Some like it cold', www.economist.com/business/2003/10/02/some-like-it-cold.

The Economist (2011, November 5). 'TCS in America: From Mumbai to the Midwest', www.economist.com/business/2011/11/05/from-mumbai-to-the-midwest.

Egan, E.A. (2000). 'Application districts: An emerging spatial form in the computer software industry', *Journal of Comparative Policy Analysis*, 2, 321–344.

Elkington, J. (1997). *Cannibals with Forks: The Triple Bottom Line of 21st Century Business*, Capstone, Oxford, UK.

Evans, P.B. (1995). *Embedded Autonomy: States and Industrial Transformation*, Princeton University Press, Princeton, NJ.

Gates, W.H. (2008). 'A new approach to capitalism in the 21st century', https://news.microsoft.com/ 2008/01/24/bill-gates-world-economic-forum-2008/.

Gertler, M.S. (2003). 'Tacit knowledge and the economic geography of context, or the undefinable tacitness of being (there)', *Journal of Economic Geography*, 3(1), 75–99.

Godfrey, J. (2015). 'Why have 9,000 Indian NGOs been deregistered?'. https://nonprofitquarterly.org/why-have-9-000-indian-ngos-been-deregistered/.

Govindarajan, V. and C. Trimble (2012). *Reverse Innovation: Create Far from Home, Win Everywhere*, Harvard Business School Press, Boston, MA.

Grabher, G., Ibert, O. and S. Floher (2008). 'The neglected king: The customer in the new knowledge ecology of innovation', *Economic Geography*, 84(3), 253–280.

Heeks, R. (1996). *India's Software Industry: State Policy, Liberalisation and Industrial Development*, Sage Publications, New Delhi, India.

Hope, N.C., Kochar, A., Noll, R. and T.N. Srinivasan (eds.) (2013). *Economic Reform in India: Challenges, Prospects, and Lessons*, Cambridge University Press, New York, NY.

InfoTech Consulting (1992). *India's Software and Services: Export Potential and Strategies*, report submitted in fulfillment of contract with the Government of India, Department of Electronics under World Bank Japan grant #2612.

Jenkins, R. (2010). 'NGOs and Indian politics', in N.G. Jayal and P.B. Mehta (eds.) *The Oxford Companion to Politics in India*, Oxford University Press, New Delhi, India.

Kapur, D. and M. Vaishnav (2016). 'Being middle class in India', www.thehindu.com/opinion/op-ed/being-middle-class-in-india/article6673580.ece#lb?ref=infograph/%200/%20News%20.

Koch, K. (1998). 'High-tech labor shortage', *CQ Researcher*, 8(16), 361–384.

Kochhar, R. (2015). 'A global middle class is more promise than reality: From 2011–2011, nearly 700 million step out of poverty, but only barely', Pew Research Center, Washington, DC. www.pewresearch.org/global/2015/07/08/a-global-middle-class-is-more-promise-than-reality/.

Kraft, P. (1977). *Programmers and Managers: The Routinization of Computer Programming in the United States*, Springer-Verlag, New York, NY.

Krishnadas, K.C. (2000). 'Indian readies laws to protect IC designs', www.eedesign.com/article/showArticle.jhtml?articleId=17405970.

Krishnadas, K.C. (2003). 'Indian EEs show you can go home again', www.eetimes.com/article/showArticle.jhtml?articleId=18309505.

Krishnan, S. and N. Hatekar (2016). 'Emergence of the new middle class in India and its structural composition: An empirical investigation from 1999–00 to 2011–12', *Conference on the Middle Class in World Society*, December 16–17, Institute for Social and Economic Change, Bangalore.

McKinsey Global Institute (2017). *Artificial Intelligence: The Next Digital Frontier?* http://www.odbms.org/2017/08/artificial-intelligence-the-next-digital-frontier-mckinsey-global-institute-study/.

Ministry of Electronics and Information Technology (MeitY). *Annual Report*, various years. https://meity.gov.in/content/annual-report.

O'Riain, S. (2004). 'The politics of mobility in technology-driven commodity-chains: Developmental coalitions in the Irish software industry', *International Journal of Urban and Regional Research*, 28(3), 642–663.

Parthasarathy, B. (2012). 'The changing character of Indian offshore ICT services provision, 1985–2010', in A. Bardhan, C.A. Kroll and D.M. Jaffee (eds.) *The Oxford Handbook of Offshoring and Global Employment*, Oxford University Press, New York, NY.

Pawar, U.S., Pal, J., Gupta, R. and K. Toyama (2007). 'Multiple mice for retention tasks in disadvantaged schools', *CHI '07: Proceedings of the SIGCHI Conference on Human Factors in Computing Systems*, 1581–1590.

Polanyi, M. (2009, orig.1966). *The Tacit Dimension*, University of Chicago Press, Chicago, IL.

Porter, M.E. (1998, orig.1990). *The Competitive Advantage of Nations*, Free Press, New York, NY.

Prahalad, C. K. (2009). *The Fortune at the Bottom of the Pyramid: Eradicating Poverty Through Profits,* Pearson, Upper Saddle River, NJ.

Salus, P.H. (1994). *A Quarter Century of Unix*, Addison Wesley Publishing, New York, NY.

Saxenian, A. (1994). *Regional Advantage: Culture and Competition in Silicon Valley and Route 128*, Harvard University Press, Cambridge, MA.

Saxenian, A. (2006). *The New Argonauts: Regional Development in a Global Economy*, Harvard University Press, Cambridge, MA.

Schware, R. (1992). 'Software industry entry strategies for developing countries: A "walking on two legs" proposition', *World Development*, 20(2), 143–164.

Sen, P. (1994). 'Software exports from India: A systemic analysis', *Electronics Information and Planning*, 22(2), 55–63.

Sharma, A. (2010). 'U.S. Senator: Infosys is a "chop shop"', http://blogs.wsj.com/indiarealtime/ 2010/08/06/us-senator-infosys-is-a-chop-shop/.

Singh, S. (2003). 'India calling', www.businessworldindia.com/Nov1003/coverstory02.asp.

Spar, D.L. and L.T. La Mure (2003). 'The power of activism: Assessing the impact of NGOs on global business', *California Management Review*, 45(3), 78–101.

Sridharan, E. (1996). *The Political Economy of Industrial Promotion: Indian, Brazilian, and Korean Electronics in Comparative Perspective 1969–1994*, Praeger, London, UK.

Srinivas, A. and M. Jayashankar (2002, February 25). 'Hard times, hard lessons: The new software Solutions', *Business World*, 24–29.

Stein, E. (2017, January 26). 'How AI is changing software development', *Communications of the ACM*. https://cacm.acm.org/news/212583-how-ai-is-changing-software-development/fulltext.

Subramanian, C.R. (1992). *India and the Computer: A Study of Planned Development*, Oxford University Press, New Delhi.

Trump, D.J. (2017). 'Presidential executive order on buy American and hire American'. www.whitehouse.gov/the-press-office/2017/04/18/presidential-executive-order-buy-american-and-hire-american.

Udell, J. (1993). 'India's software edge', *Byte*, 18(10), 55–60.

United Nations Development Program (2016). *Human Development Report 2016: Human Development for Everyone*, UNDP, New York, NY.

United States Citizenship and Immigration Services (USCIS) (2017). 'Rescission of the December 22, 2000 "Guidance memo on H1B computer related positions"', Policy Memorandum PM-602-0142. www.uscis.gov/sites/default/files/files/nativedocuments/PM-6002-0142-H-1BComputerRelatedPositionsRecission.pdf.

United States Citizenship and Immigration Services (USCIS) (2018). 'Contracts and itineraries requirements for H-1B petitions involving third-party worksites', Policy Memorandum PM-602-0157. https://www.hsdl.org/?view&did=808570.

United States Citizenship and Immigration Services (USCIS) (2020). 'Rescission of Policy Memoranda, Policy Memorandum PM-602-0114. https://www.uscis.gov/sites/default/ files/USCIS/Laws/Memoranda/2020/PM-602-0114_ITServeMemo.pdf.

Varian, H.R., Farrell, J. and C. Shapiro (2004). *The Economics of Information Technology: An Introduction*, Cambridge University Press, Cambridge, UK.

Venkatesan, R. (2013). *Conquering the Chaos: Win in India, Win Everywhere*, Harvard Business School Press, Boston, MA.

Wadhwa, V., Saxenian, A., Rissing, B. and G. Gereffi (2007). 'America's new immigrant entrepreneurs: Part I', *Duke Science, Technology and Innovation Paper No. 23*. https://ssrn.com/abstract=990152 or http://dx.doi.org/10.2139/ssrn.990152.

Index

For Product Safety Concerns and Information please contact our EU representative GPSR@taylorandfrancis.com
Taylor & Francis Verlag GmbH, Kaufingerstraße 24, 80331 München, Germany

www.ingramcontent.com/pod-product-compliance
Lightning Source LLC
LaVergne TN
LVHW021123300926
849160LV00010B/842